Hegel's Philosophy of Politics

Hegel's Philosophy of Politics

Idealism, Identity, and Modernity

Harry Brod

Routledge
Taylor & Francis Group

LONDON AND NEW YORK

First published 1992 by Westview Press, Inc.

Published 2018 by Routledge
52 Vanderbilt Avenue, New York, NY 10017
2 Park Square, Milton Park, Abingdon, Oxon OX14 4RN

Routledge is an imprint of the Taylor & Francis Group, an informa business

Library of Congress Cataloging-in-Publication Data
Brod, Harry, 1951–
  Hegel's philosophy of politics : idealism, identity, and
modernity / Harry Brod.
     p. cm.
  Includes bibliographical references and index.
  ISBN 0-8133-8317-X (HC).—ISBN 0-8133-8526-1 (PB)
  1. Hegel, Georg Wilhelm Friedrich, 1770–1831—Contributions in
political science. I. Title.
JC233.H46B76   1992
320′.01—dc20   91-40678
                                                                                        CIP

ISBN 13: 978-0-367-01244-1 (hbk)
ISBN 13: 978-0-367-16231-3 (pbk)

MIX
Paper from
responsible sources
FSC   FSC™ C013985
www.fsc.org

Printed in the United Kingdom
by Henry Ling Limited

We have shared
both laughter and tears
over the many acknowledgments by male academics
thanking their wives
for keeping the kids out of their hair
and the house neat
(and sometimes doing the typing too).

This one's for Maria,
with thanks for not
keeping the kids away
or the house in too much order,
and insisting
I partake
of real life,
a precondition
for political philosophy
and for life itself
(and for suffering through it all with me).

And of course for Artemis and Alexi too.

Contents

Acknowledgments

This study started ten years ago as a doctoral dissertation completed in the Philosophy Department at the University of California at San Diego. At a particular point back then when I was lost in the German woods and could no longer see the forest for the trees, my advisor, Robert Pippin, offered suggestions that enabled me to find a path through my confusion. His comments were consistently both prodding and encouraging. Gerald Doppelt, Frederick Olafson, and Stanley Moore also played positive roles in my education at UCSD.

Early research for this work was supported by a Fulbright-Hays – Deutscher Akademischer Austauschdienst grant, which enabled me to study at the Hegel archives at the Ruhr-Universität Bochum, and by a Fellowship from the University of California.

Much has transpired since then, and my work has taken me in some very different, unanticipated directions. Yet I like to think that all my work, no matter how far afield others may think it is, still bears the imprint of someone who has tried to learn something about dialectical thinking from Hegel. Part of my original motivation for writing a dissertation on Hegel was a growing realization that many philosophers whose work I greatly admired, among them Herbert Marcuse, had themselves devoted a considerable amount of time to studying Hegel. Marcuse's comment that an early version of part of this work was "not bad" meant a great deal to me, as did the honor of his friendship.

The comments of anonymous reviewers have also been helpful. An earlier version of part of this study appeared as "The 'Spirit' of Hegelian Politics: Public Opinion and Legislative Debate from Hegel to Habermas" in Peter G. Stillman, ed., *Hegel's Philosophy of Spirit* (Albany: State University of New York Press, 1987).

Harry Brod

Introduction

Interpretive Frameworks

What must a political philosophy *do*? To what practical and theoretical needs does it respond?

One approach to the history of political philosophy is to treat it as a set of answers to a set of universal questions. Each of the "greats" in the Western tradition is then held to have given a distinctive set of answers to these perennial questions of philosophy.

But another, and I think more correct and profound view is that the "greats" of the philosophical tradition are "great" not because they offered distinctive *answers* but because they posed distinctive *questions*. I believe that all of the major figures of Western political philosophy can be said to have redefined for their time what the essential questions of political philosophy *were*. Is the central problem of political theory that of securing individual rights (Locke)? Or making possible the living of the good life (Aristotle)? Or promoting the peace and welfare of the community (Mill)? And so on.

This work is a study of Hegel's political philosophy. My central contention is that many interpretations of Hegel have foundered on an inadequate understanding of what questions Hegel thought a political philosophy in his time needed to answer and how it had to go about answering them.

A comparison between English-language and German-language secondary literature on Hegel's political philosophy reveals that substantially different interpretive styles or programs predominate in each camp. The former tends to take a more pragmatic, institutional approach, seeking Hegel's position on such standard substantive issues of political theory as identifying the locus of sovereignty, the nature of legislative authority, questions of distributive economic justice, relations between church and state, and so on. The tendency here is to discount

Hegel's claims to have systematized political philosophy in some distinctive way, his claim to be approaching the subject matter of politics with categories that more accurately and fully capture the essentials of political life than do the categories of any other theoretical framework. Applied to Hegel's mature, systematic expression of his political philosophy, the *Philosophy of Right*, this approach attempts to disentangle the content of Hegel's political thought—the what—from the form in which he said it—the how. Those who share this interpretive style often come to the disparaging conclusion that "the arrangement [of topics] hopelessly dislocated the subject-matter"[1] or, at a minimum, that "Hegel's political thought can be read, understood, and appreciated without having to come to terms with his metaphysics."[2]

Quite a different emphasis and context of discussion is evident in most of the German-language literature on Hegel's political philosophy. Here one finds a great deal of attention being paid to the programmatic, metatheoretical dimensions of Hegel's thought, while relatively little attention is paid to how Hegel's systematic conception of political philosophy is applied in detail to political life. Although more faithful to the avowed intention of Hegel's *Philosophy of Right* and more attentive to Hegel's expressed wish that the work be understood as part of a wider philosophic system, those who have appreciated the importance of examining Hegel's political doctrines within the philosophical framework in which they are formulated (for example, Joachim Ritter, Jürgen Habermas, Manfred Riedel) have been too content to convey their theses in sweeping generalizations, with the result that their analyses have not been refined and substantiated by a close look at Hegel's proposals regarding the concrete institutions of political life—the kind of close examinations more typically found in English-language commentaries. These latter commentaries, however, all too often bring to the discussion of Hegel the categories of their own philosophical frameworks rather than Hegel's own concepts. Consequently, Hegel's distinctive claims are often too facilely assimilated to more familiar claims made in the liberal or Marxist traditions.

This study attempts to synthesize a concern for Hegel's overall conception of the task of political philosophy with a concern for the details of the political institutions proposed in the *Philosophy of Right*. This dual emphasis is necessary to fulfill both of the above-mentioned interpretive projects. That is to say, Hegel's grand view of the nature of political philosophy cannot be fully understood without seeing how that view is embodied in the political institutions of the Hegelian state, and the institutions of the Hegelian state cannot be properly understood without reference to the underlying philosophical conceptions that generate them.

An interpretation of Hegel's political philosophy that attempts to do justice to both the macro and micro levels of Hegel's writings needs to be constructed with the help of analytical tools that will both separate and integrate these dimensions, as required in particular contexts. One such distinction is that between the "deep" and "surface" structure of the *Philosophy of Right*.[3] It is both a programmatic work, developing criteria and standards for modern political philosophy, and a pragmatic work, seeking to apply and instantiate those standards. This study attempts in its earlier chapters to articulate the programmatic, deep structure of Hegelian political theory and attempts in its later chapters to use this deep structure as a set of guidelines by which to understand the intentions and specifics of the political structures Hegel discusses. At times, the success of Hegel's political philosophy will be assessed by measuring the latter against the demands of the former.

Method and Substance of the *Philosophy of Right*

For one example of what it means to claim that Hegel's political philosophy has been misinterpreted because non-Hegelian categories are often brought to the interpretation, consider briefly Hegel's much-discussed treatment of the issue of poverty in civil society, a question more fully discussed in Chapter 5. Hegel can be, and has been, correctly criticized for propounding a system that allows such great inequality of wealth to exist. But this line of criticism, as just as it is, is insufficient as an interpretation of Hegel. It does not take into account that the "problem of poverty" from a Hegelian perspective is a problem different from the "problem of poverty" from a liberal or Marxist perspective.

As will be made clear during the course of this study, Hegel's philosophy is in important ways an idealist political philosophy in that its primary concern is with the consciousness of the citizens in the Hegelian state, with their conception of themselves as political agents. But this does not simply assimilate Hegel into the Romantic tradition or into the mold of his German idealist contemporaries, with their emphasis on subjectivity, sentiments, and personal morality as the basis of political life. Although the intention of Hegel's political philosophy is idealist in the sense just described, this idealism goes hand in hand with an analysis that differentiates Hegel from his contemporaries by showing that modern political consciousness grows out of distinct historical, political, and economic processes. To emphasize the distinctly Hegelian nature of Hegel's approach to the problem of poverty is to call attention to Hegel's arguments that the dominant strain of political thought in the modern world has a decidedly economistic, even hedonistic, bent, a bias that Hegel argues is both theoretically and historically insufficient as a basis for political theory.

Furthermore, as we shall see, one of Hegel's primary concerns is to explore the interrelations between the historical and theoretical deficiencies of economistic models of politics. For Hegel, the problem of poverty is not fundamentally that one group does not have the economic goods allotted to another group, but rather that by the standards of self-worth generated by civil society, one group is denied access to a conception of human selfhood and independence deemed necessary by that society. The problem of poverty is for Hegel a problem of creating an adequate political sense of self, not a problem of distributive economic justice. Without the background of Hegel's conception of what the appropriate questions for political philosophy are and with a contemporary concept of "poverty," one can only be baffled by the inadequacy of Hegel's proposed solutions to the problem. With this background, Hegel still remains open to criticism, but to a more informed criticism, a kind of criticism not possible if one remains solely within the framework of the "problem of poverty" as defined by liberal or Marxist notions of the economic responsibilities of the state.

To return to the claim made earlier regarding the necessity of the dual perspective of this study, not only does the general framework of Hegel's thought enter into the interpretation of specific issues in this way, but Hegel's philosophical construction of the *Philosophy of Right*, his claim to have articulated a certain kind of necessary political rationality, cannot be fully understood without seeing how it entails that the strictly economic considerations that arise in the sphere of civil society must be outside the scope of political philosophy per se.

I cited the example above as one case that demonstrates the value of the approach taken in this study. It shows how Hegel can be more clearly under stood by understanding how macro-level questions of Hegel's methodology impinge on micro-level questions of his substantive doctrines. At other points in this study, I will argue the inverse of this thesis—that we gain a clearer understanding of Hegel by seeing when questions of Hegel's methodology should *not* enter into discussions of his doctrines. The most striking example here is the question of Hegel's

relationship to liberalism. The Hegelian political logic is decidedly an-
tiliberal. Hegel in many different ways criticizes the individualism of
liberal accounts of the nature of political life. His thought is totalistic
in that it moves from considerations of the whole to considerations of
the role of the individual in that whole rather than constructing the
whole out of its individual parts.

Hegel's mode of reasoning has wrongly led many to believe that his
system is totalitarian, that he leaves no room for the individual and is
opposed to the classical liberal individual freedoms of thought, expression, assembly, and so on. What has often been missed is that although
Hegel's mode of discussing these freedoms is hostile to the liberal mode,
his conclusions are not hostile to these liberal doctrines, and he does in
fact espouse these freedoms. In this case, questions of method, of competing paradigms of the logic of political discourse, must be carefully
sorted out from questions of political doctrine in much the same way
that contemporary philosophers have learned to distinguish between
metaethical questions about the nature of moral discourse and normative ethical questions about moral actions. Most of Chapters 4 and 5
will be devoted to these questions. In particular, I shall argue that the
Hegelian transition from civil society to the state can be understood as
a kind of perspectival shift from an economic standpoint, which Hegel
criticizes, to a standpoint adequate to political philosophy, and that the
civil society-state relationship in Hegel cannot be properly understood
if one imports the connotations these terms carry in liberal or Marxist
literature.

History and Structure

The earlier chapters of this study examine one crucially important
element in Hegel's philosophical conception of the nature of political
life. We have already mentioned Hegel's criticisms of some of the dominant tendencies of modern political philosophy. Taking note of these
criticisms, many commentators have claimed that Hegel's political philosophy represents a deliberate retreat from modernity, a return to the
classical conceptions of the civic virtue found in an ethical community
as a basis for the political association.

It is vitally important to understand that Hegel would not accept
such a characterization. In his mind, he is not retreating from modernity but revealing hidden undercurrents of modern political life, dimensions of modernity not visible to most people in the modern era
because they all too uncritically accept a modern worldview that is

blind to its own historical presuppositions and components. In Hegel's eyes, his system is not antithetical to but is rather a fulfillment of the historical forces that created the modern political world, although he readily admits that to see this requires a philosophical reinterpretation of those historical forces. Such a reinterpretation is precisely the task of Hegel's philosophy of history, the study of which is a necessary prolegomenon to a proper appreciation of the *Philosophy of Right*. Without this reference to the *Philosophy of History*, Hegel's *Philosophy of Right* necessarily appears as just one individual's quasi-utopian recommendations set up against the recommendations of other thinkers, and Hegel's claims for the necessity of his work cannot be properly evaluated. Not only would this violate the intentions of the *Philosophy of Right* but also it would disregard Hegel's many other references throughout his work to the historical genesis of his system.

An examination of Hegel's philosophy of history and of the distinctive way in which his views on history determine the philosophical structure of the *Philosophy of Right* are the primary concerns of Chapters 1–3. Against views that hold that historical considerations are irrelevant to the substantive or logical content of the *Philosophy of Right* or that the form of logical deduction in which Hegel presents his views is an unfortunate distortion of the material in the text, I shall argue for a strong sense in which Hegel's analysis of history shapes the basic philosophical enterprise of the *Philosophy of Right*. I argue that at key points the form of the work, when correctly understood, significantly illuminates, and is at times a very part of, its doctrines.

It breaks no new ground to show that at certain points the lessons Hegel learns from history affect the content of his political philosophy, as one might do if one were writing an intellectual biography of Hegel. Like most social theorists, Hegel draws conclusions from his analyses of events in the past, such as the deaths of Socrates and Robespierre, conclusions that are integrated into and find expression in certain of his doctrines. What I argue is that Hegel's analysis of historical developments, culminating in the French Revolution and its aftermath, enters into his philosophy in a much more fundamental way, shaping the basic structure and intent of his philosophic system. The key factor in Hegel's analysis of history is his claim that the modern era has come to be essentially characterized by the emergence of a new form of rational, universalist consciousness, which finds expression in the *Philosophy of Right* and the modern attempt to found political institutions on the self-consciousness of the members of those political systems.

The interpretation of Hegel's understanding of the general framework of political discourse in the modern world, which I develop in Chapters 1–3, forms the background for the examination of those sections of the *Philosophy of Right* in which Hegel expounds his own positive political doctrines, which I undertake in Chapters 4–7. There I argue that the guiding feature of Hegelian politics, an essential aspect of what I call Hegel's idealism, is Hegel's attempt to delineate a system of political institutions that progressively engender in the citizens of the Hegelian state an ever-more- conscious awareness of their roles as political agents.

Students of Hegel are aware of the tremendous value he placed on self-consciousness, on the idea that there is intrinsic value in, and one might say an innate drive toward, human beings coming to full consciousness of the totality of their situations.

I shall show that the underlying thrust of the institutions of the Hegelian state is to create in citizens' minds an ever-greater consciousness of the foundations of modern political life, foundations discussed in the earlier parts of both this study and the *Philosophy of Right*, and of their own natures as rational political/historical agents. As the author of a recent book on Hegel's *Philosophy of Right* notes: "The individuals who comprise the state must be in some sense conscious of its rationality. It is, I think, quite remarkable that this feature of Hegel's political thought has been so persistently ignored or underplayed."[4]

The later chapters of this study essentially follow the flow of Hegel's exposition in the *Philosophy of Right*. They can therefore be read as a kind of commentary or guide to the text. The relation of the earlier to the later chapters is in part that of means to ends. Many fundamental philosophical distinctions articulated by Hegel, such as those of reason vs. understanding, logic vs. history, or description vs. prescription, are dealt with only insofar as they have direct bearing on Hegel's political theory. The exposition here makes no claim or attempt to do full justice to the complexities of these issues. I acknowledge that there are other readings of Hegel on these issues. In what follows, I explicitly defend my reading against others only when necessary for my purpose of demonstrating the necessity of understanding Hegel's philosophy of politics as a prerequisite to understanding his political philosophy. For the most part, I take the stance that the proof is in the pudding, so to speak. My principal defense of my reading of Hegel's metatheory in the earlier sections is the sense this reading makes of his political theory in the later sections.

The central "moment" of Hegel's tripartite division of the political realm into the spheres of family, civil society, and state is also the

central focus of this book. As we shall see, for Hegel civil society is the
sphere of life that is new and distinctively modern. It follows for him,
then, that modern political philosophy differs from previous theories
by being distinctively grounded in and concerned with civil society.
Hegel thereby initiates a transformation of political philosophy in which
modern political theory moves toward the social sphere, becoming, as
the field is often designated today, "*social* and political theory."

Hegel conceptualizes this transformation as a product of his historical epoch. The Hegelian concept of *Sittlichkeit*, often translated as
"social ethics" or "ethical community," situates politics in the context
of collective social consciousness. As we shall see in Chapter 6, this
inaugurates a conception of politics today most closely associated with
the writings of Jürgen Habermas, in which the political sphere is seen
as the sphere of conscious, collective, discursive will formation.[5] I call
this focus on the consciousness of the citizens of the state Hegel's political "idealism." The "social-intersubjective" aspect of Hegel's concept
of *Geist* (Spirit), situates this *Sittlichkeit* and "idealism" as historical
creations.[6]

With its emphasis on the social sphere, Hegel's theory leads toward
the "third way" sought for in much contemporary political theory, a
third way between the anarchic individualism of unregulated market
structures and the repressive collectivism of unopposed state power.
The significance of this for the contemporary search for a "third way"
in Eastern Europe is addressed in the concluding chapter. Here, too,
distinguishing Hegel's method from his substantive doctrine is essential
in coming to terms with his theory. Although Hegel's political philosophy has often been criticized as "statist" because the state appears as
the highest embodiment of political rationality, it is in another important sense antistatist in that it shifts the center of gravity of social and
political theory away from the (political) state toward (civil) society,
or at least away from the state as it is conventionally and narrowly
understood.[7]

I have attempted in this study to approach Hegel's political philosophy through a reading of the *Philosophy of Right*, clearly the principal
text for his political philosophy. As I argue in the following pages,
though, I do not believe this text can be entirely severed from other
Hegelian texts, such as the *Phenomenology of Spirit* and the *Science of
Logic*. But I tend to refer to these other works primarily when necessary
to elucidate the *Philosophy of Right*. Although I readily admit that a
full comprehension of Hegel's political philosophy requires greater attention to the interconnections of these texts, I do not pursue these

interconnections here in any systematic way. This study follows the *Philosophy of Right* in that, like the *Philosophy of Right*, it connects Hegel's political philosophy more to the *Philosophy of History* than to any other Hegelian work. A central focus here is an emphasis on the intrinsic interconnection between historical and philosophical argumentation in Hegelian political philosophy, a topic relatively neglected in many studies of Hegel's philosophy, but one essential to understanding Hegel's philosophy and its influence.

The contrast between my treatment and that of other commentators remains for the most part in the background of this work. This is a book on Hegel, not on the history of Hegel interpretations. I have ventured to specifically refute or differentiate my views from those of others only on occasions when I felt some particular view of some commentator had come to so generally infuse the common understanding of Hegel's philosophy that it had to be specifically addressed in order for the reader to be able clearly to entertain my view. Even here, I have been primarily concerned not so much with refuting others as with clearing conceptual space so that I might plausibly present my line of argument, with the reader then enabled to make informed choices between my views and those of others.

Hegel's own introductions have the reputation of being incomprehensible unless one has already read the work being introduced. I hope my own Introduction, with its inescapably high level of generality and sketchiness of detail, is not so true to the problematic aspects of the Hegelian mode that it cannot serve as a useful indication of and guide to what follows.

Notes

1. George H. Sabine, *A History of Political Theory*, 3d ed. (New York: Holt, Rinehart and Winston, 1961), p. 637.

2. Z. A. Pelczynski, in *Hegel's Political Writings*, trans. T. M. Knox (Oxford: Oxford University Press, 1969) (hereafter *Polit.*), p. 136.

3. Cf. Adriaan Peperzak, *Philosophy and Politics: A Commentary on the Preface to Hegel's Philosophy of Right*, (Dordrecht: Martinus Nijhoff, 1987), p. 99: "In the words of the *Philosophy of Right*: the philosophical concept penetrates through the outer surface at which consciousness initially remains and gets down to the rational core (or 'inner pulse'), and only then discovers that 'the infinite wealth of forms, shapes, and appearances' (in spite of all possible criticism) does indeed have its being thanks to that core and its dynamic."

4. Peter J. Steinberger, *Logic and Politics: Hegel's Philosophy of Right* (New Haven: Yale University Press, 1988), p. 209.

5. Richard R. Weiner, *Cultural Marxism and Political Sociology* (Beverly Hills: Sage Publications, 1981).

6. See Robert R. Williams, "Hegel's Concept of Geist," in *Hegel's Philosophy of Spirit*, ed. Peter G. Stillman (Albany: State University of New York Press, 1987), pp. 1–20.

7. See Z. A. Pelczynski on Hegel's concept of the "political state" in "The Hegelian Conception of the State," in *Hegel's Political Philosophy: Problems and Perspectives*, ed. Z. A. Pelczynski (Cambridge: Cambridge University Press, 1971), pp. 1–29.

1

The Historical Basis
of Political Philosophy

It is a commonplace that Hegel incorporated the dimension of historical development into his philosophy to a degree greater than any of his predecessors. It is also generally appreciated that the decisive historical event of his own time that shaped Hegel's thought and with which he struggled to come to terms in his philosophy, and especially in his political philosophy, is the French Revolution. What is often not sufficiently understood is the profound and precise way in which Hegel's analysis of the revolution determined his political thinking. By way of contrast, one may note that Sartre, for example, relates the events of World War II to the development of his philosophy.[1] Yet, in the case of Sartre, although this is an important historical and biographical fact *about* his philosophy, this relationship to a specific historical period is not *part of* his philosophy. The case of Hegel is different. What must be appreciated, and what this study hopes to make clear, is that intrinsic to Hegel's system is a crucial self-conscious reference to the impact of the French Revolution and the kind of philosophy that Hegel insists must consequently be developed in its aftermath.

Many commentators have taken note of the fact that the revolution was important for Hegel. Yet, although there is widespread agreement as to the French Revolution's importance for Hegel's thinking, there is widespread disagreement as to precisely which aspect of Hegel's thought most clearly shows the impact of the events of the revolution. To take some illustrative examples, Steven Smith has seen in Hegel's interpretation of the revolution "an epitaph for republicanism."[2] A long line of differing views precedes him. Georg Lukács stresses Hegel's economic theories as stemming from considerations related to the revolution,[3] while Sidney Hook expounds on Hegel's analysis of the revolution as a litmus test of Hegel's liberalism and connects the topic to the logical categories of Hegel's *Logic*.[4] Herbert Marcuse sees Hegel's credentials as a critical social theorist established here.[5] Jürgen Habermas sees the issue as being Hegel's stance toward political action in general.[6] Others interpret Hegel's stance toward the revolution as a sign of his Prussianism or nationalism.[7] Lewis White Beck stresses the importance of Hegel's Lutheranism and his philosophy of religion in coming to terms with Catholic France.[8] Manfred Riedel brings out connections with Hegel's philosophy of nature,[9] and Joachim Ritter sees the French Revolution as decisive for Hegel's metaphysics.[10]

These examples should suffice to give some indication of the wide and diverse range of topics that could be and have been considered under the rubric "Hegel and the French Revolution." As Stanley Rosen notes: "An adequate discussion of Hegel's attitude toward the French Revolution would encompass his entire teaching."[11]

The aim of this study is to examine the internal appropriation of the revolution by Hegel's political philosophy rather than the external influence of the revolution on that philosophy. Our concern will not be so much with the influence of the revolution on the development of Hegel's thought but rather with the explicit view of the revolution taken by Hegel's mature thought. For that reason, there will be far more references to Hegel's treatment of the revolution in the *Philosophy of Right* than in the *Phenomenology*. It may be well to note also at this point that my chief concern is to elucidate the structure of Hegelian political thought, which allows and necessitates explicit, self-conscious references within that thought to the genesis of that thought in world-historical processes. Consequently, there will be little in the way of an independent evaluation of the accuracy of Hegel's analysis of the revolution and its causes and effects. Such a project, though of obvious importance, falls outside the scope of this study, whose main concern is with Hegel as a philosopher, not as a historian.

Given the thesis that the key to understanding Hegel's political philosophy lies in understanding his philosophical appropriation of the events of the French Revolution, a discussion of his political philosophy must begin with a brief discussion of his philosophy of world history. This discussion must elucidate the way in which history grounds political principles.

The Concept of World History

For Hegel the concept of history as world history has a specific meaning. If we were today to use the terminology of "world history," we would use it rather indiscriminately, as being synonymous with everything that has ever happened on the globe. In this sense, an attempt to give a complete account of world history is obviously doomed to failure—all historical accounts are necessarily incomplete, omitting a great deal. For Hegel, however, the concept of world history arises out of the meaning of events as they are organized in a coherent narrative rather than as they are arranged in a bare succession. Some events are quite definitely more world-historically significant than others, and some do not properly enter into the scope of world history at all.[12] (Biographies of famous figures, for example, are not properly the subject of world history for Hegel. It is important to see that for him this kind of data is omitted for conceptual rather than for merely pragmatic reasons. The unwieldiness or bulk of such a comprehensive history is not the issue here.) One can compose many histories—of particular regions of the world or of particular fields of human endeavor—as Hegel himself presents histories of art, religion, and philosophy. Yet for Hegel none of these merits the title of world history per se; none of these is the focus of the philosophy of history. Only the political history, which we are concerned with here, warrants that distinction. Why?

At the outset of this discussion, Hegel calls attention to the German word *Geschichte* for reasons similar to those that prompt Heidegger to make the same reference a century later—to point out the connection between the objective and subjective components of history. That is, the fact that human beings have an objective history is grounded in the structure of human consciousness such that human beings can abstract themselves from and relate themselves to the world that surrounds them. So far, what we may call Hegel's concept of "historicity" accords with Heidegger's.[13] Yet what remains for Heidegger a purely metaphysical truth that opens up the human being to Being is for Hegel historically-politically grounded. Hegel proceeds to argue that the specific kind of reflection required to provide the motive force of history, as well as the existence of historical chronicles, depends on the existence of a state. This section of the Introduction to the *Philosophy of History*, though somewhat lengthy, is worth repeating here.

In our language the term *history* unites the objective with the subjective side, and denotes quite as much the *historia rerum gestarum*, as the *res gestae* themselves; on the other hand it comprehends not less what has *happened*, than the *narration* of what has happened. This union of the two meanings we must regard as of a higher order than mere outward accident; we must suppose historical narrations to have appeared contemporaneously with historical deeds and events. It is an internal vital principle common to both that produces them synchronously. . . . it is the State which first presents subject-matter that is not only *adapted* to the prose of History, but involves the production of such history in the very progress of its being. Instead of merely subjective mandates on the part of government—sufficing for the needs of the moment—a community that is acquiring a stable existence, and exalting itself into a State, requires formal commands and laws—comprehensive and universally binding prescriptions; and thus produces a record as well as an interest concerned with intelligent, definite—and, in their results—lasting transactions and occurrences.[14]

Historical consciousness revolves around the political sphere because in this sphere a community is created that is conscious of its continuity over time and requires and produces an enduring record of its actions. Hegel is not engaged in reducing all history to political history, nor is he saying that history is simply a record of the intentions of historical agents. Hegel does believe, however, that history as the history of states is the guiding, central thread around which any comprehensive historical account must be organized.

It should be stressed that Hegel claims to be accurately representing historical developments and not presenting a fanciful construction of history. Hegel has on occasion been charged with a willful disregard for historical facts.

The ideas contained in them [Hegel's *Lectures on the Philosophy of History*] clearly came from Hegel's own speculations, not from a close acquaintance with the materials for the history of the periods he is discussing. History is used by him to illustrate, to enforce, to bear out, to "prove" an elaborate theory of world development, a theory peopled and operated by abstract entities. It is not history that Hegel is writing, but philosophical poetry with historical overtones.[15]

As I said earlier, I am not passing judgment on Hegel's expertise as a historian, but I am concerned to maintain that it is history that he is writing and not poetry. Hegel accepts the obligation of demonstrating, by a faithfulness to empirical facts, that the organizing principles he uses to write history are the correct ones and that when properly employed, they produce a coherent and comprehensive account.

The Nature of Historical Analysis

On the one hand, then, Hegel's account of history must be strictly empirical, and he cannot import into this account his own philosophical concepts. But there is another side to the story. A straightforward narrative account, as history is usually conceived, could hardly provide material for a claim that the course of history demands a certain kind of political philosophy. Hegel's account of history, then, must have a decidedly philosophical bent. But does not the idea that history has a specific story to tell (what Hegel calls "the only thought which philosophy brings with it to the contemplation of history"[16]) vitiate Hegel's claim to be an empirical historian and justifiably resurrect the charge that Hegel's *Philosophy of History* is "a priori historiography"? How, then, can these conflicting demands on Hegel's philosophy of history be reconciled? How can an analysis of history be guided by the philosophic commitment to the proposition that the examination of history will yield political principles appropriate to a philosophy that captures the spirit of the current era and at the same time be guided by a scientific commitment to examine the facts of history without prejudice?

The answer to this question depends on the application of a common Hegelian line of argument, articulated also in numerous other contexts in the Hegelian corpus, attacking the idea that there is any such thing as a pure, unmediated empiricism of raw facts.[17] Hegel argues that in order to apprehend the facts, all historians must bring with them their basic concepts of the nature of the historical process. Therefore the discovery of philosophical concepts operating in his philosophy of history cannot be used as an argument against his account in favor of any others. The question of the suitability of his narrative can only be settled by an examination of the narrative itself and not by hurling an a priori charge of unwarranted a priorism at Hegel.

Every historical analysis must have an identifiable object of study, be it the fall of Rome, Italian Renaissance music, the entire scope of Western philosophy, and so on. The question here is how this object of study is apprehended by the historian. It is not the question of what constitutes explanation in history. Hegel is not concerned here with whether an explanation of the French Revolution consists in subsuming it under a general law, or recreating the lived situation of the participants, or picking out antecedent events to create a causal chain. (As far as the latter goes, Hegel's attitude is that it is open to the understanding to choose any of a number of determining factors and designate it as the cause.[18]) Rather, Hegel is directing himself to a prior question. He is calling attention to the fact that all historians would agree that there is such an entity as the French Revolution, which needs to be explained. But by virtue of what is this so? What is the ground of the periodization of history?

We may begin by quoting Hegel's views of this question.

> Now it is at least admitted that a history must have an object, e.g. Rome and its fortunes, or the decline of the grandeur of the Roman Empire. But little reflection is needed to discover that this is the presupposed end which lies at the basis of the events themselves, as of the critical examination into their comparative importance, i.e. their nearer or more remote relation to it. A history without such aim and such criticism would be only an imbecile mental divagation, not as good as a fairy tale, for even children expect a *motif* in their stories, a purpose at least dimly surmiseable with which events and actions are put in relation.[19]

The analyst of history is here patently involved in a circularity. The unity that marks the period as an object of study and is therefore presupposed by the inquiry can, of course, actually be shown to exist only as its result. This circularity, however, is not peculiar to the philosophy of history. It characterizes all subject areas of philosophy. To seek to avoid it is, as Hegel puts it elsewhere, to want to know how to swim before going into the water. The philosophical solution to this problem is that the beginning is therefore provisional. Yet it is not arbitrary. The object of history, whether it be a period of a few years or a few thousand years, possesses a certain internal unity that qualitatively distinguishes it from what precedes and what follows it and gives it its meaning. This decidedly does not mean that nothing at all relevant happened prior to the beginning. There are always, for example, at least climatic or geological circumstances that affect history. The crucial point, however, is that these are of a definitely subordinate nature and do not essentially determine events and cannot be the source of meaning in history.

The passage quoted earlier reveals that for Hegel historical consciousness originated with the formation of states—that is, stable communities concerned with transmitting a permanent collective identity through time in the form of laws and institutions. States are the source of meaning in history and the subjects of the philosophy of history. Although the philosophy of history is concerned with the temporal development of reason in history, a concept designated in the most general way by Hegel's concept of world spirit *(Weltgeist)*, Hegel also maintains that this very general ethos of each historical period must be crystallized, as it were, at one particular spatial location in each epoch. Hegel is not a cosmopolitan in the manner of Kant, for example, and thus even when he is discussing the most general cultural trends of an epoch, he continually returns to examine how these principles are embodied in particular peoples and nations. Despite Hegel's idealist cultural concerns, this principle—that universal values must be particularized into tangible form in individual states—keeps Hegel focused on history as the history of politically organized communities and prevents his philosophy of history from degenerating into a general and diffuse cultural or intellectual history of the world.[20]

A Note on Historicism

Any interpretation of Hegel that stresses the historical dimensions of his thought must come to terms with the specter of "historicism," with all its multiple, nefarious connotations, which has come to loom over the history of Hegel interpretation. We have already discussed Hegel's responses to some epistemological objections to some versions of historicism, which argue against the possibility of attributing any purpose or meaning to history.[21] We must now address some common ethical and political objections to historicism. One sense of historicism that leads many to criticize any theory labeled historicist is the claim that historicism is necessarily historical relativism and therefore moral relativism. The charge is that one is here restricting oneself to the internal standards of any given period or system, and one therefore has no standpoint from which to mount any critique.

Hegel's response to this line of criticism is embedded in his notion of immanent, or internal, dialectical critique, paradigmatically expressed in the *Phenomenology*. There, every form of consciousness is tested against its own criteria of truth. Hegel's analysis reveals that every form of consciousness presents not only its form of knowing but also its criteria for evaluating its knowing, by which it claims to demonstrate the adequacy, that is, the veracity and completeness, of its knowledge. Hegel believes that those who argue that internal critique cannot be fully critical are ignoring the fact that every form of consciousness is also a form of self-consciousness. Hegel argues that they have a one-dimensional understanding of the nature of consciousness, as opposed to Hegel's philosophy, which captures the self-reflective nature of consciousness. Hegel plays off each form of consciousness against its own criteria of truth in order to reveal its inadequacies and contradictions.[22]

What prevents this from being simply a form of relativism is Hegel's contention that each form of consciousness' criteria for truth makes claims to be valid not only for that form of consciousness "in itself" *(ansich)* but also universally *(für uns;* that is, for philosophical consciousness). Every form of consciousness partakes of the universal in that it universalizes its own standards, claiming universal validity for them. Internal critique is thereby simultaneously external critique made from the standpoint of universal truths. This doubled vision is how the *Phenomenology*'s ladder to absolute knowledge can be at the same time both "phenomenology" and "science."

In its appropriation of history Hegel's political philosophy replaces the *Phenomenology*'s criteria of truth with criteria of freedom. We shall see shortly how and why Hegel believes that the contemporary period has reached adequate, universally valid conceptions of freedom. Suffice it to say here that, in analogous fashion to the *Phenomenology*, when judging an age on its own terms, Hegel is also judging it against his contemporary philosophical concept of freedom, which finds previous forms inadequate. Thus his philosophy of history and the political philosophy that follows from it can be both historically based and critical.

Even if one grants that the reasons just discussed are sufficient to grant plausibility to the project of basing a political philosophy on an analysis of history, recognizing that the precise way in which Hegel's theory arises out of historical processes has yet to be established, those critical of Hegel on this point still claim to have grounds for not accepting his theory. The above line of reasoning, if accepted, may grant plausibility to the general sort of reasoning Hegel invokes. But some of Hegel's pronouncements on the embodiment of spirit in history raise the issue of acquiescence to that which is in particularly acute form and seem to belie any truly critical intent. Can the interpretation just offered of Hegel as a critical theorist be maintained in the face of some of his most apparently conservative pronouncements?

A reading of modern discussions of this issue reveals that Joachim Ritter's essay on "Hegel and the French Revolution," published in 1957, was decisive in establishing a frame of reference for subsequent discussion of the issue. For example, Jürgen Habermas's essay on Hegel and the French Revolution is expressly written to "amplify"[23] Ritter's thesis, and Manfred Riedel refers to Ritter's work as *grundsätzlich*[24] ("fundamental"). The thrust of Ritter's essay is to disengage the discussion of Hegel's stance toward the politics of his day from the level of bandying about specific utterances of Hegel on particular political ideas and to move the discussion to look at the intention of Hegel's political thinking as a whole, with particular attention to the broad question of how Hegel conceives of the relationship between philosophy and politics. Ritter attempts to penetrate to the core of the objections to Hegel's subsumption of political philosophy under a metaphysical theory. It is Hegel's willingness to attach ethical, religious, and metaphysical significance to state power—his "deification" and "absolutization" of the state—that fundamentally gives rise to his being branded "reactionary" or "totalitarian." Because the context in which Hegel makes these pronouncements is not that of his critics, and especially because this difference has not been perceived by those critics, Hegel's remarks here have often been misinterpreted.

Much of the criticism of Hegel as conservative centers on his dictum that the task of philosophy is to comprehend "that which is." Ritter maintains that this is conservative only on a historicist reading of what is meant by "that which is," where it then implies that Hegel counsels reconciliation to everything that exists. But Ritter emphasizes the metaphysical background of Hegel's thinking, along the lines of Hegel's own elaboration of this remark in the *Encyclopaedia of the Philosophical Sciences*,[25] to recall that "that which is," for Hegel, "is reason," in precisely the same sense that the rationalist philosophical tradition since the Greeks has always maintained that it is the rational structure of the world that gives it its substantial reality and that historical, contingent realities are at best secondary in comparison to this.[26] Hegel thus follows the philosophical tradition in operating from the hypothesis that the truths of reason will become manifest during the course of his investigations. It is precisely here that he raises the ire of his liberal critics. For these critics share the assumption that modern society makes about itself, namely, that the most important thing about modernity is that it has won its liberation from past, antiquated notions of metaphysical truth and finds its fulfillment in its freedom from tradition. Hegel's political philosophy, in its attempt to understand modern political society in continuity with, and with the concepts of, the historical-philosophical tradition, flies in the face of the deepest self-image of the age. It is this challenge to the basic self-understanding of modern society, rather than any specific political opinion of Hegel's, that motivates the attack on Hegel at its most fundamental level.

Hegel is aware that this leaves him in a seemingly paradoxical position. Although he claims to justify his philosophy on the grounds that it conceptually comprehends the spirit of his time, he is also aware that his philosophy runs into conflict with the dominant self-understanding of the time. In the effort to firmly ground Hegel's philosophy in his analysis of history we will emphasize how Hegel's views on modern political theory and practice rest on his analysis of contemporary consciousness. Yet we must guard against the danger of taking this in too strong a sense. For, the question arises, if this way of viewing world affairs is in truth the contemporary worldview, would it not then follow that everyone was already thinking this way? In which case, far from a philosophy of right being necessary, it would turn out to be superfluous?

But it would be an error to suppose that Hegel is simply transcribing the prevalent patterns of contemporary thought. Rather, Hegel first has to filter out that which is true in contemporary consciousness from that which is false. "What lies between reason as self-conscious mind and reason as an actual world before our eyes, what separates the former from the latter and prevents it from finding satisfaction in the latter, is the fetter of some abstraction or other which has not been liberated (and so transformed) into the concept."[27]

Philosophy and Right

The first task of the *Philosophy of Right*, the most comprehensive, systematic exposition of Hegel's political thought, is therefore a negative one—to rid the mind of abstractions that, though admittedly founded in certain aspects of ethical practice, nevertheless intervene between that mind and the objective world and prevent the reason of the former from recognizing itself in the latter. This task is the function of the first two parts of the *Philosophy of Right* ("Abstract Right" and "Morality"). These sections are methodological fictions, designed to show that these abstract standpoints in themselves lead to dead ends, but that they also open up onto the concrete starting point. This is why the third section ("Ethical Life") appears as a new beginning, as well as a result of the earlier sections. It is in truth the first real beginning.[28]

The political issue here is the ambiguous character of public opinion. When we come to examine the role of public opinion in the proper functioning of the state, we shall see that the role of the conscientious politician vis-a-vis public opinion is analogous with that of the philosopher vis-a-vis ordinary consciousness— not only in the sense that each must bring to universal form those aspects of their objects that are of lasting value but dispersed amidst the profusion of transitory opinions, but also that their activities have an educational character, conducted with an eye toward pedagogical effectiveness. The theme of education figures prominently in Hegel's political theory. The educative character of civil society makes possible the transition from civil society to the state, from political economy to political philosophy.

> In these circumstances (civil society), the interest of the Idea—an interest of which these members of civil society are as such unconscious—lies in the process whereby their singularity and their natural condition are raised, as a result of the necessities imposed by nature as well as by arbitrary needs, to formal freedom and formal universality of knowing and willing—the process whereby their particularity is educated up to subjectivity.[29]

Here we also find the theme of a necessary connection between philosophy and the state. Philosophy is practiced in and receives support from public institutions (the universities) in contrast to, for example, the Greeks, for whom philosophy was a private affair. The state cannot be indifferent to philosophy because there exists in the state "a need for a deeper education and insight, a need which the state required philosophical science to satisfy."[30] Philosophy is to serve the state, not in the form of obedience or subservience, but in the form of adherence to its own nature, insofar as both philosophy and the state embody principles of rationality. This is reflected in the pedagogical character of the *Philosophy of Right* as a whole, which is structured so as to lead ordinary consciousness to a philosophic standpoint. In this respect, it is more akin to the *Phenomenology* than to any of the other works that Hegel himself published. This is what prompts the inclusion in the *Philosophy of Right* of a discussion of the actual stages of history, which was omitted in the *Encyclopaedia* treatment of the same subject matter, for this elaboration helps to elucidate the process of the formation of consciousness.

This study concentrates on the positive exposition of Hegel's philosophy in the third part of the *Philosophy of Right* and not on his attempt to lead ordinary consciousness out of the morass of incompletely formed conceptions. There are two reasons for this. In the first place, although it may be true that we are no less under the spell of uncritical consciousness than those of Hegel's generation, nevertheless the specific content of our misleading ideas is different from that of previous times, and Hegel's points of reference here can no longer have the same philosophic impact. In the second place, and much more pragmatically, to do justice to the earlier sections of the *Philosophy of Right* would make the present study of unmanageable size, because this would require not only extended commentary in itself but, as indicated above, would also require for a contemporary audience a prior summary of those views that Hegel is opposing. This would be especially true of any attempt to construct a dialogue between Hegel and earlier political theorists who take the findings of political economy as their basis. What would complicate the exposition here is that while this tendency is more familiar to an English- speaking audience in its original English form, where the economic base of the theory is more explicit (for example, Hobbes, Locke), Hegel has in mind its later, continental form, in which the formation of the political sphere comes more to the foreground (for example, Rousseau, Kant, Fichte). We will, therefore, concentrate our efforts on the explication of Hegel's own position, and his criticisms of other views will be referred to only as an aid to the understanding of Hegel.

A similar limitation will be applied to the examination of Hegel's *Philosophy of History*. There is ample precedent and justification for the procedure followed here of treating Hegel's lectures on the philosophy of history as an elaboration of the section on world history in the *Philosophy of Right*, because they correspond on all essential points.[31] But we will be subjecting to close scrutiny only that section dealing with the modern world, because the primary thesis we wish to propound is that the *Philosophy of Right* receives its fundamental determinations from this analysis. Here only the pragmatic justification for this restriction can be fully defended. An attempt to trace the whole course of history would again make this study too unwieldy, yet we do carry our history with us in a more fundamental sense than we carry inadequate, though previously popular, philosophical theories with us. Although this study would certainly be enriched by extending our problematic back through the philosophy of history (demonstrating how, for example, on Hegel's analysis the immediate unity of Greek political life is mirrored in Plato's thought), such an inquiry is beyond the scope of this investigation.

As we shall see, although Hegel does indeed claim to abide by and base his theory on the fundamental principles of the modern era, he will also argue that these principles are incorrectly understood by modern consciousness. The next chapter will be devoted to an exposition of Hegel's analysis of the distinctive form of modern politics ushered in by the French Revolution. We shall examine what he finds these basic principles to be and how these principles lead him to conclude that the satisfaction of the demands of modern political consciousness requires a political philosophy in the style of the *Philosophy of Right*, showing how Hegel turns the acceptance of these basic principles into the grounds for an internal critique of the self- understanding of the epoch in a way that allows him to develop a critique of modernity. The later chapters will show how the political principles that emerge from this analysis of modern political life are systematically applied in Hegel's presentation of the dialectics of civil society and the state.

Notes

1. Jean-Paul Sartre, "An Interview (1970)," in *Phenomenology and Existentialism*, ed. Robert C. Solomon (New York: Harper and Row, 1972), pp. 511-513.

2. Steven B. Smith, "Hegel and the French Revolution: An Epitaph for Republicanism," *Social Research* 56:1, Spring 1989, pp. 233-261.

3. Georg Lukács, *The Young Hegel*, trans. Rodney Livingstone (London: Merlin Press, 1975).

4. Sidney Hook, "Hegel Rehabilitated" and "Hegel and His Apologists," in *Hegel's Political Philosophy*, ed. Walter Kaufmann (New York: Atherton Press, 1970); "Hegel and the Perspective of Liberalism," in *A Hegel Symposium*, ed. D. C. Travis (Austin: University of Texas Press, 1962).

5. Herbert Marcuse, *Reason and Revolution: Hegel and the Rise of Social Theory* (Boston: Beacon Press, 1960).

6. Jürgen Habermas, "Hegel's Critique of the French Revolution," in *Theory and Practice*, trans. John Viertel (Boston: Beacon Press, 1974).

7. See the essays by Knox and Carritt in Kaufmann, *Hegel's Political Philosophy*.

8. Lewis White Beck, "The Reformation, the Revolution, and the Restoration in Hegel's Political Philosophy," *Journal of the History of Philosophy* 14:1, January 1976, pp. 51-61.

9. Manfred Riedel, *Theorie und Praxis im Denken Hegels* (Frankfurt am Main: Ullstein, 1976); *Bürgerliche Gesellschaft und Staat bei Hegel* (Neuwied: Luchterland, 1970) (chap. 2 and part of chap. 3 translated as "Nature and Freedom in Hegel's Philosophy of Right," in *Hegel's Political Philosophy*, ed. Z. A. Pelczynski (Cambridge: Cambridge University Press, 1971).

10. Joachim Ritter, *Hegel und die französische Revolution, Arbeitsgemeinschaft für Forschung Des Landes Nordrhein-Westfallen* (Geisteswissenschaften Heft 63, Köln und Opladen, Westdeutscher Verlag, 1957) (reprinted in *Metaphysik und Politik* [Frankfurt am Main: Suhrkamp, 1977]).

11. Stanley Rosen, *G.W.F. Hegel: An Introduction to the Science of Wisdom* (New Haven: Yale University Press, 1974), p. 13.

12. Cf. Walter Jaeschke, "World History and the History of Absolute Spirit," in *History and System: Hegel's Philosophy of History*, ed. Robert L. Perkins (Albany: State University of New York Press, 1984), pp. 101-121.

13. Cf. Martin Heidegger, *Being and Time*, trans. John Macquarrie and Edward Robinson (New York: Harper and Row, 1962), pt. 2, chap. 5. The similarity is also noted by Alexandre Kojève, *Introduction to the Reading of Hegel*, trans. James H. Nichols, Jr., ed. Allan Bloom (New York: Basic Books, 1969), p. 259. See Michael Allen Gillespie, *Hegel, Heidegger, and the Ground of History* (Chicago: University of Chicago Press, 1984).

14. G.W.F. Hegel, *Philosophy of History*, trans. J. Sibree (New York: Dover Publications, 1956) (hereafter *PH*), pp. 60–61. See Stephen Houlgate, "World History as the Progress of Consciousness: An Interpretation of Hegel's Philosophy of History," *Owl of Minerva* 22:1, Fall 1990, pp. 69–80.

15. Charles W. Cole, "The Heavy Hand of Hegel," in *Nationalism and Internationalism: Essays Inscribed to Carlton J. H. Hayes*, ed. Edward Mead Earle (New York: Columbia University Press, 1950), p. 69.

16. *PH*, p. 9.

17. Cf. Steven B. Smith, "Hegel's Idea of a Critical Theory," *Political Theory* 15:1, February 1987, pp. 99–126.

18. G.W.F. Hegel, *Philosophy of Right*, trans. T. M. Knox (London: Oxford University Press, 1971) (hereafter *PR*), §115A, p. 79.

19. G.W.F. Hegel, *Philosophy of Mind*, trans. William Wallace (Oxford: Clarendon Press, 1973) (hereafter *PM*), §549, p. 279.

20. See Raymond Polin, "Philosophie du Droit et philosophie de l'Histoire chez Hegel d'après les Principes de la philosophie du Droit' de 1821," in *Hegel: L'Esprit Objectif: L'Unité de L'Histoire* (Lille: Actes du IIIème Congrès International de l'association Internationale pour l'étude de la philosophie de Hegel, 1968).

21. See Maurice Mandelbaum, *History, Man, and Reason: A Study in Nineteenth-Century Thought* (Baltimore: Johns Hopkins Press, 1971).

22. See Steven B. Smith, "Hegel's Idea of a Critical Theory," *Political Theory* 15:1, February 1987, pp. 99–126.

23. Habermas, *Theory and Practice*, p. 121.

24. Riedel, *Theorie und Praxis im Denken Hegels*, p. 89.

25. G.W.F. Hegel, *The Encyclopaedia of the Philosophical Sciences*, pt. I, *Logic*, trans. William Wallace (Oxford: Oxford University Press, 1972) (hereafter *Enc. I*), §6, pp. 9–12.

26. Ritter, *Metaphysik und Politik*, p. 189.

27. *PR*, Preface, p. 12.

28. This position is also put forth by K.-H. Ilting. See "The Structure of Hegel's Philosophy of Right," in Pelczynski, ed., *Hegel's Political Philosophy*. For Hegel on morality, see Allen W. Wood, *Hegel's Ethical Thought* (Cambridge: Cambridge University Press, 1990).

29. *PR*, §187, pp. 124–125.

30. *Ibid.*, Preface, p. 8.

31. In his introduction to the four-volume edition of Hegel's *Vorlesungen über Rechts-philosophie* (Cannstatt: Stuttgart-Bad, Frommann-Holzboog Verlag, Stuttgart-Bad, 1973) (hereafter Ilting), K.-H. Ilting makes an even stronger case for according Hegel's lecture remarks equal status with the published *Philosophy of Right*. He bases his contention primarily on the publication of the *Philosophy of Right* under the Karlsbad censorship decrees and the status of the lectures as Hegel's "last words" on the subject, because he continued to give these lectures after the book was published.

2

The Philosophical Politics
of Modernity

The Present Age Characterized

In the concluding paragraphs of the *Philosophy of History*, Hegel presents a list of "the leading features in the political condition of Germany." At the end of this list, we find the statement: "This is the point which consciousness has attained." This list, then, reflects Hegel's own characterization of the most important features of the consciousness of the modern world in his own time. An analysis of Hegel's views on the politics of his era may well begin with a consideration of these factors and ask whether they share or reflect any fundamental principles. We will begin by simply stating these factors in Hegel's own terms and seek to translate them into more familiar idioms as we proceed. These factors are:

1. The existence of a code of rights.
2. Freedom of property and persons recognized as fundamental principles.
3. Offices of state open to every citizen, conditional only on talent and adaptation.
4. Government resting with official bodies, with the personal decision of the monarch being at the apex of that government, whose real strength, however, lies in the rationality incorporated in it.
5. A share in the government for all with competent knowledge, experience, and a morally regulated will.
6. The reconciliation of religion and legal right created by a religious conscience (that is, Protestantism) not hostile toward the state.[1]

The first four of these features of modern political consciousness are concerned with the institutions and laws of the state. These secure

objective freedom and embody what to Hegel are the principles of the
universality and rationality of the modern state. The last two considerations relate to Hegel's doctrine of subjective freedom, which addresses
the consciousness of the individuals within the political system.

Some general remarks about the Hegelian concepts of rationality,
universality, and subjectivity are in order here. Hegel is critical of any
kind of instrumentalist concept of reason that limits reason to a function of calculating means to the satisfaction of given ends. Hegel stands
in a rationalist philosophical tradition (along with, for example, Plato,
Spinoza, Kant) that closely ties the concept of rationality (as well as
the concept of freedom) to the idea of explicit self-determination. Rationality for Hegel has to do with the conscious determination of ends,
not the calculation of means. For Hegel to attribute full rationality to
the political sphere means that for him politics essentially involves the
highest kind of human self-determination.

I shall argue later that this entails that the kinds of arguments often
given for the grounds of the political association—arguments that tie
political life to the satisfaction of material interests—are insufficient
once one accepts this notion of rationality. For the moment, it suffices
to note the link between rationality and self-consciousness in Hegel's
thought, which goes to the heart of what I call Hegel's political idealism. It is a link that is manifest in Hegel's philosophy of history, where
the hypothesis of a rational structure to history is in part validated
by demonstrating that people and institutions in succeeding historical
periods display increasingly greater consciousness of their freedom. It
is also much in evidence in the prominence in the Hegelian state of institutions that promote citizens' involvement with the political process
rather than institutions that regulate social life independently of the
will and consciousness of the citizens.

Hegel's notion of the universality of modern political life has both
negative and positive moments. Negatively, it comes to mean that factors of birth, wealth, or belief should not impinge on political rights
(principles 2 and 3 of the six listed above). Positively, it requires that
political principles be embodied in an objective, impartially admin-
istered code of laws, not dependent on the private opinions of public
officials (principles 1 and 4 of the six above). These laws must be based
on the recognition of the rights of human beings as such and not on
special privileges attaching to any group or groups.

The political implications of Hegel's concept of universality are more
immediately obvious in the original German than in English transla-
tions. As Merold Westphal notes: "English loses etymological linkages

which are visible and audible in German between universality (*Allge-meinheit*), community (*Gemeinschaft*), and congregation (*Gemeinde*). Since Hegel takes these linkages very seriously, true universality never signifies for him abstract similarity but always concrete participation in some actual totality."[2]

Modern Rational and Universal Consciousness

All of these features of the Hegelian state must be, at least in principle, explicit to the citizens of the Hegelian state and not merely intrinsic to the system. This is the principal political consequence of Hegel's doctrine of subjective freedom, the idea that people must be aware that their freedom stems from the freedom of their own will. The citizens of the Hegelian state must come to identify with the institutions of the Hegelian state as a reflection of their own rationality. This does not mean that every individual must have a decisive say in political affairs. As we shall see, this is the kind of radical misinterpretation of what to Hegel is a sound principle of subjectivity that he links to the Terror that followed the French Revolution. Nor does it mean that an emotional, spiritual identification with the state is the basis for politics. For Hegel, subjective freedom follows the institutionalization of objective freedom, not the reverse. To understand this is again to remove some of the totalitarian overtones that have accrued to Hegel's political philosophy. Subjective freedom does entail for Hegel a certain kind of identification of one's self with the political process—but it is an identification ultimately justified by the rationality of political institutions rather than by the act of identification itself.

Hegel's most general way of referring to the emergence of the principles of rationality, universality, and subjective freedom as characteristic of the modern world is in reference to the progressive development of the realm of spirit (*Geist*) through history as it wins its freedom from its natural origins. "The history of the world is the discipline of the uncontrolled natural will, bringing it into obedience to a universal principle and conferring subjective freedom. The East knew and to the present day knows only that one is free; the Greek and Roman world, that some are free; the German world knows that *all* are free."[3]

At the core of modern political theory and practice, argues Hegel, lie the principles that political life must in some way be based on the consciousness of human beings as such in the modern era and that these principles must be embodied in public laws and codes. This leads Hegel to reject as entirely inappropriate and insufficient for a modern political philosophy several different kinds of paradigms for political thinking that had previously been advanced. He explicitly rejects as candidates for the foundations of political theory an appeal to tradition or custom as justifying a political practice or institution, as in the patriarchalist tradition of paternal authority in the family being extended to provide a justification for political authority; or an appeal to religion, as in the standard arguments for the divine rights of kings; or an appeal to feelings or sentiments, as in romantic arguments that base the coherence of the body politic on supposed instincts for social solidarity or an intuitive moral rectitude; or an appeal to analogies with nature, as in attempts to ground property rights in natural, biological needs. Only universal principles rationally arrived at can satisfy the demands of modern political consciousness.

A crucial consequence follows: In modern times concepts and theories play an unprecedentedly active and important role in political affairs. "The consciousness of the spiritual is now the essential basis of the political fabric, and *Philosophy* has therefore become dominant."[4]

The French Revolution received its inspiration and impetus from philosophy (though in a decidedly qualified sense, as we shall see later). The revolution was primarily responsible for bringing to the world recognition of the importance of the role of thought in political life. As Hegel expresses it in the oft-quoted passage from the *Philosophy of History*:

> Never since the sun had stood in the firmament and the planets revolved around him had it been perceived that man's existence centers in his head, i.e., in thought, inspired by which he builds up the world of reality. Anaxagoras had been the first to say that *nous* governs the world, but not until now had man advanced to the recognition of the principle that thought ought to govern spiritual reality. This was accordingly a glorious mental dawn.[5]

The introduction to the historical scene of the principle that the social world is to be ordered according to the dictates of reason marks a decisive watershed in history from which there can be no regression to previous eras, according to Hegel. The spirit of the time has elevated itself to the level of the universal, and only truths presented in this form will now be accepted.

This creates the need for a political philosophy in a particularly acute way. Although it remains true that every age has its political philosophy, only in the modern age does the demand for a political philosophy—that is, the demand that political principles be expressed in solely rational, universal form—stem from the nature of the political sphere itself. The need for a philosophy of right is now no longer simply a philosophical requirement (for example, in response to the demands for systematization made by the philosopher) but is now a political requirement as well.

> In modern time general principles rule. . . . In as much as it is the culture of the time which has elevated itself to this form, it is an especial need of thought to know and conceptualize the right. Thought, then, has raised itself to the essential form, and the right must also be grasped this way (as thought).[6]

> Law must be known by thought, it must be a system in itself, and only as such can it be recognized in a civilised country. . . . It is just systematization, i.e., elevation to the universal, which our time is pressing for without any limits.[7]

Form and Method in the *Philosophy of Right*

This brings us to the single most important characteristic of Hegel's *Philosophy of Right*—that feature of the book that Hegel himself says is the most important aspect of the work but that has been either ignored or misunderstood since his time. This critical factor is the *form* of the *Philosophy of Right*. In Hegel's own words: "the whole, like the formation of its parts, rests on the logical spirit. It is also from this point of view above all that I should like my book to be taken and judged. What we have to do with here is philosophical *science*, and in such science content is essentially bound up with form."[8]

This remark is usually taken to be a declaration by Hegel that he is more concerned with his metaphysical philosophic system than with the subject matter of politics in this work. Reaction to this stance then ranges from the attempt to simply disregard the form of the work and extract some content from it (typical of the English-language commentators on Hegel mentioned in the Introduction);[9] to an acceptance of this stance at its face value, coupled with the evaluation that Hegel was right that he was primarily a metaphysician and that his system cannot and should not be applied to actual political questions; to the judgment that whatever valid political insights Hegel may have had are obliterated by his commitment to his philosophic system (the most well known such critique is, of course, that of Marx).[10]

Situating this remark in the context of Hegel's analysis of his historical period suggests another reading of what is meant by the statement that the form of the work is its most important aspect. This analysis suggests that rather than being a departure from the realm of actual political practice into the abstract realm of a philosophic system, this perspective is Hegel's deepest response to the political conditions of his time. On his analysis, these conditions demand precisely such a systematic presentation of political principles.

Hegel on many occasions stresses that his system is in its entirety a historical product (see, for example, the preface to the *Phenomenology* or the introduction to *Lectures on the History of Philosophy*). The uniqueness of Hegel's period, such that it could generate a philosophic system like Hegel's and the age's and his system's claims to absolute knowledge, lies in this period having reached a point at which universal principles are the guiding ones of the era. Hence contemporary politics is more self-consciously guided by universal principles and ideals than at any other time.

Much the same sort of interpretive error, again mistaking a historical for an atemporal truth, is often made in comments regarding another remark made by Hegel in an aphorism relevant to the discussion here. In the preface to the *Philosophy of Right* Hegel says, "What is rational is actual and what is actual is rational."

This, too, is often taken as a glaring example of the unwarranted intrusion of metaphysical absolutism into political theory, as representing a glorification and sanctification of given reality. Misinterpretations of Hegel could have been avoided were this sentence only read in conjunction with the immediately following one: "On this conviction the plain man like the philosopher takes his stand, and from it philosophy starts in its study of the universe of mind as well as the universe of nature."[11]

Because Hegel is well aware that ordinary people do not take their stand on the basis of the abstruse doctrines of Hegelian metaphysics, these doctrines cannot be what is at issue here. Rather, Hegel is attacking those who would look for reason in the scientific study of nature but would surrender the social realm to the workings of opinion, caprice, chance, and feelings. His point is that he, as well as the ordinary person in modern times, would insist on the idea of political rationality, on the importance of searching for rational principles manifestly operating in the spiritual and political world. What seems like an abstract metaphysical remark is grounded in an analysis of contemporary consciousness.

This is extremely important for the understanding of Hegel's philosophy. Much is often made of the formal or transcendental nature of Hegel's dialectical method, and it is often suggested that Hegelian philosophy demands the application of this same method at all times.

But our analysis here suggests rather that to understand Hegel, and especially to continue to philosophize in a Hegelian tradition, is to understand that this philosophizing is not simply a matter of applying a method, be Hegel's method described as dialectical, phenomenological, or whatever, but rather allowing the method itself to be formulated on the basis of one's analysis of one's own historical period, with a view toward responding to the most deeply experienced spiritual needs of that period. To interpret Hegel's dictum that "philosophy is its own time apprehended in thought" without taking into account what can be called this historical deduction of Hegel's transcendental method belies the vitality of his thought. The very structure of his thought is explicitly formulated in the spirit of the time.

For this reason, the philosophical form of the *Philosophy of Right* is definitely not extraneous to the subject of the work. In a real sense, the form *is* the content of the *Philosophy of Right*, in that the form of the book presents a political system developed solely from a philosophic analysis of the concept of right. This form thus gives voice to the basic premise of Hegel's political philosophy, namely, that the political principles of the modern era must be developed solely from reason.

The task of Hegel's *Philosophy of Right* is thus to develop what might be called a logic of political life that elaborates the rational structure of present political institutions and practices. This account must not only satisfy the criteria of universality and rationality but also must meet the other criterion for an acceptable political philosophy in the modern era, namely, the demand for subjective freedom. This component of modern consciousness is reflected in the last two of the six features of modern political conditions with which this chapter began, and to which we may now turn.

The Concepts of Right and Will

The principle of subjective freedom antedates the French Revolution. It makes its first, prefigurative appearance in Christianity but only really enters the social and political world with the advent of the German Reformation. For Hegel, Christianity establishes the principle that human beings are free in their inner essence, simply as human beings. In what Hegel uses as an example of the long time span it may take for an idea to work itself out in history, he notes that it took until the time of the Reformation for this principle to be applied to the social and political world.[12]

The political consequences of this principle are that the objective, intrinsic rationality of political institutions must also be part and parcel of the consciousness of the citizens. The citizens of the modern state must be able to affirm that they have freely chosen those activities that they pursue in accordance with the laws of the state, in whose rationality they find their own reflected. The laws and institutions of the state must be seen as stemming from the consciousness of its members, not externally imposed.

Applied to the philosophical political project of the *Philosophy of Right*, this means that not only must the concepts of the *Philosophy of Right* be systematically developed from reason alone but they must also be concepts that develop from the experiential consciousness of individuals in the modern era. The conceptual development of the *Philosophy of Right* must be demonstrably immanent to consciousness. This is the underlying reason for the *Philosophy of Right* beginning with an explication of the structure of individual consciousness and only arriving at the level of social consciousness through the contradictions generated at this earlier level. The development of political concepts must begin with the starting point of natural, individual consciousness.

Here, too, the choice of starting point is dictated by historical, not atemporal, standards. A philosophy that seeks to be true to, and therefore accepted by, contemporary consciousness must begin its phenomenological description of experience with what contemporary consciousness will recognize as a legitimate starting point. We begin with what appears to modern consciousness as the indisputable, immediate self-certainty of the individual natural will, because modern consciousness takes this as its obvious starting point for philosophical discussion. In the important interpretation of the *Phenomenology* by Alexandre Kojève, history is said to enter the *Phenomenology* only with the dialectic of lordship and bondage.[13] This interpretation must be severely qualified. Although it may be said that history only enters explicitly into the *Phenomenology* at that point, we must also say that the absence of history at the outset is itself a historical phenomenon. It is Hegel's bow to the ahistorical consciousness of his historical period.

The *Philosophy of Right*, then, must proceed via the unfolding of a concept that can fulfill both the objective and subjective requirements of modern political consciousness—a concept that is at the same time both universal and immanent to consciousness. Hegel finds such a concept in the concept of the free will.

The concept of right has its "point of origin"[14] in the concept of the will. The will is the form that thought takes as it is oriented toward acting in the world, for the will and thinking "are surely not two faculties: the will is rather a special way of thinking, thinking translating itself into existence, thinking as the urge to give itself existence."[15]

For further elaboration of the philosophical background of this concept of the will, Hegel refers the reader to his *Encyclopaedia*. There one finds the concept of the will situated as an aspect of mind. More specifically, the concept of the will is situated as the transition between the concepts of cognition and volition.[16] As such, Hegel can develop this concept in a way that allows him to mediate what to his mind are two distinct tendencies in the history of ethical and political philosophy—on the one hand, an objectivist, cognitivist, universalist approach and, on the other hand, a subjectivist, voluntarist, particularist approach to the problem of the freedom of the will.

In what, then, does the freedom of the will consist? One answer is that given by Kantian ethical theory, according to which the freedom of the will lies in its ability to abstract from all determinations, to be purely by itself. This is the universality of the will. "The will contains (a) the element of pure indeterminancy or that pure reflection of the ego into itself which involves the dissipation of every restriction and every content either immediately presented by nature, by needs, desires, and impulses, or given and determined by any means whatsoever. This is the unrestricted infinity of absolute abstraction or universality, the pure thought of oneself."[17]

On this account, the freedom of the individual lies in the universality of the individual will. But the problem of characterizing the freedom of the will appears at the level of political theorizing about society as a whole as well. Here, the problem is one of characterizing and identifying the locus of the general will. The general will determines the collective identity of the social whole. Put another way, the general will is that in virtue of which a society finds its identity as a particular society and is able to act as a unit.

Here, too, a universalist and a particularist strain emerge from the history of philosophy. The universalist approach to this problem is best exemplified by Plato's philosopher-ruler or Rousseau's legislator. Here, a society receives its identity and freedom through an individual or group freed from the particularist concerns of those within the body politic. By virtue of this removal from the realm of the particular, these individuals or groups gain access to universal insights into the nature of the society and are then free to act accordingly.

The other answer to the problem of the freedom of the will is that adopted by empirical psychology at the level of the individual and by

liberal, majoritarian-democratic political theory at the level of society.
According to this tendency, the will is free because of its determinacy,
its ability to choose any one particular. "(b) At the same time, the
ego is also the transition from undifferentiated indeterminacy to the
differentiation, determination, and positing of a determinacy as a content and object. . . . This is the absolute moment, the finitude or
particularization of the ego."[18]

Here, my personal freedom lies in my ability to freely choose among
any of a range of choices presented to me. At the social level, the
general will is held to emerge out of the summation and reconciliation
of particular wills of individuals in the body politic. No individual or
group is held to have any special universal or rational insight into the
structure of the whole, nor is it even necessary or desirable that any
individual or group enjoy this capacity.

Hegel opts for neither of these positions but rather attempts to synthesize these two strains into a concept of the rational will that preserves what is valid in each conception. The unity of these two moments
produces a concept of true individuality (that is, individuality according to its concept, as the mediation of universality and particularity).[19]
"(c) The will is the unity of both these moments. It is particularity reflected into itself and so brought back to universality, i.e., it is
individuality."[20]

The bulk of Hegel's introduction to the *Philosophy of Right* consists
of an explication of the concept of the will, designed to show that the
fully developed concept of the will generates a fully developed concept
of freedom, including elements that insure that this freedom has both
objective and subjective actuality.[21] Here, again, the form of the *Philosophy of Right* is the key to understanding its content. The entire
description of political institutions characteristic of the modern state is
carried out as an immanent development of the concept of the will, now
understood to be the concept of freedom. Hegel argues that if this description can accurately capture the essentials of the modern state, this
would then mean that this state embodies the realization of freedom.

What Hegel has in mind here has two dimensions. It can be understood from both a logical and a psychological point of view. From a
philosophical, logical perspective, it may perhaps best be understood as
a form of transcendental argument. This sort of transcendental inquiry
into the nature of political freedom is an inquiry into the presuppositions necessary for there to be such a thing as freedom in the realm
of politics. Hegel is articulating the structure of consciousness and its
world necessary for there to be a subject of "right." The hypothesis

that there is indeed such an object is the concept of "right" itself, the single philosophical presupposition that the science of right brings to this study.

It is this that enables what is essentially a descriptive work like *Philosophy of Right* to have a normative legitimating or justifying function. If a system of right can be fully described using only the rational development of the concept of freedom, argues Hegel, this would show that this system of right not only does not restrict freedom but is in fact the realization of it and hence legitimate. "An existent of any sort embodying the free will, this is what right is."[22]

From a psychological point of view (in Hegel's terms, from the point of view of experiential, phenomenological consciousness), describing the subject of right as a development of the will means that political institutions will confront individuals as not foreign but familiar. The point of helping individuals feel "at home" in political institutions is not simply to reconcile them to these institutions but also to empower them to subject these institutions to the critique of their rational wills.[23]

Synchronic and Diachronic Development

It would be helpful at this point to summarize the argument thus far. We have attempted to take seriously Hegel's own descriptions and assessments of his work. Hegel emphasizes both the historical roots of his philosophy as well as the fact that it is grounded in reason alone. These two claims seem at first glance to be at odds with each other, to say the least. How can the same philosophic system be rooted both in what seems to be the contingent progression of history and in the necessary development of reason?

A close look at Hegel's analysis of his historical period provides the solution to this dilemma. The modern period is characterized by the ascendancy of the principles of universality and rationality. Not only does this mean that the political sphere, as the arena par excellence for consciously universal activity, comes to the fore in the modern age and that the modern world is thus preeminently political but it also means that within this political sphere there is a marked need for political principles to be expressed and known in universal, solely rational form. Thus, the specific nature of the contemporary need for a political philosophy in this historical period is precisely that this philosophy be developed from thought alone, independently of appeals to tradition, religion, sentiment, or nature. Only such a deduction of a system of

right can satisfy the principle, historically arrived at, that thought is
to provide the foundation for the right.

The German subtitle of the *Philosophy of Right* identifies it as a work
in *Naturrecht und Staatswissenschaft*—that is, "Natural Right [or Law]
and Political Science." The work integrates not only the "natural"
and the "political" but also "law" and "science."[24] Hegel's analysis
of modern consciousness grasps the inner link between modern law
and modern science. The shift from the classical ancient conception
of natural law to the modern conception initiated by Hobbes is a shift
from a substantive to a procedural conception of natural law.[25]

That is, consulting classical natural law directly told one what to
do in a given situation, yielding immediate directives for action; but
consulting modern natural law tells one how to proceed, how to go
about determining what should be done, either on one's own or in
and through political society. Similarly, the Baconian shift to modern
science is a shift from direct theoretical knowledge of nature to ex-
perimental procedure. In both cases, modernity means methodological
self-consciousness— its defining characteristic for Hegel. This is part of
what Hegel means by his dictum in the *Phenomenology* that everything
now depends on grasping substance as subject; the form or method of
thought is its claim to knowledge in modernity. Hegel establishes as
the foundation of his philosophy of politics what one writer recently
referred to as "the connection between two modern principles: the primacy of method in inquiry and the primacy of procedural legitimacy
in politics."[26]

The question of the sense in which the progression of concepts of the
Philosophy of Right (or, for that matter, of any or all of the rest of
the Hegelian system) is said to be "necessary" is one of the most vex-
ing questions of Hegel interpretation. Steven Smith has distinguished
three possible interpretations of what Hegel might mean. The first, and
weakest, sense is "a kind of hermeneutic or logographic necessity." In
this sense, the progression is necessary only hermeneutically, so that we
may understand these concepts. Smith views this sense as "too loose to
satisfy Hegel's more stringent criteria" that the necessity be intrinsic to
the concepts themselves, not just imported to them by the analysis.[27]
The second sense is a sort of "practical necessity." But this sense can
apply only to those things under the domain of what the philosophical
tradition has identified as "practical reason," that is, things "within
our power to produce or prevent." But history for Hegel is not sufficiently subject to our self-conscious intentions for this sense of necessity
to cover Hegel's meaning. Smith opts for his third sense to explicate

what Hegel means, and this study adopts his view. The third, "more distinctively 'Hegelian'," sense is one "which might be called rational or teleological necessity." In Smith's words: "To say that 'reason rules the world' is not to say that individuals act to maximize their preferences, but that there is some general kind of shape, plan or pattern to history without which there would be no means of organizing the empirical substance of inquiry into a meaningful whole."[28]

For a philosophical deduction such as Hegel offers to serve its legitimating purpose, clearly the rational analysis of the concept of right must yield a system of right that essentially corresponds to the system of right brought into being by historical circumstances. Without this correspondence, one could not establish the reconciliation of reason and history in the modern period that makes Hegel's philosophical project plausible. The political philosophy of the *Philosophy of Right*, then, must encompass both the logical and historical deductions of the political principles it espouses and show that their end results correspond.[29] Hegel finds this correspondence in the fully developed concept of the modern state founded on the rational will of its members. This convergence of the synchronic and diachronic developments of the modern state, both that from the concept and that from history, is what Hegel calls the "idea of right." The first sentence of the body of the *Philosophy of Right* defines the idea of right as its subject matter, and what it means is then elaborated on in the addition to that paragraph.

The subject matter of the philosophical science of right is "the Idea of right, i.e. the concept of right together with the actualization of that concept."[30] "The Idea of right is freedom, and if it is to be truly understood, it must be known both in its concept and in the determinate existence of that concept."[31]

The modern state as the realization of the categories of freedom in legal and ethical form then emerges from history and philosophy as "the actuality of the ethical idea."[32] In terms of its logical form, this is the political embodiment of the identical subject-object also sought by absolute idealism in the metaphysical realm. Here universal ends are known and willed.

Now, if one could simply read off the features of the rational state from the tableau presented by modern history, the task of the *Philosophy of Right* would indeed be an easy one. However, as noted earlier, the story is not quite that simple. The history that yields the philosophic concept of the modern state is not quite simply the history that one follows in the daily newspapers, notwithstanding Hegel's insistence that philosophers should take their orientation from events as they actually occur.[33] To bring forth its results in their full significance, history requires conceptualization by the philosopher of history.

This complicates matters a great deal. As a philosopher of history, Hegel has an understanding of the relationship between philosophy and history that differs from that of modern consciousness. As we have seen, modern consciousness works within a framework of an absolute opposition between philosophy and history. The demand that political theory be generated from reason alone means that this philosophy must be independent of and make no appeal to history. Yet, on Hegel's analysis, this discontinuity and opposition between history and philosophy is itself a product and part of the development of history. This means that modern political consciousness is divorced from and does not understand its own origins. This results in a one-sided and abstract understanding of the implications and consequences of the fundamental political principles of the modern era. Although Hegel continues to ground his theory in what he maintains are the basic principles of the modern era—the principles of universality, rationality, and subjective freedom—he is also critical of the way these principles are misappropriated by modern political consciousness. He is especially critical of the hasty, immediate application of these principles in the French Revolution.

Hegel's analysis of history leads him to see that the opposition between philosophy and history, though real and important, is not absolute. This opposition results from the spirit of the time's antipathy to history. This hidden dialectic of philosophy and history, however, is not the only element of the modern era that operates behind the backs of the agents of modernity, brought to consciousness only by the philosopher. Hegel's philosophical perspective leads him to develop all the basic principles of the modern era differently from the manner in which the dominant consciousness of the modern era would develop them.[34] In this way, Hegel can offer a critique of many dominant political ideas of the modern period and at the same time claim that he is being faithful to the consciousness of the modern era, which insists that these basic principles be rationally developed. Hegel argues that the philosopher is in a better position to provide this service to modernity than the ordinary citizen. The consciousness of the modern era contains many unresolved tensions. These contradictions of modernity form the subject of the next chapter.

Notes

1. *PH*, pp. 445-446.
2. Merold Westphal, "Hegel's Radical Idealism: Family and State as Ethical Communities," in *The State and Civil Society: Studies in Hegel's Political Philosophy*, ed. Z.A. Pelczynski (Cambridge: Cambridge University Press, 1984), p. 287.
3. *PH*, pp. 445-446.
4. *Ibid.*, p. 104.
5. *Ibid.*, p. 446.
6. Ilting, vol. 3, pp. 98-99.
7. *PR*, §211A, pp. 271-272.
8. *Ibid.*, Preface, p. 2.
9. Introduction.
10. Karl Marx, *Critique of Hegel's Philosophy of Right*, ed. Joseph O'Malley (Cambridge: Cambridge University Press, 1970).
11. *PR*, Preface, p. 10.
12. *PH*, pp. 416-417.
13. Alexandre Kojève, *Introduction to the Reading of Hegel*, trans. James H. Nichols, Jr., ed. Allan Bloom (New York: Basic Books, 1969).
14. *PR*, §4, p. 20.
15. *Ibid.*, §4A (addition to paragraph 4), p. 226.
16. *Enc. I*, §232, pp. 370-71.
17. *PR*, §5, p. 21.
18. *Ibid.*, §6, p. 22.
19. For a contemporary application of this concept of individuality with specific reference to Hegel, see Shierry M. Weber, "Individuation as Praxis," in *Critical Interruptions: New Left Perspectives on Herbert Marcuse*, ed. Paul Breines (New York: Herder and Herder, 1972).
20. *PR*, §7, p. 23.
21. For a comprehensive account of the role of this concept of the will in Hegel's philosophy, see Bernard Quelquejeu, *La Volonté dans la Philosophie de Hegel* (Paris: Editions du Seuil, 1972).
22. *PR*, §29, p. 33.
23. See Donald J. Maletz, "Hegel on Right as Actualized Will," *Political Theory* 17:1, February 1989, pp. 33-50.
24. On the former see Manfred Riedel, *Between Tradition and Revolution: The Hegelian Transformation of Political Philosophy*, trans. Walter Wright (Cambridge: Cambridge University Press, 1984), especially pp. 162-166.
25. See Frederick A. Olafson, "Natural Law and Natural Right," *Society, Law, and Morality: Readings in Social Philosophy*, ed. Frederick A. Olafson (Englewood Cliffs, N.J.: Prentice-Hall, 1961).

26. William Connolly, "Introduction: Legitimacy and Modernity," *Legitimacy and the State*, ed. William Connolly (New York: New York University Press, 1984), p. 10. Connolly is here discussing a point made by Sheldon Wolin in "Max Weber: Legitimation, Method, and the Politics of Theory" in the same volume.

27. Steven B. Smith, *Hegel's Critique of Liberalism: Rights in Context* (Chicago: University of Chicago Press, 1989), pp. 205–206.

28. *Ibid.*, p. 206.

29. Werner Maihofer proposes a similar distinction between Hegel's *Begriff des Staats* and his *Prinzip des Staats*. See "Hegels Prinzip des modernen Staats" in *Materialien zu Hegels Rechtsphilosophie*, ed. Manfred Riedel, vol. 2 (Frankfurt am Main: Suhrkamp, 1975).

30. *PR*, §1, p. 14.

31. *Ibid.*, §2A, p. 225.

32. *Ibid.*, §140A, p. 257.

33. See Hegel's references to the reading of the daily newspaper as "the morning prayer of the realist." Quoted in Jean Hyppolite, *Studies on Marx and Hegel*, trans. John O'Neill (New York: Harper and Row, 1973), p. 36.

34. Cf. David Kolb, *The Critique of Pure Modernity: Hegel, Heidegger, and After* (Chicago: University of Chicago Press, 1986).

3

The Contradictions of Modernity

Hegel expresses his analysis of the consciousness of the modern world in three distinct and parallel modes of discourse: historical (via his reading of the historical origins of the French Revolution), philosophical, or logical in Hegel's terms (via his contrast between the thought processes of reason and the understanding), and political (via his contrast between the perspectives of civil society and the state). Although the latter political analysis is worked out in some detail in the appropriate sections of the *Philosophy of Right*, the philosophical and historical analyses must be pulled together from several sources, though most of the relevant material for the latter is in the *Philosophy of History*. This chapter draws out the general principles of Hegel's political philosophy from his historical and philosophical analyses of modernity. (His specific political program will form the subject of succeeding chapters.) These principles will then emerge as criteria to evaluate the institutions of civil society and the state, as will be shown in the following chapters.

From Religion to Revolution

Hegel devoted most of his discussion of the historical background of the French Revolution to an analysis of the development of that form of subjective consciousness that finds political expression in the revolution. The exposition of this analysis which follows pays particular attention to the role Hegel assigns to religion. This is a much-neglected aspect of Hegel's political thought, but his argument against an individualistic morality and for a conception of social ethics is incomprehensible without this component.

Although Hegel notes cases where religion played a directly political role (for example, religious wars), of far greater importance is the gradual diffusion throughout a culture of the spiritual values embodied in religious doctrines. I do not mean to endorse the so-called "theological" interpretations of Hegel, whereby all of history for Hegel is claimed to be nothing other than the revelation of the divine spirit as manifest in Christianity. Hegel is far more of a rationalist philosopher than he is a theologian. Even his "theological" writings, including the early manuscripts unpublished in his lifetime,[1] are more properly classified under the heading of sociology of religion than of theology.[2] The role of religion in Hegel's rational unfolding of history has often been misunderstood, largely along the lines of the split of Hegel's followers into left-wing and right-wing camps soon after his death. This split has left its legacy to contemporary interpretations of Hegel, such that left-wing or political interpretations of Hegel tend to be uncomfortable with the religious dimensions of Hegel's thought and practically ignore it,[3] while right-wing or theological interpretations of Hegel ignore the fact that Hegel was far more interested in the ethics than in the metaphysics of religious doctrines.[4]

The proper situating of Hegel's religious philosophy vis-a-vis his political philosophy is one result that emerges from an examination of Hegel's history of the modern period. In addition, the lessons Hegel draws from his reading of history form the basis for his arguments regarding the abstract versus the truly rational interpretations of the modern principles of subjective freedom, universality, and rationality. This chapter will proceed by first tracing the relevant aspects of the history of the modern period as Hegel presents it and then discussing the conclusions Hegel reaches based on this analysis.

For Hegel, the modern period begins with the Reformation—"the all-enlightening Sun."[5] Protestantism proclaims the realm of inwardness and subjectivity as the repository of the truth of the world. The external ritual and symbolism to which Catholicism had degenerated by the end of the medieval period, in Hegel's eyes, is rejected at the outset of the modern period in favor of the Lutheran doctrine that "the subjective feeling and the conviction of the individual is regarded as equally necessary with the objective side of truth."[6]

The turn to inwardness signals a rejection of the principle of hierarchy. Because all individuals in their hearts are equally filled with the divine spirit, there can be no distinction between laity and clergy as rigid as that in Catholicism. "This subjectivity is the common property of *all mankind*."[7] For Hegel, then, "this is the essence of the Reformation: Man is in his very nature destined to be free."[8]

The Protestant ethic is not, however, entirely individualistic or relativist for Hegel. As a religious consciousness, it retains a claim to the totality of objective truth, which distinguishes Protestantism from the standpoint of the immediate natural will. For the latter, what counts is simply its original conviction and self-certainty. Protestants, however, acknowledge that their insight must be reconciled with the doctrine of the church. By so doing, they abandon their particularity, and their subjective conscience passes over into the realm of free *spirit*, inasmuch as their convictions now are part of and bear upon the social world. For the individual, then, Protestantism (more properly, Lutheranism) accomplishes the reconciliation of individual autonomy of conscience and institutionalized structure. Protestants feel and acknowledge church doctrine as their own.

This idea, that human beings are as such independent and at the same time part of a world in which they feel at home, is for Hegel the primary principle of the modern world. "This is the banner under which we serve, and which we bear. Time, since that epoch [the Reformation] has had no other work to do than the formal imbuing of the world with this principle, in bringing the reconciliation implicit (in Christianity) into objective and explicit realization."[9]

The imbuing of the world with the spirit of the reconciliation of subjective and objective spirit implicitly achieved in Protestantism does not proceed in simple, linear fashion, however. This principle makes its initial appearance in a one-sided way. The principle of subjectivity is overextended. Although Luther still assumed that the truth to be recognized by individual conscience was a truth already operative in the world, this element is lost by the time a new element enters the scene of world history, the Enlightenment. "*Now*, the principle was set up that this import [the truth that activates human beings] must be capable of actual investigation—something of which I (in this modern time) can gain an inward conviction—and that to this basis of inward demonstration every dogma must be referred."[10]

In Hegel's eyes, the Enlightenment brings with it a new kind of atomistic individualism. It enthrones the reasoning powers of each empirical individual, removed from the individual's historical and social milieu, as the supreme judge of the way of the world. For this reason, the excessive individualism of modernity, which Hegel finds manifest in the French Revolution and elsewhere, is ascribed by Hegel to the Enlightenment rather than to the Reformation.

In working out the inner truth of the Enlightenment, a dialectical reversal again takes place. Though it began by unreservedly heralding a new age of subjectivity and inwardness, the Enlightenment ended by ushering in a new era dominated by a materialist ideology subservient to given, objective reality. The Enlightenment set up "the so-called immediately enlightening truths of the healthy human understanding"[11] as the sole and ultimate standard for truth. But this understanding cannot penetrate beyond its own immediacy, beyond a naturalistic intimacy with its surrounding environment, argues Hegel. Superstition and faith in a world beyond may have been overcome by the Enlightenment only to be replaced by faith in a secular form of received wisdom. The natural, individual will cannot maintain itself as ultimate arbiter of reality, and surrenders judgment to an objective standard in the name of utility. Thus the development of a notion of subjectivity, which began in the Reformation as the sanctification of the inner, spiritual dimension against the claims of the external world, ends by reestablishing a naive materialism.[12] (In linking the Enlightenment to materialism, Hegel has in mind primarily the French Enlightenment. The French Enlightenment was positioned much more radically in opposition to religion, which it saw as the remnants of naive superstition, than was the German Enlightenment, which was aimed more at a rationalization of religion. Compare Voltaire and Lessing, for example.)[13]

The same kind of dialectic, from radical subjectivity to a new submission to the given, can be traced in Hegel's analysis of the course of the French Revolution itself. In one sense, the revolution represented the triumph of subjectivity over the external world. It was perceived, especially in Germany, as a philosopher's revolution, heralding the new age of the rule of reason. Hegel was not alone in taking this stance.[14] Yet, a careful reading of Hegel's analysis of the revolution reveals important qualifications in Hegel's attitude toward the relationship between philosophy and the revolution. In the first place, it should be noted that Hegel's attitude toward the assertion that the revolution received its inspiration from philosophy is decidedly ambivalent.

> It has been said that the French Revolution resulted from philosophy, and it is not without reason that philosophy has been called "Weltweisheit." ... We should not therefore contradict the assertion that the revolution received its first impulse from philosophy. But this philosophy is in the first instance only abstract thought, not the concrete comprehension of absolute truth—intellectual positions between which there is an immeasurable chasm.[15]

This is at best a lukewarm endorsement of the proposition that the revolution stemmed from the influence of philosophy. Hegel's hesitation is twofold. First, the philosophy in question is the philosophy of the Enlightenment. This philosophy developed its principles in a one-sided, abstract way, and therefore does not warrant the label of being a true philosophy. In the modern era, this appellation is reserved for Hegel's own system. Second, even the principle of subjectivity, which the revolution took as inspiration from the Enlightenment, is not properly a product of the Enlightenment but was appropriated by it from the Reformation.

Hegel's hesitation about proclaiming that it was the revolution and its preceding philosophy that introduced the principle that subjective reason should reign in the political world shows up elsewhere as well. Hegel's reference to the revolution bringing into reality Anaxagoras's idea of *nous* governing the world has already been quoted.[16] After proclaiming this a "glorious mental dawn," the passage continues: "Emotions of a lofty character stirred men's minds at that time; a spiritual enthusiasm thrilled through the world, as if the reconciliation between the divine and the secular was now first accomplished."[17]

The tentativeness of the last affirmation—"as if" this reconciliation were now first accomplished—is noteworthy. It reflects Hegel's ambivalence. On the one hand, it was the French Revolution that really accomplished this because only with the revolution did the spiritual nature of modernity become an active political force capable of restructuring the world in accordance with the principles of the modern era. On the other hand, this revolution did not arise in a vacuum and overturn all that passed before it. Indeed, it built on and presupposed a long development of world history. But this is something to which the revolution is blind. The revolution shares the Enlightenment's hostility to tradition and religion and consequently does not acknowledge its debt to history. (It is difficult to avoid seeing in Hegel's remarks here a form of self-criticism of his own youthful enthusiasm for the revolutionary spirit.)[18]

The revolution's lack of historical perspective is to Hegel's mind intrinsically connected to its chronic instability. Constitution follows constitution, and no result achieved by the revolution remains secure. The principle of subjective freedom is interpreted by the revolution in too radically autonomous a fashion. Individual wills are sundered from all context. The valid principle that reason is to rule the world is misinterpreted by the revolutionaries to mean that each individual's reason must have a determining impact on events; the idea that politics should be based solely on rational principles is given a too immediate, individualistic, and voluntaristic interpretation by the revolution. Hegel identifies Rousseau as the theoretician who best expressed this flawed, though pivotally important, viewpoint. In a lengthy addition to paragraph 258 of the *Philosophy of Right*, in which Hegel defines what he means by the rationality of the state, Hegel offers an analysis of Rousseau's theory that highlights this problematic.

> He [Rousseau] reduces the union of individuals in the state to a contract and therefore to something based on their arbitrary wills, their opinion, and their capriciously given express consent; and abstract reasoning proceeds to draw the logical inferences which destroy the absolutely divine principle of the state, together with its majesty and absolute authority. For this reason, when these abstract conclusions came into power, they afforded the prodigious spectacle of the overthrow of the constitution of a great actual state and its complete reconstruction *ab initio* on the basis of pure thought alone, after the destruction of all existing and given material. The will of its re-founders was to give it what they alleged was a purely rational basis, but it was only abstractions that were being used; the Idea was lacking; and the experiment ended in the maximum of frightfulness and terror.[19]

The valid principle that the will is the foundation of the modern state is misinterpreted to mean that the state must be founded on the express consent of its members. But this is far too ephemeral a foundation, argues Hegel, because the individual will is given over to caprice and inclination. Only the rational will, correctly understood and developed in philosophy and history, can be the basis for a stable political union. Lacking the proper mediations between the subjective wills of the citizens and the collective institutions of the state, the attempt of the revolution to rebuild society from the ground up necessarily ends in the chaos of the Terror. The historical perspective that the revolutionaries lacked would have made them aware that the radical restructuring of society that they favored was not the work of a moment, however passionately inspired by revolutionary zeal, but of a much longer span of time. Indeed, it presupposes the entire development of world history, which the revolution takes itself to be repudiating.

Before a government that is accountable to the will of its citizens can be established, those citizens must first have developed a disposition favorable to the very idea of government. This means that the recognition of the autonomy of the individual will in accordance with the demands of subjective freedom must be tempered with a willingness to have one's will expressed within and through an institutional framework. This reconciliation of objective structure with subjective freedom is precisely what Hegel attributes to Protestantism, and is what he has in mind in his declaration that "with the Catholic religion no rational constitution is possible."[20] He thus indicates that France's Catholicism is one of the reasons for both the revolution's necessity in France and its failure, because Hegel regards Catholicism as hostile to the political sphere on account of its otherworldliness. "It is no use to organize political laws and arrangements on principles of equity and reason, so long as in religion the principle of unfreedom is not abandoned."[21]

Operating on the basis of abstract principles that posit the will of the individual in its immediate, arbitrary form rather than in its intrinsic, rational form as their starting point, "disposition and religion were not taken into account"[22] by the French Revolution at its outset. Consequently, a purely external system of checks and balances of power was set up. Under such circumstances, the element of subjectivity can make its entrance only in a negative way, as suspicion and mistrust. Eventually, during the course of the revolution this subjective element, previously excluded because of the legalistic attitude toward political affairs of the constitution, which had been established without reference to the subjective disposition of the citizens, comes to predominate. But because of the revolution's abstract opposition between religious conscience and political rationality, the subjective element does not become an added element of civic virtue but rather becomes an extremist concept of virtue that stands in opposition to the possibility of effective government. The Reign of Terror represents for Hegel the absolute reign of the subjective concept of virtue. This standpoint lacks any concept of mediation and can deal with conflict in only one way—the lengthy process of conscientious accommodation to law is reduced to one single stroke of the blade at the guillotine. "Virtue and terror are the order of the day; for subjective virtue, whose sway is based on disposition only, brings with it the most fearful tyranny. It exercises its power without legal formalities, and the punishment it inflicts is equally simple—death."[23]

Hegel argues that such an arrangement cannot last long. It is self-destructive, eventually destroying even its own leaders. On Hegel's analysis, the eventual ascension to power of a strong, centralized government is the inevitable outcome of the shortcomings of the revolution. Napoleon emerges not so much as the countertendency to the revolution but as its stabilizer, as one who saves it from devouring itself. Having secured the revolution, Napoleon set out to extend it beyond the

boundaries of France. But, here again, the dialectic between the opposing principles of legal constitutionalism and rationality versus religious
consciousness and the disposition of the people plays itself out again.
The attempt to impose constitutions on other nations fails. These constitutions do not match the spirit of the people.[24] Traditions cannot be
supplanted by acts of will.

Even in those cases where opposition to the establishment of successful constitutional government is not religiously or traditionally based,
Hegel still finds the basic flaw to be that the proper attitude toward
government does not prevail. Hegel holds it impossible to establish effective government where individuals insist that their personal voices be
efficacious. As strange as it sounds to modern ears, which equate constitutionalism with liberalism, it is liberalism that Hegel identifies as the
culprit here. (Not without good historical reasons, we should add. In
Hegel's day, liberalism was still associated with radical, direct democracy and could plausibly be identified as being in the generally Jacobin
camp. The association of liberalism with representative democracy was
a phenomenon of the mid- and later nineteenth century.) Hegel lists
what he takes to be the permanent contributions of the political perspective of the era inaugurated by the revolution, and then argues that
liberalism sees any established government as being only a faction and
not representative of the will of the people as a whole, and therefore
illegitimate.

> Not satisfied with the establishment of rational rights, with freedom of person
> and property, with the existence of a political organization in which are to
> be found various circles of civil life each having its own functions to perform,
> and with that influence over the people which is exercised by the intelligent
> members of the community, and the confidence that is felt in them, "Liberal-
> ism" sets up in opposition to this the atomistic principle, that which insists
> upon the sway of individual wills; maintaining that all government should
> emanate from their express power, and have their express sanction. Asserting
> this formal side of freedom—this abstraction—the party in question allows no
> political organization to be firmly established.[25]

Hegel goes on to pinpoint this oscillation between the one and the
many as the primary political problem of the current period. "This
collision, this nodus, this problem is that with which history is now
occupied, and whose solution it has to work out in the future."[26]

History shows the general outline of the problem and the principles to be used in its solution. But the detailed working out of this solution is a task yet to be accomplished. In a rough way, this is the major feature of the relationship between Hegel's *Philosophy of History* and his *Philosophy of Right*. The principles that have been the motive force of history function as criteria for the establishment of the rational political state in the *Philosophy of Right*. Having traced their historical genesis, it is also necessary that we state these principles on their own philosophical terms as they emerge from Hegel's analysis.

The Nature of Revolutionary Action

The French Revolution marks a decisive turning point in world history in that it declares that from this time on universal, rational principles will be the sole determinants of political life. Hegel attempts to ground this declaration in the nature of the historical world itself, showing how the revolution represents the culmination of world history. The motivation for this attempt had already been articulated by Hegel in the Preface to his *Phenomenology of Spirit*.[27] Without this grounding, this reference to its own process of becoming, the assertions of the revolution appear as just one set of principles espoused by one group, facing other principles equally sincerely and passionately propounded by another group, both laying claim to objective validity. Hegel argues that this historical perspective is crucial to the revolution's securing and permanently establishing its results. But it is precisely here, in his attempt to champion the revolution, that Hegel encounters the sharpest resistance from the proponents of the revolution. His insistence on a historical perspective flies directly in the face of the most basic component of the revolutionaries' own understanding of what it is they are setting out to accomplish. In the eyes of the revolutionaries, the revolution's greatest achievement is precisely to have set humanity completely free from its history, once and for all. From this perspective, an appeal to history is a betrayal of the revolution.

A good example of the attitude toward modern revolutions that Hegel is criticizing can be found in the opening pages of Marx's "The Eighteenth Brumaire of Louis Bonaparte."

> The tradition of all the dead generations weighs like a nightmare on the brain of the living. And just when they seem engaged in revolutionising themselves and things, in creating something entirely new, precisely in such epochs of revolutionary crisis they anxiously conjure up the spirits of the past to their

service and borrow from them names, battle slogans, and costumes in order
to present the new scene of world history in this time- honored disguise and
this borrowed language.[28]

Marx here reveals himself as much more a child of the Enlightenment, as much more uncritically enthralled by the ahistorical ideology
of modernity, than Hegel. The past is discussed here in entirely negative terms, as blocking the process of "creating something entirely new."
The image of revolution as creation *ex nihilo*, which appears from time
to time in Marx's writings, is part of a conception of politics that Hegel
argues makes lasting change impossible because it obliterates any foundations upon which a social structure could be built. This Hegelian line
of criticism of Marx has not been lost on later generations of Marxists.
It permeates Horkheimer and Adorno's *Dialectic of Enlightenment*,[29]
and it has entered into debates about Marxist attitudes toward third
world revolutions, including criticism of Marx's tendencies to see im-
perialism as a positive, modernizing force in the third world.[30] Other
dominant modern political ideologies could also benefit from Hegel's
insight into the necessity of integrating traditions of the past into radical change rather than simply cutting the future off from the past. The
inability of modern politics to divorce religion and politics, for example, with anything approaching the degree of separation of church and
state espoused by modern political theories is too much in the air at
the present time to require further comment.

The issue being wrestled with here is complex. On the one hand,
Hegel seems right to insist that an awareness of its own past is an
essential component of any successful political program. He has identified, in particularly strong terms, a distinctive liability of modern consciousness to see itself as always producing something startlingly new,
something entirely unconnected to what has gone before. This form
of blindness ironically results in the continual return of the past that
modernity attempts to repress. On the other hand, it also seems true
that reliance on the past does stifle innovation and change. This charge
becomes even more acutely posed when one remembers that for Hegel
much of past history is entwined with a religious consciousness, which
claims eternal validity and immutability for its tenets. In this connection, it is important to remember that for Hegel "the true theodicy, the
justification of God in history,"[31] is the demonstration of the rational
structure of history. In combating the "a-theism" of the modern world,
Hegel takes himself to be combating the "a-historicism" of the modern
world. The connection between religion and politics in the *Philosophy*

of Right is more appropriately understood as a way of restoring a historical dimension to political theory than as a sanctification of existing social structures.

The task for political theory, following Hegel, is to sort out the progressive from the regressive in the historical past. As we shall see in the following chapters, this perspective figures prominently in Hegel's attempt to find political institutions that can mediate between individuals and their society. Hegel turns to the corporations as intermediate institutions whose roots are in a now obsolete feudal economic order but which are capable of being reoriented to serve a necessary function in the modern state. Interpreting Hegel against this background enables one to see that much of the criticism of Hegel's use of the corporations in his ideal of the modern state is simply one instance of the modern antipathy toward traditional institutions, which Hegel is criticizing here. The interpretation developed here enables one to understand that, in and of itself, the fact that Hegel's political philosophy is historically grounded is not sufficient ground to claim Hegel either as a proto-Marxist revolutionary or as a neo-Burkean conservative, as some have tried to do. The perspective of this study attempts to focus attention on the specifics of Hegel's approach to history to see precisely how history enters into his philosophy. With this in mind, we may return to the specific question of how the era ushered in by the French Revolution figures in Hegel's political philosophy.

One way of approaching this issue is to pose the question, What is the real nature of revolutionary action? To modern political consciousness, revolution is a radical act of autonomous self-creation that signals a decisive new beginning. Hegel's conception of revolution, however, takes its distance from this Enlightenment-influenced concept and returns to the classical, Greek idea of revolution. A revolution is in some sense a realignment which brings the world into proper order, a return (revolution) to a natural harmony.[32] For the former, reference to the past undermines the revolution by misdirecting its attention. For the latter, reference to the past strengthens the revolution by revealing its roots. This attitude on Hegel's part is revealed when, for example, he cautions against regarding the constitution of the state as something created by human artifice for the needs of the moment but rather argues that it be regarded as divine, that is, as stemming from the rational unfolding of history, which for Hegel "is the true *Theodicea*, the justification of God in history,"[33] as noted above. "In any case, however, it is absolutely essential that the constitution should not be regarded as something made, even though it has come into being in time. It must therefore be treated rather as something simply existent in and by itself, as divine therefore, and constant, and so as exalted above the sphere of things that are made."[34]

Such a statement, when taken out of context, of course brings down upon Hegel's head the full wrath of secular modernists. But, again, Hegel's basic target here is that "atheism" of the modern world that sees only contingency and not rationality in history. This stance does not preclude rational criticism of existing states. One requirement for effective political action for Hegel, then, is that it must be historically self-conscious. It must be aware of its own origins, for otherwise it cannot secure its results against the further passage of time. As one writer on the subject of the relationship between tradition and revolution appropriately puts it, invoking a Kantian metaphor: "Tradition without revolution is admittedly empty, but revolution without tradition is clearly blind."[35]

Hegel's attempt to secure the revolution by placing it in the objective course of the world does have its price, however. As Jürgen Habermas puts it, Hegel "has to legitimize the revolutionizing of reality without legitimizing the revolutionaries themselves."[36] That is, although Hegel supports the principle that reason is to rule, he sees only chaos resulting when individuals are told that their reason is to rule. This seems to close the door to any element of revolutionary subjectivity, of human participants actually entering the scene to radically change the course of events. And without this moment, no revolution, even a rationally necessary one, can take place.

There is much to be said for this strain of criticism, but recalling the difference between Hegel's and the dominant modern conception of what a truly revolutionary act consists of can help to put this criticism in its proper perspective. To the extent that this criticism views revolutionary action par excellence as individuals choosing their destiny in a historical vacuum and setting out to make it a reality, Hegel's analysis reveals this image of revolution as being ideologically blinded by the modern antipathy toward history. With this as one's model of revolutionary action, no revolution can succeed, argues Hegel, for it is ignorant of its own basis and hence unable to establish new roots that will enable it to survive. But should a rational analysis of history reveal the necessity of introducing revolutionary new principles, as was the case prior to the French Revolution, Hegel is in a position to be able to affirm the necessity of the revolution but at the same time criticize its excesses—that is, those actions that aim to shove aside the historical process by acts of will.

To the extent that this criticism addresses more than Hegel's attitude toward the French Revolution, however, and addresses the issue of a Hegelian stance toward revolution in general, and especially in the modern age, different problems are raised. On the one hand, if the French Revolution's role was to dramatically announce the principles of modernity—political rationality, a universal code of rights based on the freedom and dignity of persons as such, and so on—then no more announcements in the form of violent revolutions should be necessary, because all that really remains is to bring the world into accordance with its own principles. On the other hand, should it be rationally demonstrated that a revolution was called for, Hegel's theory seems committed to endorsing it, with the proviso that the program of the revolution build on historical traditions.[37] (That Hegel himself was by temperament conservative and would have been loath to admit any such consequence is not the issue here.)[38]

Hegel himself, then, was not a reactionary. His endorsement of the Restoration was to his mind not a betrayal of the revolution but a championing of the historical dimension of the Restoration that was lacking in the Revolution. A distinction between the content (principles, goals) of the revolution and the form (actions, means) taken by the revolutionaries can help to clarify this. Hegel consistently supported the content of the revolution but criticized its form, primarily because this form was unable to secure the content.[39] It will be helpful to approach this issue using other Hegelian terminology, namely, Hegel's doctrine of the relationship between essence and appearance as that doctrine is developed in his *Science of Logic*.

Identity and Difference

The dominant mode of consciousness of the era approaches the problem of the relationship between essence and appearance through the faculty of thought that Hegel calls the "understanding." Taking his point of departure from Kant's use of these terms, Hegel considers the understanding to be a mode of thought that operates with rigid, fixed oppositions between the different concepts it employs. It is analytical, breaking up a phenomenon into its constituent parts and examining each element separately, in isolation from the rest. When some feature of a phenomenon is declared to be the essence of that phenomenon, the understanding holds it apart from those aspects of the phenomenon that are seen as accidental predicates, mere appearances. Essence and appearance are indifferent to each other.

In contrast to the understanding, Hegel holds up the process of reason. Reason seeks unity, interconnectedness. The truly rational interpretation of the relationship between essence and appearance is summarized in the sentence "Essence must appear" (*Das Wesen muss erscheinen*).[40] That is, essence shows itself through its appearances; appearances are the appearances of essence. The essence of something is not some additional thing that lies behind or beyond that thing but it is rather the way in which the thing appears as what it is.

The ahistorical attitude of the modern world stems from the modern world understanding itself through the categories of the understanding rather than through the processes of reason. Modern consciousness correctly sees that a new plateau in the history of the world has been reached, that the essence of what it is to be a free, rational human being is manifest in the political world for the first time. But modern consciousness incorrectly concludes from this that all of past history is to be jettisoned as irrelevant. Hegel, however, insists that the present era embodies the essential truth about humanity and its freedom only because these principles of modernity have been implicitly operative throughout history. They can now be observed to have been the telos of history because now, for the first time, a rational eye can look back upon the history of the world.

A rational philosophy (that is, Hegelianism) sees the continuity between the revolution and its past. A key feature of the Hegelian dialectic is this ability to see the continuity between the continuous story of the past and modernity's break with tradition—in the more abstract terminology of Hegel's logic, the identity of identity and difference. Put another way, the cornerstone of Hegel's interpretation of modern consciousness is that this consciousness sees itself as being radically autonomous, free from all traditional moorings. Yet Hegel's philosophy attempts to demonstrate that this radical opposition between the historical past and the present era is simply a particular historical form of the continuing historical- philosophical tradition, from which modernity views itself as having laboriously won its freedom. This is the ideological form taken by consciousness under the general conditions of the bifurcation (*Entzweiung*) of the world into discreet, disparate realms characteristic of the modern era as it comprehends itself using the categories of the understanding.[41]

Just as modern consciousness fails to find reason in history, so too it fails to properly situate subjective freedom of conscience within an objective, institutional framework. Here, too, Hegel attempts to mediate these oppositions. The problem of politics, for Hegel as for the classical tradition he invokes, is that of situating the individual within an ethical community. Much of Hegel's political theory, indeed much of his entire philosophical system, can be read as an extended critique of individualism in all its forms. Hegel relies on the ideal of a community that encompasses the totality of one's relationships, an ideal he finds embodied in the modern world in religious consciousness, to combat the atomistic individualism of the Enlightenment. True individualism, for Hegel, results not from separating individuals from their history and affiliated groupings but from individuals who incorporate within their activities the particularities of their origin and the universal elements of their goals.[42]

The loci par excellence of this atomistic individualism are those areas of life that Hegel conceptualizes under the heading of "civil society," whose creation "is the achievement of the modern world which has for the first time given all determinations of the Idea their due."[43] On the one hand, Hegel evaluates civil society in terms of its own categories of economic activities. But Hegel's version of the British political economists' hidden hand of reason is not that the economy regulates itself unconsciously but rather that economic realities lead individuals into organizations that bring them to an explicitly universal, political perspective. Just as, in accordance with Hegel's doctrine of essence, reason appears in history, so too the political realm must emerge out of prepolitical areas of life. In the final analysis, then, civil society is evaluated not in its own terms but in terms of the criteria for a rational political state that have emerged from Hegel's analysis of history. The ahistoricity of civil society, its self-understanding as being based on laws of nature, is revealed as stemming from the same defects of the understanding already discussed. Hegel's dialectic of civil society discloses that, though originally appearing as an autonomous sphere, civil society only truly attains its significance in terms of the distinction between civil society and the state. This dialectic is the subject of the next chapter.

Notes

1. Many of these writings have been translated by T. M. Knox and Richard Kroner as *G.W.F. Hegel: Early Theological Writings* (Philadelphia: University of Pennsylvania Press, 1971).
2. See Walter Kaufmann, "The Young Hegel and Religion," in *Hegel: A Collection of Critical Essays*, ed. Alasdair MacIntyre (Notre Dame: University of Notre Dame

Press, 1976); and Georg Lukács, *The Young Hegel*, trans. Rodney Livingstone (London: Merlin Press, 1975).

3. For example, Herbert Marcuse's excellent *Reason and Revolution: Hegel and the Rise of Social Theory* (Boston: Beacon Press, 1960) hardly mentions Hegel's philosophy of religion, and Lukács's *The Young Hegel* restricts Hegel's interest in religion to his early years.

   As Lukács tells the tale of Hegel's early development, the villain in the piece is Schelling, whose subjective idealism was the principal deleterious influence on Hegel, preventing his objective idealism from maturing into an early version of dialectical materialism.

4. See, for example, Gustav E. Mueller, "Hegel's Absolute and the Crisis of Christianity," in *A Hegel Symposium*, ed. D. C. Travis (Austin: University of Texas Press, 1962).

5. *PH*, p. 412.

6. *Ibid*, p. 416.

7. *Ibid*, p. 416.

8. *Ibid.*, p. 417.

9. *Ibid.*, p. 416.

10. *Ibid.*, p. 442.

11. G.W.F. Hegel, *Lectures on the History of Philosophy*, trans. E. S. Haldane and Frances H. Simson (New York: Humanities Press, 1974) (hereafter *Hist.*), vol. 3, p. 384.

12. See G.W.F. Hegel, *Phenomenology of Mind*, trans. J. B. Baillie (New York: Harper and Row, 1967) (hereafter *Phen.*), chap. 6, pp. 559–598.

13. *Hist.*, vol. 3, p. 386. Cf. also Judith N. Shklar, *Freedom and Independence: A Study of the Political Ideas of Hegel's Phenomenology of Mind* (Cambridge: Cambridge University Press, 1976), p. 166.

14. See George Armstrong Kelly, *Idealism, Politics, and History: Sources of Hegelian Thought* (Cambridge: Cambridge University Press, 1969); G. P. Gooch, *Germany and the French Revolution* (New York: Russell and Russell, 1966); and Harold Mah, "The French Revolution and the Problem of German Modernity: Hegel, Heine, and Marx," *New German Critique* 50, Spring/Summer 1990, pp. 3–20.

15. *PH*, p. 446.

16. Chapter 2.

17. *PH*, p. 447.

18. See Shlomo Avineri, *Hegel's Theory of the Modern State* (Cambridge: Cambridge University Press, 1974), pp. 62–72; and Ritter, *Hegel and the French Revolution*, pp. 193-196.

19. *PR*, §258A, p. 157.

20. *PH*, p. 449.

21. *PM*, §552, p. 287.

22. *PH*, p. 450.

23. *Ibid*, pp. 450–451.

24. *Ibid.*, p. 451. The influence of Montesquieu is apparent here; cf. *PR*, §274A, p. 179.

25. *Ibid.*, p. 452.

26. *Ibid.*, p. 452.

27. *Phen.*, pp. 75–130.

28. Karl Marx, "The Eighteenth Brumaire of Louis Bonaparte," in *The Marx-Engels Reader*, ed. Robert C. Tucker (New York: W. W. Norton and Company, 1972), p. 437.

29. Max Horkheimer and Theodor W. Adorno, *Dialectic of Enlightenment*, trans. John Cumming (New York: Herder and Herder, 1972).

30. See Shlomo Avineri, ed., *Karl Marx on Colonialism and Modernization* (New York: Anchor-Doubleday, 1969).

31. *PH*, p. 457.

32. See George Grant, "Revolution and Tradition," in *Tradition and Revolution*, ed. Lionel Rubinoff (Toronto: Macmillan of Canada, 1971), pp. 82–83. See also Steven B. Smith, "Hegel and the French Revolution: An Epitaph for Republicanism," *Social Research* 56:1, Spring 1989, pp. 236–238.

33. *PH*, p. 457.

34. *PR*, §273A, p. 178. Cf. Ilting, vol. 1, pp. 195–197.

35. Rubinoff, *Tradition and Revolution*, p. 13.

36. Jürgen Habermas, "Hegel's Critique of the French Revolution," in *Theory and Practice*, trans. John Viertel (Boston: Beacon Press, 1974), p. 126.

37. Extending Hegel's theory into the future raises as many questions as it answers. To do justice to the issues raised here would require a full discussion of Hegel's *Owl of Minerva* metaphor of philosophy comprehending the world only after the fact and the controversial "end-of-history" thesis. Some of this will be found in Chapter 7 in the "End of History" section.

38. On Hegel's fear of new revolutions toward the end of his life, see Franz Rosenzweig, *Hegel und der Staat* (Munich: Verlag R. Oldenbourg, 1920), vol. 2, pp. 220–221. Cf. also Ritter, *Hegel and the French Revolution*, p. 193.

39. This has been recognized by diverse commentators. See for example Alfred Stern, "Hegel et les idées de 1789," *Revue Philosophique de la France et de l'Etranger* 128, July-December 1939, pp. 353–363.

40. G.W.F. Hegel, *Science of Logic*, trans. A. V. Miller (New York: Humanities Press, 1969) (hereafter *Logic*), p. 479. (*Wissenschaft der Logik*, ed. Georg Lasson [Hamburg: Felix Meiner Verlag, 1967], vol. 2, p. 101.)

41. For elaboration of this perspective, see Joachim Ritter, "Hegel und die französische Revolution," *Metaphysik und Politik: Studien zu Aristoteles und Hegel* (Frankfurt am Main: Suhrkamp, 1977).

42. Marx learned this well from Hegel. "To be avoided above all is establishing 'society' once again as an abstraction over against the individual. The individual is the social being." Karl Marx, "Economic and Philosophic Manuscripts," in *Writings of the Young Marx on Philosophy and Society*, ed. Lloyd D. Easton and Kurt H. Guddat (New York: Doubleday, 1967), p. 306.

43. *PR*, §182A, p. 266.

4

Property and Personhood

"Civil society is the [stage of] difference which intervenes between the family and the state. . . . Moreover, the creation of civil society is the achievement of the modern world which has for the first time given all determinations of the Idea their due."[1] So writes Hegel in his introductory, and most general, characterization of the nature of civil society. But why is it of such paramount importance that the modern world has created as a separate sphere of ethical life a realm that intervenes between the family and the state? And why is civil society a sphere also characterized by Hegel as "the external state, the state based on need, the state as the Understanding envisages it"?[2] The answers to these questions lie in Hegel's conception of civil society as the sphere of the formation of the distinctive consciousness of modernity, the sphere of education and culture (*Bildung*). "Through civil society education [*Bildung*] comes about in general. Education, with respect to the individual, is a general way of determining oneself according to universal maxims and forms, of behaving and acting in a universal way. This form of universality comes about through civil society, and civil society is therefore necessary simply 'that spirit exist as free spirit.' "[3]

From a philosophical perspective, the processes at work in civil society can be seen as producing a sort of phenomenology of ethical consciousness, leading the individual from an immediate, natural standpoint through a series of mediations to a universal, political standpoint. "The interest of the Idea—an interest of which these members of civil society are as such unconscious—lies in the process whereby their singularity and their natural condition are raised, as a result of the necessities imposed by nature as well as of arbitrary needs, to formal freedom and formal universality of knowing and willing."[4]

The Family

The starting point for this movement of ethical consciousness lies within the natural unity of the family, echoing for Hegel the way in which classical political philosophy began with the Greek citizen's immersion in the natural unity of the polis. The many accounts of Hegel's political philosophy that neglect this aspect and focus their treatment only on the origins of the state in the second moment of ethical life, the sphere of civil society, miss important elements of his theory.[5] The question of how one's conceptualization of the family relates to one's conceptualization of the state and political life in general has its own history within the history of political theory. Hegel's treatment of the family can be best appreciated in this context.

For classical Greek philosophy, the family is the natural starting point for political theory because it represents the most immediate, natural form of association. Even those who reject the family as a model for political life nonetheless take it as their initial frame of reference. While Aristotle in Book I of the *Politics* takes pains to distinguish political association from the kind of association found in a household, the household is nonetheless the starting point of the discussion.[6] Although Plato in the *Republic* ultimately comes to identify the family as the locus of the kind of privatized, individualized concerns deleterious to the welfare of the polis, and he therefore attempts to remove as much as possible of the vestiges of family life from the lives of the Guardians, the consideration of the nature of justice, here too, still begins with a discussion of the nature and justice of Cephalus's household duties.[7]

This approach to political philosophy persists through the medieval period. Whatever the eventual substantive position taken with regard to the goods or evils of family life, considerations of the family as an early form of association and as a natural model for political theory play an important methodological role in the major tradition of political philosophy.[8] This situation changes in the seventeenth century, in the early period of modern political theory.

We may recall that in describing his own method, Aristotle says: "Just as, in all other fields, a compound should be analysed until we reach its simple and uncompounded elements (or, in other words, the smallest atoms of the whole which it constitutes), so we must also consider analytically the elements of which a polis is composed."[9]

Twenty centuries later, Thomas Hobbes applies Galileo's "resolutive-compositive" method to break the political association down into its constituent components and arrives not at families but at isolated individuals.[10] Hegel's rejection of modern methodological individualism in favor of Aristotelianism on this point will prove crucial in his doctrines of corporatism and political representation, which we will discuss in later chapters. For Hegel, the state is an association *of associations*, not an association of individuals. The first such association is the family.

The individualist methodological stance becomes more pronounced as the modern period progresses, though the story is not without its twists and turns. Although Hobbes on a few occasions allows himself the use of analogies between natural patriarchal authority and constituted monarchical authority, the thrust of his well-known arguments that political authority arises by covenant and not by nature is to disallow such analogies. At his most consistent, Hobbes maintains a continuity between familial and political bonds not by treating commonwealths as extended families but by reading the language of rights and consent back into the matrix of family relations, as when he discusses the mutual rights of parents and children vis-a-vis each other.[11]

John Locke, however, felt that the tradition of seeing the family as a basis for political thought, of basing political right on patriarchal right, could not be so simply disposed of. Locke felt it necessary to meet the challenge of patriarchal theory head on and devoted the entirety of his *First Treatise on Government* to a refutation of Sir Robert Filmer's *Patriarcha, or the Natural Power of Kings*. (The title page of the original printing of the two treatises states: "In the Former, The False Principles and Foundation of Sir Robert Filmer, and His Followers, Are Detected and Overthrown. The Latter is an Essay Concerning the True Original, Extent, and End of Civil-Government.")[12] With respect to our own distance from the tradition of familially based political theory, it is noteworthy that Locke's *First Treatise* is rarely read today and that attention to Locke's political theory is almost exclusively focused on the *Second Treatise*.

By the time Rousseau took pen in hand, he felt justified in writing, after the first few pages of his article on Political Economy, with regard to a subject to which Locke had devoted an entire book: "I thought these few lines would suffice to reject the odious system that Sir Robert Filmer tried to establish in a work entitled *Patriarcha*, which two famous men have already overly honored by writing books to refute it."[13]

Rousseau specifically excludes families from the extreme picture of asocial individuals he draws in the "Discourse on the Origin of Inequality." Despite Rousseau's doctrine of the natural feelings of sympathy for others to be found in the state of nature, no affective ties bind people into families until after the introduction of a rudimentary form of private property.[14]

The same disregard for family life is evident in Kant's political writings. Kant, too, does not consider the family as a natural form of social unity. In Kant's references to the family or marriage, such as they are, he speaks of marriage in terms of the partners' rights to one another's bodies.[15]

The distinctive features of Hegel's treatment of the family stand out most clearly when viewed against the background of these trends: the classical tradition of conceptualizing the family as a natural unit in one way or another relevant to political life, giving way to the modern tradition of political philosophy, which concerns itself with the associations of propertied individuals removed from the context of familial, personal life. These features disclose fundamental themes of Hegel's political philosophy and of his attempt to reconcile the insights of antiquity with those of modernity.

The family, for Hegel, is the embodiment of a natural ethical unity. The language of individual rights, the terms of discourse of civil society, enters into the family "only when the family begins to dissolve."[16] Hegel thus begins with the classical standpoint—the consideration of the familial social unit as an organic whole not reducible to the individuals within it.

Hegel's general antipathy toward abstract individualism is evident in all of his writings, from the abstract formulations of the *Science of Logic* to the historical examples in the *Philosophy of History*. His understanding of the relevance of the family for political philosophy embodies his insistence that consciousness of oneself as an individual can never be an initial given but can emerge only as a result of a process of differentiation from the starting point of one's initial environment. Hegel's theory here articulates a critique of modern political philosophy. In starting with fully formed adult individuals, modern political philosophy is blind to the developmental socializing processes that take place in the family, processes necessarily presupposed by this individualism.

But then Hegel makes his decisive departure from the classical conception. The family as such does not enter into the arena of political life. It generates no further, larger associations that build on the ethical ties of the family, at least not directly. Rather, the function of the family in Hegel's political philosophy is to produce that propertied individual who serves as the foundation for modern political theory. But these Hegelian propertied individuals, ready to enter into the contracts of civil society, are different in one important way from their Lockean or Hobbesian counterparts, who enter into contracts directly from the state of nature. These Hegelian individuals have an ethical component to their consciousness, not in the sense of being able to intuit or deduce the laws and rights of nature, but in the sense of having a predisposition to think of themselves as an integral part of a larger social unit. They know that the property of which they are the proprietors is not theirs by individual acquisition but is theirs as embodying a social product, as "family capital,"[17] in Hegel's words. Hegel also differs from Locke in that he explicitly acknowledges that these individuals who leave the family for civil society are male. For Hegel, women's proper sphere remains domestic. We shall discuss the implications of this in the concluding chapter.

There is a certain politicization of life in Hegel's philosophy. As we have seen, many political theorists conceptualize the family as pre- or nonpolitical. Hegel concurs insofar as he is treating the family as phenomenologically experienced, arguing that internal family relations should not be politicized and conceptualized in terms of rights. At the same time, however, Hegel argues that when the family is fully philosophically conceptualized and set in a larger context, we can see that there are essential political dimensions to family life in the transmission of capital and in the inculcation of ethical consciousness, what we might today call socialization for citizenship. The family as an institution provides a stable, continuing source of capital on which the economic system of civil society can be built and a nascent civic-mindedness on the basis of which the political state can be secured.

Whereas for Locke the rights of inheritance are discussed in terms of one individual handing down accumulated property to another,[18] for Hegel the transmission of property from the individuals of one generation to the individuals of another is mediated through the institution of the family, so that this property retains its social dimension. This theme plays a role in Hegel's discussion of the way in which property rights contribute to the proper functioning and stability of the state. As we shall see later on, Hegel rejects any political theory that makes the securing of property rights the principal basis or task of the state. This is not to say that Hegel thinks economic considerations are irrelevant to the state, but he does think they are insufficient as a foundation for political theory because such a conception does not do full justice to the nature of human dignity. Hegel reverses the means-ends relationship that obtains between property rights and the establishment of the state in classical liberal contractarian theory. For Locke, for example, the state secures natural property rights. For Hegel, on the other hand, property rights secure the stability of the state.

For property rights to play this role in the Hegelian state, Hegel must build on a social conception of property rights, in contrast to the individualist conception of property rights in liberal theory. The roots of this social view of property are in Hegel's doctrine of Abstract Right in the first section of the *Philosophy of Right.* In view of their importance, Hegel's arguments there warrant more detailed examination.

Property Rights I: Hegel and Locke

In the exposition that follows, I shall continue to use Locke as the most appropriate foil against which the distinctive features of Hegel's views clearly emerge, because Locke's is the most influential and well-known defense of property rights as conceptualized along the lines that Hegel is criticizing. The choice of Locke here might be questioned, because Hegel does not mention Locke by name in his discussion. But one should remember that Hegel rarely mentions other philosophers by name. On the whole, he usually mentions specific names only when he is either crediting someone with being the first to establish some principle or when he is engaged in some specific dispute with one of his contemporaries. Otherwise, his usual tack is to sketch the position he is criticizing and leave it up to the reader to fill in the appropriate names of those who hold such a position. In this case, it seems clear that Locke's account fits the description of the kind of theory Hegel is attacking.

A word of warning, or perhaps apology, seems due to committed Lockeans here because Locke as seen through Hegelian eyes may seem different from Locke as seen through Lockean eyes. This should not be surprising. If the Hegelian perspective on political theory is indeed distinctive, one could expect that other theories would appear different in its light. Indeed, this is one of the rewards of studying Hegel's political philosophy. It allows one to view other positions in a different context than that in which they are usually appraised, especially because Hegel, more than any other philosopher, developed his own positions via critiques of the views of other philosophers. Although I think the account of Locke given here can be reconciled with other, perhaps more familiar, readings of Locke's arguments defending private property rights, such a reconciliation is outside the scope of this study. My primary interest here is to bring out the salient features of Hegel's own views and the grounds of his criticisms of other views of the nature of property rights.

Hegel's analysis and defense of private property rights is one of the most politically important consequences of his philosophic commitment to idealism. Hegel's metaphysical deduction of private property rights in the "Abstract Right" section of the *Philosophy of Right* follows directly from his identification of the will as the source of right. Hegel's identification of politics as the sphere of the will, part of the realm of "objective spirit," is intended to give political institutions the essential function of mediating between two dimensions of human beings: (1) their properties as purely "natural" creatures, acting out of particular desires, inclinations, talents, and so on (along the lines of Hobbesian psychology or the *homo economicus* of classical political economy) and (2) their properties as purely "cultural" creatures, completely given over to the formal universality of the Kantian moral will or to the contemplation of the universal truths of art, religion, and philosophy.

Hegel considers property rights to be essential to the free and full development of human personality. Locke's defense of private property presents a materialist, consequentialist argument for private property rights. In contrast, Hegel presents an idealist argument that makes the right to private property intrinsic to the nature of freedom as such. For Hegel, a Lockean view of property is literally degrading to human beings in that it treats them as beings on a grade lower than human dignity requires; it treats them on the level of biological, animal nature rather than on the level of human, spiritual nature. Locke's account of property is based on the natural dimensions of human beings—their having bodies and biological needs. Hegel's account is based on the spiritual dimensions of human beings—their possession of minds and wills. The contrast is made clear by simply juxtaposing the relevant passages from Locke and Hegel. Following is first Locke, then Hegel:

> Men, being once born, have a right to their preservation, and consequently to meat and drink and such other things as nature affords for their subsistence. . . . Every man has a property in his own person; this nobody has any right to but himself. The labor of his body and the work of his hands, we may say, are properly his. Whatsoever then he removes out of the state that nature has provided and left it in, he has mixed his labor with, and joined it to something that is his own, and thereby makes it his property.[19]

> A person has as his substantive end the right of putting his will into any and every thing and thereby making it his, because it has no such end in itself and derives its destiny and soul from his will. This is the absolute right of appropriation which man has over all "things." . . . If emphasis is placed on my needs, then the possession of property appears as a means to their

satisfaction, but the true position is that, from the standpoint of freedom, property is the first embodiment of freedom and so is in itself a substantive end.[20]

Although the Lockean problematic is focused on the distribution of goods, the Hegelian problematic is focused on the productive activity of the self. On the Lockean model, a self that is already fully constituted in the state of nature stands ready to appropriate and internalize the objects it needs for biological subsistence. On the Hegelian model, both the human self and the external world become reciprocally constituted as self-subsistent when natural objects become the property of human will.

For Hegel, making the things of the world subject to the human will demonstrates the dignity of human personality over and above biological nature. In one sense, it demonstrates the truth of idealism as well. "The free will, therefore, is the idealism which does not take things as they are to be absolute, while realism pronounces them to be absolute, even if they exist only in the form of finitude. Even an animal has gone beyond this realist philosophy since it devours things and so proves that they are not absolutely self- subsistent."[21]

This "refutation" of realism (what we would be as likely to call naturalism or materialism) through the eating habits of animals is little more than a reversal of Johnson's famous refutation of Berkeley's idealism by kicking a stone. Nonetheless, there are important questions at issue here.[22] For Hegel, the right to property enters into the very definition of selfhood in a way not found in Locke, because the act of appropriating objects is an act more fundamentally formative of the self for Hegel than it is for Locke. Hegel's theory of selfhood, or personality, based in the will, has been described by one commentator as "a purposive conception of the self" that "suggests the possibility of self-transcendence through action."[23]

To maintain such a conception, Hegel must adhere to a strict separation between the properly human and the merely biological aspects of human nature, and he must assign property rights to the former aspect. Hegel's strategy here has both positive and negative features. On the one hand, it provides him a firm foundation for the inalienability of property rights, and it lays the foundation for his social conception of property rights. On the other hand, the rigidity of the separation between biological and human nature carries over into the rigidity of the separation between the economic activities of civil society and the political activities of the state. As we shall see later on, one result of this is that Hegel's political theory cannot properly solve some of the economic issues that it should be expected to solve, even if one accepts the Hegelian principle that economics cannot be the basis of political theory.

Hegel insists that the human will must be actively involved whenever we properly speak of rights. This leads him to analyze every dimension of property rights as a further development of the concept of the will, including even the sense in which we may be said to have rights in or to the use and preservation of our own bodies. For Locke, we have property even in our own bodies.[24] But we are not the only ones who have property in our bodies, because for Locke the prohibition against suicide and injuring oneself or others stems from the rights God has to our bodies. "For men being all the workmanship of one omnipotent and infinitely wise Maker—all the servants of one sovereign master, sent into the world by his order, and about his business—they are his property whose workmanship they are, made to last during his, not another's pleasure."[25]

In contrast, Hegel refuses to speak of humans having rights in or over themselves or their bodies. "To speak of a right over one's own life that a person has is a contradiction, because this would mean that a person has a right over himself."[26]

For Hegel, this Lockean language impermissibly objectifies human beings. To speak this way is to treat persons as things or animals, because only over such entities do human beings have property rights. A person is by nature that kind of entity over which no entity, even oneself, can have property rights. Rather than speaking of rights *in* our bodies, it would be more appropriate to say that for Hegel we have rights *through* our bodies. Hegel systematically rejects any kind of instrumentalist account of the relationship between ourselves and our bodies. To use one of Hegel's own examples, an assault on one's body is not experienced as damage to one's property but rather as a direct injury to one's self as a person. Our bodies are the embodiment of our wills, and it is through them that the will reaches out to the world.

Hegel draws several political consequences from this, the most important being the denial that the enslavement of one human being to another can ever be justified. Hegel criticizes materialist justifications of property rights for their failure to recognize that slavery is by its very nature an affront to human dignity. By basing property rights on natural needs, a materialist justification treats human beings as members of the animal rather than of the specifically human realm. As a result, it leaves the door open to human beings being treated as natural objects. Hegel is not here accusing Locke or others of advocating slavery nor even of not being able to muster sound arguments against slavery from their points of view.[27] His argument is that the terms of discourse and the context in which such arguments are given are inappropriate to the subject. With a proper (Hegelian) understanding of the nature of human dignity, arguments for slavery are absolutely ruled out of court, and arguments against slavery almost need not be given because it is immediately obvious that slavery is an injustice.

> The alleged justification of slavery (by reference to all its proximate beginnings through physical force, capture in war, saving and preservation of life, upkeep, education, philanthropy, the slave's own acquiescence, and so forth), as well as the justification of a slaveownership as simple lordship in general, and all historical views of the justice of slavery and lordship, depend on regarding man as a natural entity pure and simple, as an existent not in conformity with its concept (an existent also to which arbitrariness is appropriate). The argument for the absolute injustice of slavery, on the other hand, adheres to the concept of man as mind, as something inherently free.[28]

To distinguish a naturalist, or materialist, view of property rights from his own spiritualist, or idealist, view, Hegel distinguishes possession from property. I may have possession of some object through my body, but I have no property in it unless I recognize my will objectified in this object.[29] Even this distinction, however, does not exhaust Hegel's account of the true nature of property rights. Hegel's idealist account of property rights immediately develops into a social account of property rights. For Hegel, then, properly speaking, Locke never reached the level of property *right* at all. Locke is speaking only of legalized possession, which may be backed by the force of the state but lacks a properly ethical, political dimension. Rights are for Hegel essentially intersubjective. Rights of any kind constitute relationships not between persons and things but among persons, that is, among embodied wills.[30]

By emphasizing that property represents recognition of the externalization of the will, Hegel is able to introduce a social dimension into the institution of private property at the very outset. Although initially it suffices that I recognize my own will in my property, this subjective recognition is insufficient to ground property rights because it is too tenuous and unstable. These rights require the institution of contracts to secure their existence. In Lockean liberalism, property is fundamentally conceived of as a relation between persons and things, and the rights of others appear primarily as limitations on mine. In contrast, in Hegel's analysis it becomes clear that property rights exist only within a system of mutual recognition of the wills and rights of others, such that the rights of others are the ground for the realization of the rights of any individual. This leads Hegel to his doctrine of contract. "This relation of will to will is the true and proper ground in which freedom is existent.—The sphere of contract is made up of this mediation whereby I hold property not merely by means of a thing and my subjective will, but by means of another's will as well and so hold it in virtue of my participation in a common will."[31]

As important as the situating of property right in the realm of spirit and not in the realm of nature is for Hegel, it is equally important that property right is not assigned to the realm of morality. The liberal tradition tends to see political rights and duties as a species of moral rights and obligations. For Hegel, however, the sphere of right, as a sphere of ethical life, is properly one of intersubjectivity, whereas morality remains individualistically subjective. Hegel's arguments to this effect are in the section on "Morality" in the *Philosophy of Right* and lead beyond the scope of this study. For our purposes, it is sufficient at this point to note the distinction Hegel makes between contracts and promises in the section of the *Philosophy of Right* currently under examination.

> The difference between a mere promise and a contract lies in the fact that a promise is a statement that I will give or do or perform something in the *future*, and a promise still remains a subjective volition which because it is subjective I can still alter. A stipulation in a contract, on the other hand, is itself already the embodiment of the will's decision in the sense that by making the stipulation I have alienated my property, it has now ceased to be mine, and I already recognize it as the property of another.[32]

The central point here is the unalterableness of the contract, the fact that the will expressed in a contract has a public character that gives it objectivity. Similarly, in Hegel's treatment violation of contract, or "Wrong" is not treated as a moral category. (Hegel's term is *Unrecht*, literally "unright" or "nonright.") Rather, it is treated as a consequence of the fact that individual wills following particular inclinations inevitably come into conflict with the general principles of adhering to contracts, principles that they acknowledge as the necessary framework

for their own activities.[33] Here, too, the social dimension, the conflict
between individual action and its institutional framework, takes prece-
dence over the moral dimension, the conflict between the action and a
maxim subjectively held by the same individual. Indeed, for Hegel the
entire moral dimension of the will is generated by an attempt to resolve
at an individual level conflicts generated in social interaction.[34] Morality results from the internalization of social tensions, and it cannot be
held to apply to human beings in any pristine state of nature.

This view departs from the contractarian tradition of political theory,
which generates a political system out of the failure to adhere to the
moral law or through tensions and contradictions in the moral law
in a state of nature. In his presentation concerning contract, Hegel
makes his first extended references in the *Philosophy of Right* to a theme
of major importance in his political philosophy: his criticism of the
contractarian tradition for basing political obligations on contracts and
individual consent, which reduces public law to the status of private
law.

> The intrusion of this contractual relation, and relationships concerning pri-
> vate property generally, into the relation between the individual and the state
> has been productive of the greatest confusion in both constitutional law and
> public life. Just as at one time political rights and duties were considered and
> maintained to be an unqualified private property of particular individuals,
> something contrasted with the right of the monarch and the state, so also in
> more recent times the rights of the monarch and the state have been regarded
> as the subjects of a contract, as something embodying merely a common will
> and resulting from the arbitrariness of parties united into a state.[35]

Throughout the section on "Abstract Right" in the *Philosophy of
Right*, Hegel has taken great care, as we have seen, to separate the
realm of property rights from both that of nature, with its concomitant materialism, and that of morality, with its concomitant subjective
universality. In this section, Hegel has offered a thorough analysis of
property right as a medium for human intersubjectivity.

This social conception of property enables property to play the mediating role that it assumes in the later "Ethical Life" section of the
Philosophy of Right. It allows Hegel to maintain that although a valid
conception of right demands that everyone have property (because it is
an essential component of free personality), this conception also demonstrates the vacuousness of the demand that everyone have equal property. To make such a demand is again to overlook the ontological gap

between human freedom and nature. It treats human beings as essentially bound to the particularities and vicissitudes of nature.

> Of course men are equal, but only *qua* persons, that is, with respect only to the source from which possession springs; the inference from this is that everyone must have property. Hence, if you wish to talk of equality, it is this equality which you must have in view. But this equality is something apart from the fixing of particular amounts, from the question of how much I own. From this point of view it is false to maintain that justice requires everyone's property to be equal, since it requires only that everyone shall own property. The truth is that particularity is just the sphere where there is room for inequality and where equality would be wrong.[36]

The sharpness with which Hegel draws the distinction between equal property rights and rights to equal property is particularly noteworthy in this passage. This is not the more familiar claim that equal property rights do not require that everyone have equal property. This claim is compatible with a situation in which everyone's property is in fact equal. Hegel holds the much stronger position that a valid conception of property rights specifically excludes a situation wherein all have equal property. There must be, on Hegel's analysis, opportunity for arbitrary inequalities to have their way. The full significance of this shall emerge shortly, but we can briefly say a fundamental consideration is that these natural inequalities allow a differentiated economic structure to emerge in civil society. The Hegelian state operates by giving conscious, political significance to these natural, economic differences. If these natural inequalities were not allowed the room to have their effect within the Hegelian political system, the Hegelian state would be reduced to the homogeneous, leveling universality he criticizes rather than rising to the articulated universality he claims to have achieved.

Property Rights II: Hegel, Liberalism, Marxism

This question of the nature of property rights is an important area of contention in modern political philosophy and often serves as a dividing line between widely accepted liberal and socialist views of property rights. Thus, it will sharpen our understanding of Hegel's relation to both camps to note that Marx's critique of capitalist private property relations contains both Lockean and Hegelian components. We may recall that Locke's premise that one makes something one's property by mixing the labor of one's body with it leads him eventually to the position that property should accrue to me in proportion to the labor I invest in its creation. Marx retains this conception from Locke. Within Marx's system, this conception yields the concept of exploitation, where what is wrong with capitalist production is that workers are not rewarded by the system in proportion to the value their labor creates.

From Hegel, Marx retains the idea that the possession of property as the externalization and objectification of my will is a necessary part of the free development of my personality. Within Marx's system, this conception yields the concept of alienation, where what is wrong with capitalist production is not the violation of some principle of distributive justice but rather the violation of the essence of a free human being.[37]

Taking note of this element of Marx's theory can prevent a common misreading of Marx from an exclusively Lockean perspective, where Marx is taken to justify a system referred to either as state socialism or state capitalism, depending more on the political predilections of the speaker than on the nature of the system in question. Such a system concentrates decision-making power in the hands of a centralized bureaucracy. It thus ignores the elements in Marx's theory that lead him to call for radical economic democracy, because these elements ultimately derive from the Hegelian idea of property as embodied social recognition rather than from the Lockean idea of property as a means to the satisfaction of material needs.

For most of us, "Marxism" and "materialism" are closely related terms.

Yet the analysis I have presented here demonstrates that Marx builds upon Hegel's idealist conception of personal property, while he rejects the political consequences Locke and others drew from a materialist conception of property. To see this clearly, we must recall that for Locke property rights over external objects derive from our ownership of our own bodies—that is to say, ownership of the relevant means of production in the original state of nature. Locke's state of nature is not static. As the story unfolds, money is introduced, and labor, rather than being seen as an expression of one's personality à la Marx, comes to be seen as a salable commodity like any other, such that the fruits of the labor of someone in the employ of another belong to the employer, not the laborer. By the time one reaches Locke's full account of civil society, this defense of property rights becomes the doctrine that the propertied classes must consent to any alienation of their property—No Taxation Without Representation in its practical, American form.

One result of Locke's treatment is that the distinction between rights in one's personal possessions and rights in productive property is obscured, because the transition from one to the other is accomplished so gradually from the initial state of nature to fully constituted government. This is a crucial distinction maintained by Hegel and by Marx as well. Hegel argues that every individual is entitled to sufficient property *(Vermögen)* to establish oneself with permanent capital and attain social and legal standing (primarily through membership in a corporation). But he insists that this requirement is of an entirely different conceptual order from the question of one's personal possessions and argues that the economic and legal system must remain indifferent to this latter question regarding equality of possessions.

It is often overlooked that Marx, too, is not concerned with the question of equality of personal possessions. Although countercultural communes of the 1960s, for example, often invoked Marx in defense of a policy of communally shared possessions, this policy cannot in fact be derived from Marx's theory. His theory argues only for social ownership of the social means of production, for reasons having to do with the Marxist conception of democracy already alluded to, and not for the sharing of personal property. Far from arguing against the institution of personal property rights, Marx makes the loss of personal property an important element of his critique of capitalism. In the first instance, capitalism increasingly robs workers of goods under their personal control ("the more objects the worker produces, the fewer can he possess.")[38] More important, loss of control over the object of production is a loss of the worker's own essence; workers lose their specifically human capacities and become more animalistic.[39]

This is Marx's most radical critique of capitalism, and it is incomprehensible without its Hegelian component, namely, the idea that property rights are essential to human freedom as such and not merely for the satisfaction of needs. If Marx had accepted the latter as the justification of private property rights, there would be no grounds for the Marxist critique of capitalism if the workers' material needs were being met. Furthermore, there would be no grounds for the more recent developments in the Western Marxist critique of capitalism that lay more stress on factors of subjectivity and alienation than Marx himself did. This is the legacy of Hegelian idealism at the core of Marxist materialism.

Marx rejects in Hegel the idea that the economic realm of civil society remains in the sphere of nature, of necessity not susceptible to the kind of political restructuring that would allow economic activities to

be transformed into a realm of freedom. This explains why Marx ultimately calls for the overcoming of the civil society–state dualism and
why Hegel ultimately rejects the standpoint of civil society in favor of
the state.

Civil Society, History, and Nature

The next chapter will trace the steps by which the economic perspective of civil society leads to the political perspective of the state. But
before we return to pick up the thread of what was earlier called the
phenomenology of ethical consciousness leading from the family to the
state, having now examined the philosophical underpinnings of Hegel's
analysis of property, which plays a key role in this development, we
must first clarify a seemingly glaring incongruity in Hegel's analysis.
If, as was just stated, the problem with the economic level of activity
in civil society is that it remains bound to the realm of nature, what
then was the purpose of the analysis we have just finished tracing, which
sharply separates the sphere of property from that of nature? Is the
earlier, "Abstract Right" section of the *Philosophy of Right* superseded
by the connection made between the sphere of civil society and nature
in the "Ethical Life" section of the *Philosophy of Right*? It seems clear
that, on the one hand, the doctrine of property that Hegel brings to
his analysis of civil society commits him to rejecting any connection
between the sphere of civil society and the realm of nature. Yet, on
the other hand, Hegel's ultimate rejection of the standpoint of civil
society depends precisely on such a connection between civil society
and nature. What sense, then, can be given to Hegel's claims that the
economic sphere of civil society both is and is not the sphere of natural
relations?

The answer to this question will lead us to the deepest level of the
question of the relationship between philosophy and history and will
reveal the full significance of the passage quoted at the beginning of this
chapter, that "civil society is the [stage of] difference which intervenes
between the family and the state."

It will be necessary now to recall salient points from the preceding chapters. The dominant form of consciousness of the modern era
is characterized by the point of view Hegel describes as that of the
understanding. Hegel has in mind here principally the standpoint of
modern scientific rationality, which attempts to explain phenomena
through laws stemming from inductive generalization. This mode of
thought separates the phenomena it considers into discrete entities,

held in isolation from each other and reflecting the general bifurcation (*Entzweiung*) of the modern world into separate realms of existence. In the face of the political era initiated by the French Revolution, which claims that now for the first time in history reason is to structure the world, this dominant mode of modern consciousness sees past history and tradition as irrelevant to the new world of reason. For modern consciousness, political theory must now depend solely on the nature of reason itself, and it is this demand that motivates the structure of the *Philosophy of Right*. Although acceding to this demand, Hegel at the same time argues that this represents a misunderstanding of the relationship between philosophy and history, and that a properly rational philosophy would see that this discontinuity between philosophy and history is itself a historical phenomenon. The autonomy of political philosophy is seen to depend on the rationality of a historical epoch that grants this autonomy, an epoch whose characteristic form of consciousness nonetheless remains blind to the connection between philosophy and history, preventing modern political consciousness from fulfilling its project of rationally reconstructing the world. With this in mind, we must now turn our attention to the parallels between the ahistoricity of modern philosophy and the ahistoricity of modern civil society.

The idea that the workings of civil society are in some sense "natural" and are as such essentially independent of historical processes is taken over by Hegel from the British political economists. Hegel primarily cites Adam Smith and James Steuart in this regard, but he also mentions J. B. Say and David Ricardo, who in turn adopted the idea from the French Physiocrats.[40] Hegel calls political economy "one of the sciences which have arisen out of the conditions of the modern world."[41] He praises it as "a credit to thought"[42] because of its ability to find necessary and universal laws amidst a maelstrom of arbitrary activities. Although Hegel incorporates the essential findings of the political economists into his system fairly intact, in true dialectical fashion this appropriation of political economy is at the same time a limitation of the scope of its truth, established by situating it within a larger context. Although Hegel views political economy as the science of the understanding par excellence, he is sharply critical of attempts to view political economy as a true system of philosophy. "The recent science of political economy in particular, which in Germany is known as rational economy of the state, or intelligent national economy, has in England especially appropriated the name of philosophy."[43]

The level of universality reached by the laws of political economy remains limited by the particularities of the realm of nature political economy begins with. Taking its point of departure from the desires, inclinations, particular abilities, and contingencies of the individual, natural will, political economy cannot reach the level of autonomy that for Hegel is the hallmark of a true system of philosophy. In contrast to philosophy, which as a manifestation of reason seeks to show the unity and interconnectedness of the universal and the particular, political economy, as a manifestation of the understanding, is content to demonstrate only an external reconciliation of the universal and the particular. The laws of political economy are laws which do not enter the consciousness of the individuals in civil society and therefore appear not as forms of freedom but as dictates of necessity.[44] From the point of view of political economy, the natural needs that form the basis of the sphere of civil society are prior to and are the basis of the political sphere. Modern consciousness views the sphere of politics as generated through the labor and the interactions human beings undertake to satisfy these needs. "This system [civil society] may be prima facie regarded as the external state, the state based on need, the state as the understanding envisages it."[45]

It is at this point that Hegel's dialectical reversal takes place. It appears to modern consciousness that the sphere of civil society based on nature precedes the political sphere. Hegel argues that in reality the political sphere of the modern state precedes the creation of the economic sphere. Civil society, as the sphere in which "natural" relations are seen to flourish, is itself a creation of historical, political processes, which create this sphere along with the concomitant, distinctively modern way in which it comprehends itself through the categories of a naturalistic, ahistorical "science" of Political Economy. In the modern world, argues Hegel, the autonomy of civil society is not a natural phenomenon but a political one, granted by the state in response to the nature of modernity.

This nature of modernity is expressed in its most general form in the famous dictum in the *Phenomenology* that "everything depends on grasping and expressing the ultimate truth not as substance but as subject as well."[46] Translated into the political categories appropriate to our discussion here, this means that in the modern era politics must be founded on human subjectivity (that is, the will) and not on "natural law." Hegel distinguishes two senses in which laws may be said to be natural. If "natural" is meant in a genetic sense, then such laws cannot be ultimately binding on human beings because humans are "spiritual" beings, as we have seen. But if "natural" is meant in a teleological sense, describing laws befitting the fully developed nature of the being in question, then it is permissible to speak of "natural," binding political laws if these laws stem from the will and express the nature of human freedom.[47]

In this latter sense, civil society is natural, and it is in this sense that civil society is so importantly the creation of the modern world. Civil society allows whatever union is to be found among individuals to emerge with natural necessity from the free interplay of their differences, in accordance with the laws of the marketplace. In giving "all determinations of the idea their due," modernity for the first time allows human subjectivity to plumb its full depth in the world. This is the foundation of politics in the modern world, in which "the consciousness of the spiritual is now the basis of the political fabric."[48]

The creation at the beginning of the modern period of civil society as an autonomous sphere in which natural desires and subjective inclination have full reign results from the dissolution of the immediate bonds between private and public law, and between the family and the state, which were characteristic of the feudal period.[49] This separation is for Hegel characteristic of modernity, and is the historical basis for the assertion that "civil society is the [stage of] difference which intervenes between the family and the state."[50] This irruption of civil society between family and state as the sphere of free individuality is the historical basis for the concurrent change in the conceptualization of the family vis-a-vis political theory discussed earlier. Hegel is concerned with the origins of both civil society and the new mode of scientific explanation that accompanies it. As always, for Hegel, new forms of social organization are accompanied by and intrinsically and essentially related to new kinds of claims to philosophical truth. Hegelian philosophy is distinctively oriented to investigating these relationships.

Hegel's particular form of idealism, focused as it is in his political philosophy on the self-consciousness of the citizens of the modern state, is focused in a unique way specifically on the interplay between the material and ideological foundations of modern consciousness. Hegel's analysis here reveals the intrinsic connection between the modern era's self-understanding in terms of political economy in the economic sphere and in terms of contractarian political theory in the political sphere. In both cases, property relations are seen as natural and as the basis of all other social, political relations. Although he makes both these points, Hegel does not himself give particular emphasis to their interconnection, even though this interconnection follows directly from his account of both theoretical frameworks, in large part because the economic presuppositions of contractarian theory are more visible in its earlier, British form (for example, in Hobbes and Locke), while Hegel has in mind primarily its later, continental form (for example, in Rousseau and Kant), where the formation of the political sphere comes more to the fore.

If one can for a moment speak of a Hegelian transition from a state of nature to a state of civil society analogous to the transition in the contractarian tradition, one could say that the interpretation developed here shows that although for Hobbes and Locke this transition is motivated more by considerations related to economic security and property, for Hegel it is motivated more by political considerations related to sovereignty and personhood, in a way that brings Hegel closer to Rousseau and Kant in their use of the contractarian mode. But, without of course developing anything like a Marxist conception of ideology, Hegel shows political economy and contractarian political theories to be marked by the same features to which Marx would later call attention as the distinguishing characteristics of ideological theories. That is to say, ideological theories are theories that capture and reflect essential aspects of the social reality that generates them, but in a static, reified way that hides its historical dimensions. For Hegel, this historical dimension must be preserved precisely to prevent these theories from overstepping their limits. The danger facing modernity is that all relations, including familial, political, and ethical ones, will be reduced to the level of civil society, to the level of needs, contracts, and atomistic individualism, leading at best to a lack of the kind of political, ethical identity needed for the proper functioning of the state (see Chapter 5) and at worst to the kind of chaos that followed the radical subjectivism and voluntarism of the French Revolution (see Chapter 3).[51]

Despite Hegel's designating of civil society as the basis for the consciousness of the modern political era, he nonetheless attempts to demonstrate in his analysis of civil society that though originally seen as an independent sphere, in actuality it depends on the political authority of the state for its sustenance. In making the transition from civil society to the state, he says:

> Since the state appears as a result in the advance of the philosophic concept through displaying itself as the true ground [of the earlier phases], that show of mediation is now cancelled and the state has become directly present before us. Actually, therefore, the state as such is not so much the result as the beginning. It is within the state that the family is first developed into civil

society, and it is the Idea of the state itself which disrupts itself into these two moments.[52]

His analysis of civil society reveals Hegel at his most materialist moments. The political self-understanding of the revolutionaries of the French Revolution is here shown to be, in its extreme subjectivity and ahistoricity, a theoretical manifestation of the economic base of modern society. But it would be a mistake to see in this, as some have done, an early version of historical materialism.[53] To take this view is to remain within the naturalist, economistic framework, which is indeed the foundation of modern consciousness but which Hegel's philosophy attempts to show is ignorant of the historical presuppositions of its perspective and thus unable to bring its desired ends to fruition.

We may now answer the question, posed earlier, regarding the extent to which the connection between the economic activities of civil society and the realm of nature in the "Ethical Life" section of the *Philosophy of Right* vitiates the earlier strict separation of property, as a spiritual phenomenon, from the realm of nature in the "Abstract Right" section. We may now say that, when properly understood, property is indeed part of the spiritual, ethical nature and not part of the natural dimension of human beings. In the sphere of ethical life, Hegel accepts from political economists the identification of property rights and economic activity as natural because this is the basis of modern consciousness in its own eyes. The phenomenological aspect of Hegel's method commits him to beginning with this naturalistic standpoint, in accordance with the dictates of the consciousness of modernity. His dialectic of civil society, however, is intended to demonstrate that, if followed through to its completion, this standpoint transcends itself, at which point consciousness sees that its supposed natural independence was predicated on civil society being part of a larger political and, ultimately, historical process.

Hegel's transition from civil society to the state cannot then be understood in terms of the distinction, common to contractarian theory, between the state of nature and the political state. For Hegel, the entire Lockean regulatory apparatus is encompassed within the sphere of civil society under the headings of "The Administration of Justice" and the "Police."[54] Rather, the transition to the state represents a transition to a different philosophical mode of conceptualizing the relationship between the individual and the state. It represents a shift in viewpoint comparable to the transition from the natural standpoint to the standpoint of science accomplished in the course of the *Phenomenology*, a development phenomenologically experienced as being propelled by external necessity but retrospectively comprehended as an internal development.

In contrast to the classical liberal distinction between civil society and the state, Hegel's distinction between these two terms comes much closer to Rousseau's distinction between government and sovereignty, between the collective will of the body politic considered as the compilation of all the individual wills of the society, as the will of all (*la volonté des tous*), versus this collective will considered as the truly universal general will (*la volonté generale*), a distinction which Hegel himself, interestingly enough, misses in Rousseau, whom he interprets simply as a contractarian theorist.[55] (Hegel refers to the United States as a nation constructed from the point of view of civil society, not yet "a real state,"[56] and we shall examine the meaning of this more closely further on.)

In what follows, we shall see how Hegel gives an account of the progression from civil society to the political state in terms compatible with both the economistic categories of civil society itself and the political categories appropriate to the standpoint of the state. Parallel to this objective, institutional side of the dialectic of civil society, we shall find a subjective side relating to the consciousness of the individuals in civil society. Here will be found, in Hegel's analysis of the crucial educative role of labor, many of the themes presented in Hegel's dialectic of lordship and bondage in the *Phenomenology*, to which section Hegel himself makes reference,[57] such as the increasing gap between desire and satisfaction and between nature and culture, and the function of labor in terms of the externalization and universalization of the will.

Notes

1. *PR*, §182A, p. 266.
2. *PR*, §183, p. 123.
3. Ilting, vol. 4, p. 483 (my translation).
4. *PR*, §187, pp. 124–125.
5. For example, George H. Sabine's *History of Political Theory*, 3d ed. (New York: Holt, Rinehart and Winston, 1961) and Raymond Plant's *Hegel* (Bloomington: Indiana University Press, 1973) are representative in that they pay scant attention to Hegel's views on the family.
6. Aristotle, *Politics*, ed. and trans. Ernest Barker (New York: Oxford University Press, 1962), pp. 1–7.

7. Plato, *Republic*, trans. Francis MacDonald Cornford (New York: Oxford University Press, 1973), pp. 2–7, 156–168.

8. See Gordon J. Schochet, *Patriarchalism in Political Thought* (New York: Basic Books, 1975).

9. Aristotle, *Politics*, p. 2.

10. See the Introduction to Thomas Hobbes, *Leviathan*, ed. C. B. MacPherson (Middlesex: Penguin Books, 1975), pp. 25–30.

11. Quoted in Schochet, *Patriarchalism*, pp. 227–243.

12. Reproduced in John Locke, *Two Treatises of Government*, rev. ed., ed. Peter Laslett (New York: New American Library, 1965), p. 169.

13. Jean-Jacques Rousseau, "Discourse on Political Economy," in *On the Social Contract*, ed. Roger D. Masters, trans. Judith R. Masters (New York: St. Martin's Press, 1978), p. 211.

14. Jean-Jacques Rousseau, "Discourse on the Origin of Inequality," in *The Social Contract and Discourses*, trans., G.D.H. Cole (New York: Everyman-Dutton, 1950), pp. 234–239.

15. Immanuel Kant, *Gessammelte Schriften*, vol. 19, PrAkAus., p. 543, R7879.

16. *PR*, §159, p. 110. I am indebted to Shlomo Avineri for emphasizing this point during a seminar at the University of California, San Diego, in the spring of 1979.

17. *PR*, §170–172, pp. 116–117.

18. John Locke, *The Second Treatise of Government*, ed. Thomas P. Peardon (Indianapolis: Bobbs-Merrill, 1952), pp. 40–43.

19. Locke, *Second Treatise*, pp. 16–17.

20. *PR*, §41–45, pp. 40–42.

21. *Ibid.*, §44A, p. 236.

22. There are parallels between Hegel's and Locke's disagreements on the nature of property rights and their disagreements over the nature of perception. In both their respective political philosophies and their epistemological doctrines, Locke stresses the senses as recipients of objects from the external world, while Hegel stresses the intellect as forming the external world. Compare Book 2, Chapter 9 ("Of Perception") of Locke's *Essay Concerning Human Understanding* with Section A, Chapter 2 ("Perception") of Hegel's *Phenomenology of Mind*. For an extended discussion of the correspondences between metaphysical and political appropriations of the objects of nature in modern philosophy, see William Leiss, *The Domination of Nature* (Boston: Beacon Press, 1974).

23. Adrian M. S. Piper, "Property and the Limits of the Self," *Political Theory* 8:1, February 1980, p. 50.

24. Locke's theory of property is rooted in this "possessive individualism," as has been persuasively demonstrated by C. B. MacPherson in *The Political Theory of Possessive Individualism* (London: Oxford University Press, 1964).

25. Locke, *Second Treatise*, pp. 5–6.

26. Ilting, vol. 3, p. 261.

27. For Locke on slavery, see Robert J. Loewenberg, "John Locke and the Antebellum Defense of Slavery," *Political Theory* 13:2, May 1985, pp. 266–291; and James Farr, "'So Vile and Miserable an Estate': The Problem of Slavery in Locke's Political Thought," *Political Theory* 14:2, May 1986, pp. 262–289.

28. *PR*, §57, p. 48.

29. *Ibid.*, §45, p. 42.

30. See Peter G. Stillman, "Hegel's Analysis of Property in the *Philosophy of Right*," *Cardozo Law Review* 10:5–6, March/April 1989, pp. 1031–1072.

31. *PR*, §71, p. 57.

32. *Ibid.*, §79, p. 61.

33. *Ibid.*, §82, p. 64.

34. On this both the *Phenomenology* and the *Philosophy of Right* agree. Compare the transition from "Absolute Freedom and Terror" to "Morality" in the former with the transition from "Abstract Right" to "Morality" in the latter.

35. *PR*, §75, p. 59. "At one time" refers to feudalism. Central to Hegel's analysis of feudalism is this idea that under the feudal system political rights were regarded as the personal possessions of individuals rather than as stemming from public law.

36. *PR*, §49A, p. 237.

37. The tensions between these two elements in Marx's theory are discussed in Stanley Moore's *Marx on the Choice Between Socialism and Communism* (Cambridge: Harvard University Press, 1980). One virtue of Moore's treatment is that it demonstrates that these tensions are not resolved simply by making a distinction between a young, Hegelian, idealist, philosopher Marx and a mature, materialist, political economist Marxist.

38. Karl Marx, "Economic and Philosophic Manuscripts," in *The Marx-Engels Reader*, ed. Robert C. Tucker (New York: W. W. Norton and Company, 1972), p. 58.

39. *Ibid.*, p. 60.

40. See Georg Lukács, *The Young Hegel*, trans. Rodney Livingstone (London: Merlin Press, 1975); Raymond Plant, "Hegel's Social Theory," *New Left Review*, 1977, nos. 103–104; and Paul Chamley, *Economie Politique et Philosophie chez Steuart et Hegel* (Paris: Librairie Dalloz, 1963).

41. *PR*, §189A, p. 126.

42. *Ibid.*, §189A, p. 268.

43. *Enc. I*, §7, p. 14.

44. See Raymond Plant, "Hegel and the Political Economy," in *Hegel on Economics and Freedom*, ed. William Maker (Macon, Ga.: Mercer University Press, 1987), pp. 95–126.

45. *PR*, §183, p. 123.

46. *Phen.*, p. 80.

47. *PR*, §3, pp. 15–20.

48. *PH*, p. 446.

49. See Manfred Riedel, "'State' and 'Civil Society': Linguistic Context and Historical Origin," chap. 6 in *Between Tradition and Revolution: The Hegelian Transformation of Political Philosophy*, trans. Walter Wright (Cambridge: Cambridge University Press, 1984).

50. See the first page of this chapter.

51. See Joachim Ritter, "Hegel und die französische Revolution" in *Metaphysik und Politik: studien zu Aristoteles und Hegel* (Frankfurt am Main: Suhrkamp, 1977).

52. *PR*, §256A, p. 155.

53. This approach is taken, for example, by Lukács in *The Young Hegel.*

54. *PR*, §209–249, pp. 134–152. On the nineteenth century German usage of "Police" as a synonym for "public authority," see Plant *Hegel*, pp. 166–168.

55. *PR*, §258A, p. 157.

56. *PH*, p. 85.

57. *PR*, §57A, p. 48.

5

The Dialectic of Civil Society

Economic Needs

An essential component of Hegel's philosophical anthropology emerges out of what Hegel treats as the first aspect of civil society, the "System of Needs." For the first time the subject under consideration is the nature of human beings as such. "In [abstract] right, what we had before us was the person; in the sphere of morality, the subject; in the family, the family-member; in civil society as a whole, the burgher or *bourgeois*. Here at the standpoint of needs . . . what we have before us is the composite idea which we call *man*. Thus this is the first time, and indeed properly the only time, to speak of *man* in this sense."[1]

The essential concept in this philosophical anthropology is that of need. In the first instance, the concept of need is a natural, biological concept in that the immediately relevant requirements are for food, drink, and biological sustenance. At the same time, the mode in which human beings satisfy these basic needs serves to distinguish humans from animals. Humans must produce the objects that satisfy their needs by a transformation of nature—for example, food must be cooked, shelters built, clothing manufactured, and so on. These requirements of human life set in motion a process by which human needs become increasingly particularized, leading to an ever-increasing specialization of the skills needed to produce goods for human consumption. This in turn produces a growing fragmentation of the labor process, rendering people more interdependent and increasingly substituting culture for nature as the appropriate human milieu.

Other, more subjective, factors enter into the dialectic of need and labor as well—factors that "become themselves a fruitful source of the multiplication of needs and their expansion."[2] Humans are not driven to the objects that will satisfy their needs by instinct or by mere physical proximity to these objects. Rather, humans make judgments and form opinions that particular objects will satisfy their needs. These judgments are social in character. They are made on the basis of individuals' desires for both universality and particularity: to attain equality with others through acquisition of the same or equal goods and to assert oneself in some distinctive way against others through the possession of objects distinctively and uniquely one's own.

The labor undertaken to satisfy these desires in civil society has a corresponding dual structure. It has a universalizing component that equally integrates all into a system of interdependence and a particularizing component that gives people a specific, differentiated place within that system. Work is a system of "practical education"[3] that instills in people the idea that they should acquire a specific occupation. Furthermore, it instills the spirit of cooperation, because one's work must conform to that of other workers. Finally, it fosters the acquisition of socially recognized skills that eventually become matters of habit.

Increasingly, the system becomes more "abstract" as the division of labor becomes more specialized, and workers become more and more dependent on machines and on each other. But work in civil society never becomes so "abstract" and homogeneously universal that it loses its rootedness in the processes of nature. Although the system does create commonality, arbitrary "differences in the development of natural, bodily, and mental characteristics" still "are conspicuous in every direction and on every level, and, together with the arbitrariness and accident which this sphere contains as well, they have as their inevitable consequence disparities of individual resources and ability."[4]

In his exposition, Hegel intertwines the themes of the universalizing and the particularizing tendencies of labor in civil society—with good reason, given the position he ultimately wishes to defend. Hegel wants to endorse the freedom offered to the individual when occupations can be freely and interchangeably chosen—the idea of "careers open to talents" espoused by the bourgeois supporters of the French Revolution. At the same time, he wants to reject the kind of radical egalitarianism of the revolution that repudiates all notions of social stratification. For Hegel, it is crucial that there not be a totally fluid economic mobility but that individuals cluster into stable groupings that allow their economic and political interests to crystallize and be articulated. We shall see this more clearly later when we take up Hegel's doctrine of political representation in the state.

Immediately following his general presentation of the dynamics of work in civil society, Hegel announces that society is divided into a class structure of three major classes. "The classes are specifically determined in accordance with the concept as (a) the *substantial* or immediate [or agricultural] class; (b) the reflecting or formal [or business] class; and finally, (c) the *universal* class [the class of civil servants]."[5]

Hegel offers brief descriptions of the nature of each class at this point, but his full presentation of the class structure of civil society comes later, and we shall discuss it at that time. Of particular importance in the present context is that for Hegel it is crucial that in civil society the proper reconciliation of universality and particularity must take place not merely from the perspective of the philosopher. This reconciliation must increasingly be accomplished intentionally by the individuals themselves.

> What happens here [class differentiation] by inner necessity occurs at the same time by the mediation of the arbitrary will, and to the conscious subject it has the shape of being the work of his own will.[6] . . . In this class-system, the ethical frame of mind therefore is rectitude and *esprit de corps*, i.e., the disposition to make oneself a member of one of the moments of civil society by one's own act, through one's energy, industry, and skill, to maintain oneself in this position, and to fend for oneself only through this process of mediating oneself with the universal, while in this way gaining recognition both in one's own eyes and in the eyes of others.[7]

For Hegel, the foundation of modern politics that differentiates modern from classical political theory and determines the meaning of freedom in the modern world is the idea that political institutions should uphold the subjective freedom of the individual will. "The recognition and the right that what is brought about by reason of necessity in civil society and the state shall at the same time be effected by the mediation of the arbitrary will is the more precise definition of what is primarily meant by freedom in common parlance."[8]

In the above sentence, Hegel's position is expressed in a manner remarkably consistent with his overall strategy in the *Philosophy of Right*. The subjective, individualistic notion of freedom found in "common parlance" is appropriated in such a way that it is, on the one hand, given its due in a way acceptable to the common understanding of freedom—by stressing the dependence of freedom on the consent of the arbitrary, individual will—and, on the other hand, placed in a context whereby "by reason of necessity" the individual's will is situated in objective institutions that might otherwise seem foreign and alien to the individual will, thereby reconciling the individual to external laws and institutions.

Economics versus Politics

The relationship between the individual will ensconced in the "System of Needs" and the complex of political institutions described in the *Philosophy of Right* is key to understanding the work. Although one might expect the sort of philosophical anthropology and rudimentary description of an economic system that makes up the bulk of the "System of Needs" section of the *Philosophy of Right* to lead either into a fuller discussion of the economics of civil society or to the topic of the state, in fact these considerations are postponed because the system of needs first generates a legal system not yet at the level of the state. The legal system is designated by Hegel as the "Administration of Justice" and the public authority (*Polizei*, often translated as "Police"). Understanding the nature of the distinction between it and the full-fledged legal-ethical system of the political state is crucial to understanding Hegel's thought. We need here to examine more closely the substantive issues underlying Hegel's architectonic. Again, one of the methodological tenets of this study is that the form in which Hegel expresses his political thought is intimately related to its content. This is nowhere more true, and more in need of explication, than here.

Our common political vocabulary contains a number of paired terms that, although they are by no means synonymous, attempt to delimit certain kinds of activities or practices from others in roughly comparable ways. Whether or not the distinction is drawn between private and public, personal and political, individual and collective, societal and governmental, or self-regarding and other-regarding actions, the intent is to use the former concept of the pair to mark off a separate sphere in which the kind of institutionalized regulatory apparatus appropriate in the latter arena is declared inappropriate. A leitmotif in this conceptual framework is the idea that actions in the former sphere are in some way more natural or spontaneous, in contrast to the more consciously constructed actions in the latter sphere. This motif carries over into the way in which the distinction between civil society and the state is usually understood: civil society is understood as the realm of individualistic, natural economic and social interactions upon which a structure of government conventions is imposed.

The structured presentation of Hegel's *Philosophy of Right* is designed to overcome this way of understanding the civil society-state distinction. This assumed theoretical framework, by now part of the liberal heritage of Anglo-American political theory, leads a classical commentator like George Sabine to declare that in Hegel's *Philosophy of Right* "the arrangement [of topics] hopelessly dislocated the subject matter."[9] To Hegel's mind, his arrangement rather properly situates the subject matter so that it can be correctly understood. According to the conventional way of understanding the distinction between civil society and the state, that part of civil society that Hegel describes as the "System of Needs" should exhaust the sphere of civil society, and the sections on the "Administration of Justice" and the "Police" should properly come under the heading of the "State." By the same logic, freedoms of religion and public expression should be treated as part of the individual rights exercised in civil society against the state. Hegel, however, insists on treating these topics while discussing the institutions of the state. What lies behind these differences?

As we have already seen, the economic system that forms the basis of civil society is for Hegel "natural" only in a restricted sense—a sense different from that in which economic relations are natural for the contractarian tradition. For Hegel, the economy is natural in that the sphere of needs and property relations corresponds to fundamental aspects of human nature, but this sphere does not emerge from a "state of nature." Rather, the emergence of civil society as a separate sphere in which these relations are allowed full play is a historical creation—the distinctive historical creation of the political life of the modern world. Actual history plays the role in Hegel's system that is played by the hypothetical compact in social contract theories.

For Hegel, the transition from civil society to the state is not one from asocial to social life, because for Hegel there is no asocial state prior to the act of association, but rather a transition from one to another form of association, a transition from one category of organizational imperatives to another. The difference between civil society and the state is not a matter of whether or not there is an organized public body but rather a matter of the *purpose* of that body. The organization of civil society is oriented toward the satisfaction of individual, economic needs, and the organs of the state are oriented toward the satisfaction of intersubjective, political consciousness. Contractarian theories that construct the state entirely from an economistic perspective, that view the state from the standpoint of the Understanding, as Hegel puts it, merge the economic, regulatory functions of government with the political, legislative functions, a distinction that Hegel wishes to maintain.

Rousseau's distinction between government, or magistracy, and sovereignty captures much of what Hegel wishes to argue for. For Rousseau, the sovereign enacts universal laws, but the government performs particular acts. Government is "an intermediate body established between the subjects and the sovereign for their mutual communication,"[10] and it is dependent on the state; "the state exists by itself, but the government exists only through the sovereign."[11] Both Rousseau and Hegel use locutions that lead to exaggerated interpretations of their positions—Rousseau attributing infallibility and Hegel attributing divinity to the state—but the basic impulse behind their separation of government from sovereignty and civil society from the state remains clear: to insist that questions of the regulation of commerce and the protection of property are of a conceptual order subordinate to questions of the properly universal human dignity and freedom established through political association. Although for the liberal, contractarian tradition all public regulatory bodies are considered organs of the state, for Hegel and Rousseau only universal, legislative bodies are properly political, and agencies whose function it is to reconcile conflicting particular interests remain at the level of civil society.

Even those sympathetic to Hegel's political philosophy have often missed this distinction. For example, in the following passage Paul Ricoeur slips from seeing the rationality of the Hegelian state in terms of the rationality of the understanding operating in civil society to seeing the rationality of the Hegelian state in terms of a fully developed political rationality without any awareness that a substantive shift has occurred.

> If Hegel is right, the State is conciliation, the conciliation, in a higher sphere, of interests and individuals which are irreconcilable at the level of what Hegel calls civil society, which is what we would call the socioeconomic level. The incoherent world of private relationships is arbitrated and rationalized by the higher authority of the State. The state is a mediator and therefore reason. And each of us attains his freedom and rights by means of the authority of the State. I am free insofar as I am political.[12]

The equivocation between the state as arbitrator of private relationships and the state as the source of political freedom obscures precisely the important difference between the administration of justice in civil society and the higher political organs of the state that the structure of the *Philosophy of Right* is designed to emphasize.

The Example of the United States

One way to clarify the significance of this distinction is to look at certain political arrangements that in common discourse function as paradigms of the modern state but which Hegel considers to be not yet at the level of "a real state":[13] the political structure of the United States of America. Hegel describes the United States as follows:

> A subjective unity presents itself; for there is a President at the head of the State, who, for the sake of security against any monarchical ambition, is chosen only for four years. Universal protection for property, and a something approaching entire immunity from public burdens, are facts which are constantly held up to commendation. We have in these facts the fundamental character of the community—the endeavor of the individual after acquisition, commercial profit, and gain; the preponderance of *private* interests, devoting itself to that of the community only for its own advantage. We find, certainly, legal relations—a formal code of laws; but respect for law exists apart from genuine probity, and the American merchants commonly lie under the imputation of dishonest dealings under legal protection.[14]

Several features of the U.S. political system are highlighted in Hegel's remarks. These features can be brought into sharper focus when contrasted with characteristics of European parliamentary systems that are closer to the kind of political structures Hegel advocates.[15] The U.S. Constitution fuses in the office of the presidency two distinct functions that are kept separate under most parliamentary systems: head of state and head of government, usually designated as president and premier, or prime minister. In addition, U.S. political practice adds a third function to the office, which Hegel thinks should also be separate: the President of the United States is the titular head of his political party as well and thus the leader of a particular faction within the body politic. The result of this fusion of the regulatory functions of civil government and the representative functions of state authority in a single office is that the presidency structurally invites accusations of manipulating affairs of state for political partisan advantage. At the same time, the duty of the president to preside at ceremonial functions, which often requires little more than crossing the t's and dotting the i's, either detracts from and thus lessens the efficiency of the actual conduct of government or, given the more common realities of present political practices, lessens the prestige of political authority because the vice president is sent to substitute for the president. As we shall see when we discuss Hegel's doctrine of the state, Hegel advocates a system in which the monarch serves as head of state, augmented by a cabinet of ministers and a representative parliament of a particular kind. But for the moment we shall remain focused on Hegel's criticism of the kind of political consciousness created when civil society is not conceptually and structurally separated from the state.

Hegel argues that in addition to the conflation of distinct political offices, another significant problem arises when politics is seen exclusively from the point of view of civil society. What should be a distinct political identity of the citizens is reduced to a private, economic identity. Again, reference to the current U.S. political scene is illuminating. Recent political rhetoric in the United States has been filled with references to the necessity of satisfying the demands of "the American taxpayer." Although part of the stock-in-trade of U.S. politicians, this kind of locution is foreign to European ears. It is true that when he discusses the practice of taxation Hegel treats it as a praiseworthy feature of the modern state because it enables citizens to fulfill their obligations to the state while still retaining their freedom to choose the kind of work they do, as opposed to having the state decide which services citizens will perform.[16] But Hegel vigorously opposes the reduction of one's political identity to that of the "taxpayer." This is the epitome of the narrow view of political association and the reduction of public to private interests which Hegel finds objectionable and ultimately destructive to the cohesion of a political state. It engenders a loss of civic identity.

Hegel identifies two factors as contributing to this lack of civic consciousness in the U.S. political system. The first is the kind of religious consciousness predominant in the United States, a theme we will address when we discuss Hegel's analysis of the proper relation between church and state. The second anticipates Frederick Jackson Turner's thesis regarding the role of the frontier in U.S. history.[17] Expansionism mitigates against the kind of class articulation and political reflection that ground a properly articulated political structure. It is in the context of looking at the role of the open West in absorbing the discontent in U.S. political life that Hegel makes his remark: "Had the woods of Germany been in existence, the French Revolution would not have occurred."[18]

Having indicated some of the general considerations that lead Hegel to insist on the difference between civil society and the state, it is necessary that we caution against a misinterpretation of their relationship. Civil society and the state are not to be conceived of as two opposing powers, in the manner that the U.S. legislative and executive branches are thought of as separate powers when one wishes to call attention to the "balance of power" doctrine. An important goal of Hegel's political philosophy is to break away from the interest group model of politics, in which politics is seen as primarily involved with balancing competing interests against each other, and move toward a conception of politics that views different interests not as competitive with but as complementary to each other. In terms of the civil society–state relationship, by situating regulatory organs within civil society whose function it is to regulate the economy according to its own laws within civil society, Hegel saves the political organs of the state from being seen as interfering with the "natural" workings of the economy. Hegel was perceptive enough to see the mythical character of laissez-faire ideology in its pure form, based as it is on a naturalistic model of the economy that Hegel rejects. He also wished to retain the idea that the essential purpose of government in some way transcends the standpoint of economic interests. The distinction between the public authority of civil society and the political power of the state allows him to fulfill this purpose by giving both particular economic and general political concerns their own proper organs.

Although civil society and the state are thus not antagonistic spheres, one should also caution against too facilely asserting that the tensions and contradictions in civil society are completely overcome and reconciled in the state. Hegel was not that optimistic, nor is his political theory that totalistic. The contradictions of civil society that are resolved in the state are the political contradictions only—that is, those having to do with the human dignity, social standing, and identity as free legislative agents of the citizens. The state does not, nor in Hegel's eyes should it attempt to, resolve what he regards as the purely economic contradictions of civil society—those problems having to do with the distribution of wealth and the regulation of commerce. The institutions of civil society are designed to deal with the economic problems of civil society as best they can, but Hegel held out no hope for the kind of effective integration of individuals in the economic sphere that he attempted to achieve in the political arena. At the same time, these institutions are designed to progressively engender a political identity in the citizenry. Although the economy is an autonomous sphere, there is at the same time a marked politicization of all aspects of social life in Hegel's theory. These relations are complex, and demand further examination.

The Concept of Mediation

What makes the precise nature of the relationship between civil society and the state difficult to grasp in Hegel's political philosophy is that all the institutions described between the system of needs and the state have a dual role. They are at the same time situated within civil society, and consequently discussed in the economic terms appropriate to that level, and situated as mediating institutions between the system of needs and the state, and consequently discussed in the political categories appropriate to the political institutions of the state toward which they are oriented. This concept of political mediation is a distinctive Hegelian contribution to political philosophy. It can be approached from a number of different directions. It would be well to begin by recalling the doctrines Hegel is opposing here.

Hegel's objections to a more directly political treatment of social life can best be understood by recalling that for Hegel the unmediated politicization of life is precisely what is represented by the worst excesses of the French Revolution. Anarchy and terror result from the identification of the natural, immediate, individual will as a political will. Hegel's critique of this radical voluntarism has already been discussed.[19] But a reign of terror is only the most dire consequence of the excessive politicization of the individual will and does not exhaust Hegel's criticisms of this viewpoint. Far less dramatic, but also destructive of social cohesion, is another consequence of the lack of mediating institutions in political life.

This aspect of Hegel's political theory has been discussed in non-Hegelian terms by sociologist Peter Berger, who in an essay entitled "In Praise of Particularity: The Concept of Mediating Structures" in his book *Facing Up to Modernity* emerges with some conclusions that are almost a paraphrase of Hegel's views. Berger defines mediating structures as "those institutions which stand between the individual in his private sphere and the large institutions of the public sphere"[20] and gives as examples "family, church, voluntary association, neighborhood, and subculture."[21] Apropos of the contemporary situation, he writes: "The progressive disintegration of mediating structures constitutes a double crisis, on the level of individual life and also on a political level. Without mediating structures, private life comes to be engulfed in a deepening anomie. Without mediating structures, the political order is drawn into the same anomie by being deprived of the moral foundation upon which it rests."[22]

Hegel's concept of political mediation seems difficult to grasp because it is aimed at overcoming the split between the public and the private, or the individual and the collective, which is so basic to our political vocabulary. As Berger puts it, "the concept slices reality up in new ways."[23] In what he calls "a history-of-ideas treatment" Berger traces the genealogy of the concept of mediating structures.

A *locus classicus* of the concept is on the last pages of Emile Durkheim's *Suicide*, where he describes the "tempest" of modernization, sweeping away what he calls the "little aggregations" in which people existed through most of human history, leaving only the state on the one hand and a mass of individuals, "like so many liquid molecules," on the other hand. . . . If one wants to go beyond the sociological tradition, one may go back to earlier sources, which interestingly are both on the right and the left of the political-ideological spectrum. One may refer to Edmund Burke (insisting on the importance of "small platoons" as the foundation for all wider loyalties), Alexis de Tocqueville (finding in voluntary associations one of the keys to the vitality of American democracy), and Otto von Gierke (with his fixation on the alleged virtues of medieval guilds). At the same time, one may refer to sources on the left, within Marxism, and even more clearly in the anarchosyndicalist tradition.[24]

Berger argues that private life in the modern world is marked by what Arnold Gehlen calls "underinstitutionalization," while the "megastructures" of the public sphere are "in the classical Marxist term . . . alienating."[25] Berger develops his critique of modernity (which he insists is "not an attack, not a blanket rejection")[26] with an argument whose logic Hegel could unquestionably subscribe to, including the identification of the Enlightenment and liberalism as culprits in furnishing ideological justifications for the negative results of modernization.

The broad tradition of liberal ideology, all the way back to the Enlightenment, has an especially close relationship to the process of modernization. Indeed, the argument can be made that this tradition embodies the myth of modernity more than any other. It is not surprising, then, that it has been singularly blind to the importance and at times even the very existence of mediating structures. Liberalism is, above all, a faith in rationality. Its designs for

society are highly rational, abstract, universalistic. Burke, in criticizing the
programs of the French revolutionaries, aptly called them "geometrical."[27]

The question of Hegel's relation to liberalism is particularly relevant
here, because Hegel's concept of political mediation is one reason his
theory is so difficult to classify in traditional liberal categories. On
the one hand, Hegel's theory violates the liberal separation of private
from political life. It seems to encroach on the sphere of individuality and thus to carry with it an aura of totalitarianism. On the other
hand, Hegel intends his concept of mediation, at least in part, to pro-
tect liberal, pluralistic freedoms against what J. L. Talmon identified
as "totalitarian democracy,"[28] what others have sometimes called the
"tyranny of the majority." Hegel violates the traditional liberal individualist logic, but he does so in the name of many of the pluralist
freedoms liberalism has been concerned with defending.

The danger of totalitarianism for Hegel comes much more from the
unimpeded expansion of the abstract universality of civil society, which
levels all elements to a single common denominator. This universality
is based on the labor process of civil society, which reduces everything
to simple natural needs. For Hegel, the universality of the state is not
an abstract but rather what he calls a concrete universality. That is
to say, it is a differentiated universality that incorporates subordinate,
particular spheres into its general structure. The greater danger facing
modernity is not excessive politicization from above, from the state,
because this is a politicization aimed at securing individuality by establishing a stable mediated structure, but excessive politicization from
below, that is, the attempt to directly politicize the individual will in
the Jacobin style. The particular will at home in civil society continually threatens to overstep its bounds and draw the universal state down
to its level because it is "the tremendous power which draws men into
itself and claims from them that they work for it, owe everything to it,
and do everything by its means."[29]

Hegel's critique here echoes the Romantic criticism of industrializa-
tion for its leveling effects, as well as later nineteenth-century fears of
direct democracy for the same reasons. This is the negative side of
the universality of civil society. In tearing individuals loose from all
traditional ties and associations, it unleashes a tremendously expan-
sive leveling force, which by its nature is driven to expand its domain
both over the lives of individuals within the society and out to other
societies in the search for more markets and colonies.[30] This aspect
threatens to overshadow the positive achievement of an economically

based universality, which is that it lays the basis for rule by political universal law.

In order to avoid leaving the impression that Berger's essay can be read in its entirety as a contemporary equivalent to Hegel's views, it would be well for us to point out the fundamental difference between them. Berger discusses "modernization" primarily, and at times exclusively, as a political process, and his solutions are to recommend different public policies. Hegel's analysis is more multifaceted. For Hegel, the process is at least as much an economic process as a political one, and there is no hope at all of a solution at the level of conscious public policy. The only possible solution is to establish mediating institutions as part of the core structure of society, not as mere peripheral adjuncts to an unmediated megastructure.

We remarked earlier that Hegel's analysis of civil society reveals him at his most materialist moments. The particularizing and universalizing tendencies of the labor process in civil society emerge as the historical preconditions for the particular forms of both the anomie of private life and the universality of political life, which characterize modernity. Against these polarizing economic tendencies, Hegel attempts to marshal the integrating forces of articulated political structures in the social sphere and the ethical consciousness that stems from the ideal of religious community in the individual. As one commentator expresses much of what has been said so far:

> Against the danger of an unmediated politicization of civil society, which he
> sees an example of in the French Revolution. . . . In his theory of the modern
> state Hegel relies on the mediating force of restored and "modernized" prerev-
> olutionary institutions, such as the "estates," the "corporative" organization
> of social labor, the privileged position of the churches, etc. In the interest
> of preventing the immediate politicization of civil society, he appropriates el-
> ements of the prerevolutionary order, insofar as they do not contradict the
> freedom of the citizen in civil society.[31]

From the perspective of the concept of political mediation, it becomes clear why Hegel lumps together political ideologies that from the commonly assumed liberal framework seem odd bedfellows indeed: liberalism, the Jacobin reign of terror, Hobbesian or Lockean social contract theory, and Rousseau's doctrine of the general will. From Hegel's perspective, all these ideologies conceptualize the natural, individual will as a political will in a direct, unmediated fashion. They see mediating structures as the remnants of a superseded past, posing the danger of disruptive factionalism, rather than as integrating mechanisms. Perhaps the clearest expression of the view that Hegel is rejecting can be found in Rousseau, who bars all intermediate associations and factions from the society to be governed by the general will because they prevent the identification of the individual with the general will. Rousseau counsels that if they do exist, they should be made so small and numerous as to be completely ineffective.[32]

We have noted that Hegel's concept of political mediation leads him to group together political standpoints that when seen from any other perspective would seem to be poles apart, such as contractarian theories of the state and the reign of terror of the French Revolution. Hegel is not the only one to argue for such a connection. In his attempt to reconstruct the most general framework of liberal thought, Roberto Mangabeira Unger, in discussing the coercive nature of law enforcement in liberal theory, puts the point as follows:

> The ideas that there is no natural community of common ends and that group life is a creature of will help explain the importance of rules and of their coercive enforcement. But the same factors may also account for the fascination of terror, the systematic use of violence unlimited by law, as a device of social organization. The less one's ability to rely on participation in common ends, the greater the importance of force as a bond among individuals. Punishment and fear take the place of community. Moreover, when they view everything in the social world as a creation of the will, men come to believe there is nothing in society a will sufficiently violent cannot preserve or destroy. Thus, legalism and terrorism, the commitment to rules and the seduction of violence are rival brothers, but brothers nonetheless.[33]

To avoid confusion with what has been said elsewhere in this study, it should be made clear that Unger's references to the "will" refer to what Hegel calls the natural, individual, particular will, not the fully developed concept of the rational will, and Unger is thus in accord with Hegel's position.

Following the French Revolution it was proclaimed that the general will was to be the only bond in society. All mediating institutions therefore had to give way before a radical subjectivism. Hegel's fear of the terror that resulted is always in the background of his dissatisfaction with seeing society in either purely voluntaristic or purely legalistic terms. The connecting link between these two themes of excessive voluntarism and excessive legalism is the reliance of both on the concept of the natural, immediately given, individual will instead of on the culturally produced (*gebildete*), rational, collective will embodied in an ethical community (*Geist*). Intermediate, mediating institutions create organic communities that forge living links between individuals in society, thereby replacing either external force or subjective will as the only alternative way by which people may be linked.

In his own note to the paragraphs quoted above, Unger presents a remarkable pedigree for this notion, and it is worth repeating here in its entirety.

The discovery of a connection between the appeal to terror and the artificial view of society has played an important part in the criticism of liberal thought. The decisive event in this respect was the French Revolution. Both the theme of an absence of community between the Republic and its enemies and that of the subordination of society to will are already implicit in the original justification of the "Reign of Terror." See Maximilien Robespierre, *Rapport sur les Principes du Governement Revolutionnaire*, in *Discours et Rapports de Robespierre*, ed. C. Vellay (Paris, Charpentier, 1908), pp. 332–333. The idea that the disintegration of community makes fear the supreme social bond recurs in the history of the conservative attack on liberalism. See Edmund Burke, *Reflections on the Revolution in France, Works of Edmund Burke* (London, Rivington, 1801), vol. V, p. 202. The relationship of voluntarism to terror is in turn brought out by Hegel's remarks on "absolute freedom and terror." See *Phänomenologie des Geistes, Sämtliche Werke*, ed. H. Glockner (Stuttgart, Fronmann, 1927), vol. II, pp. 449–459. An analogous argument is developed by Marx and by some of his followers. See, for example, Marx's article in *Vorwärtz* of August 7, 1844; *Marx-Engels Werke* (Berlin, Dietz, 1957), vol. I, p. 392; and Lenin, *The Proletarian Revolution and Kautsky the Renegade*, in *Collected Works* (Moscow, Progress, 1967), vol. XXVIII, pp. 227–325. Still another perspective on the matter is offered by the development in social theory of the view that in "premodern" societies a clear line is drawn between what is immutable in the social order and what falls under the discretion of the rulers, whereas in modern states every aspect of social life becomes subject in principle to the political will. See Henry Maine, *Lectures on the Early History of Institutions* (London, Murray, 1897), pp. 373–386; and Max Weber, *Wirtschaft und Gesellschaft*, ed. J. Winckelmann (Tübingen, Mohr, 1972), ch. 3, 6, p. 130. In a very different context, the relationship of legalism to terrorism is highlighted by the doctrines of the Chinese "Legalists." See *The Complete Works of Han Fei Tzu*, 2 vols., trans. W. Liao (London, Probsthain, 1939); and *The Book of Lord Shang*, trans. J. Duyvendak (London, Probsthain, 1928).[34]

In Hegel's view, a stable ethical community can be established only when the social whole is the culmination of a series of intermediate social groupings and not an assembly of individuals. The individualism of civil society must give way to the collective consciousness of the state. In a nice summary of issues raised here, Jane Bennett notes that individualist theories of the state are "alert to the dangers within collectivism: an emphasis on a general will places a heavy burden on civic virtue, and excessive faith in the possibility of rational, collective self-government risks the absolute terror of authoritarianism."

Characterizing Hegel's theory as a "collectivist" one, she then goes on to note that the collectivist theory of the state identifies the following

> set of dangers in the individualist theory: to confine freedom to an economic ghetto is to risk turning citizens into mere consumers; to minimize citizens' identification with the state may be to weaken further the legitimacy of a state already conceived as hostage to a privately controlled economy; to define the state as technical coordinator is to further technocracy at the expense of democracy; to see bureaucratic power as disabling freedom obscures the connection between freedom and collective action.[35]

Given the way Hegel's concept of political mediation cuts across the political spectrum, it is no wonder that such widely divergent interpretations of Hegel's political philosophy have been offered, especially as regards Hegel's relationship to liberalism.[36] The controversy over these divergent interpretations has moved beyond the corridors of academe because in the twentieth century the debate over Hegel's political philosophy has merged with attempts to trace the intellectual origins of the German experience with National Socialism. In this context, it would be appropriate to point out that the direct, mass voluntaristic political action that Hegel is opposing has far greater affinities to the fascist mentality than to anything in Hegel's own politics.[37]

This line of argument could be summarized by saying that a careful separation and analysis of methodological and substantive issues in Hegel's political philosophy reveals that Hegel's critique of the standard liberal political logic is aimed at preserving, rather than subverting, the standard liberal pluralist freedoms (as we shall have opportunity to see again, in other areas, in the examination of the political institutions of the Hegelian state in the next chapter). Failure to make the requisite distinction between method and substance has been the cause of much misinterpretation of Hegel.

Law and the Administration of Justice

Up to this point, our discussion of the relationship between civil society and the state in Hegel's philosophy has focused on the distinction between these two spheres. The separation of the administration of justice and the police in civil society from the expressly political sphere of the state is an essential component of Hegel's ideal of the kind of human dignity to which a political philosophy must address itself. Hegel believes it essential that the tasks of economic regulation be institutionally separated from the tasks of political legislation. This alone makes possible the creation of that higher ethical community in which human beings can reach an appropriate sense of self and a concomitant political identity. Without such a separation human, as distinct from animal, nature cannot be experienced and conceptualized as such.

But this separation is by no means the whole story of Hegelian politics. Simply to leave such a dualism intact would belie the intent of Hegelian philosophy. Hegel's political philosophy also provides a ladder by which individuals can make the transition from civil society to the state. We saw the beginnings of this movement in the discussion of Hegel's concept of political mediation earlier. The remainder of this chapter will focus on the institutions of civil society as mechanisms of transition from civil society to the state.

As noted earlier, the exposition of Hegel's political philosophy is complicated by the fact that all the institutions that fall between civil society and the state have a dual role. They can be viewed in the economic categories of civil society (as we have just done) as well as in the political categories of the state (as we are about to do). In the discussion that follows, I shall attempt to sort out the underlying principles of Hegelian politics, which are in most cases more defensible than their specific instantiations. For example, Hegel's general arguments for the need for mediating institutions like the corporations are more plausible than his specific idea that all members of the same industry should be members of the same corporation, regardless of their class standing within that industry. As I argued in the Introduction, the attempt to separate general principles from their concrete applications may be un-Hegelian. It violates the claims for the necessity of the whole that Hegel makes. However, some such distinction remains necessary if one is to retain what is valuable in Hegel.

Hegel moves beyond the individualism of the system of needs in graduated stages. At the initial, economic level, the only commonality among people is that of a mutual interdependence reduced to the commonality of the least common denominator. Economic activity in civil society assumes that people have needs in common and that goods produced to satisfy these needs are interchangeable. But even this degree of universality is not at the forefront of the consciousness of economic producers and forms only the background for their activity. Greater awareness of commonality and interdependence among the citizens begins to emerge only at the level of the judicial system for the administration of justice, which begins the process of making increasingly more explicit the universality that binds people together into an ethical community. Not only is the system itself based on this greater universality but it is also structured so as to bring this universality into the consciousness of those dealing with the system.

At the earlier economic level, the well-being of the individual was left to the industriousness of that individual. The system for the administration of justice places that well-being in a social context, though at first only in a negative way. This system of justice recognizes property rights and gives them an explicitly public character, such that violations of these rights appear now not just as acts against the individual but as acts against the social order as a whole. Society's general interest in securing individual rights stems from the recognition that these rights are based in the universal nature of human beings as such. "A man counts as a man in virtue of his manhood alone, not because he is a Jew, Catholic, Protestant, German, Italian, etc."[38]

Not only must the law be equally applicable to all, it must be equally known by all. Hegel inveighs against the tendency of the legal profession to make knowledge of the law a particular possession of one group rather than spread to it throughout the political community. Just as the law must not be posted so high that people cannot read it, it also must not be buried so deeply in legal tomes that people cannot find it.[39] The codification of the law needed to satisfy modern political consciousness should be complete and systematic but not overly technical.

In a note on the nature of the completeness which a legal system should strive for, Hegel clarifies in an important way the extent to which a legal system is subject to philosophical elucidation. Because the practice of law includes the subsumption of an endless array of particular cases under general principles, it might seem to follow that no system of law can ever be complete because there will always be a need to expand the principles involved to cover these new cases. It might seem reasonable, then, to opt against the codification of law in favor of a more flexible, unwritten system. Hegel argues that such a view misunderstands what is meant by a systematic codification of law. This misunderstanding rests "on a misconception of the difference between the universal of reason and the universal of the understanding, and also on the application of the latter to the material of finitude and atomicity which goes on forever."[40] The completeness and appropriateness of a code of law from a philosophical perspective rests on it being based on rational principles whose necessity is demonstrated through their forming a logically interconnected system broad enough to encompass the essential principles of right engendered by the historical epoch. Philosophy recognizes the role of contingency in actual life and allows for a wide area of subjective discretion in judicial decision making within the broad outlines that a philosophy of right provides. Thus a philosophically sound system of law not only allows for but requires a certain degree of indeterminacy. To demand that philosophy legislate on all specifics is not to make a demand for a more rigorous philosophy but rather to misunderstand the nature of philosophy. In the same vein, Hegel in the Preface to the *Philosophy of Right* criticizes Plato and Fichte for prescribing details in their philosophy that they should have left to be decided on nonphilosophic, pragmatic grounds.

> The infinite variety of circumstance which is developed in this externality by the light of the essence glinting in it—this endless material and its organization—this is not the subject matter of philosophy. To touch this at all would be to meddle with things to which philosophy is unsuited; on such topics it may save itself the trouble of giving good advice. Plato might have omitted his recommendation to nurses to keep on the move with infants and to rock them continually in their arms. And Fichte too need not have carried what has been called the "construction" of his passport regulations to such a pitch of perfection as to require suspects not merely to sign their passports but to have their likenesses painted on them. Along such tracks all trace of philosophy is lost, and such supererudition it can the more readily disclaim since its attitude to this infinite multitude of topics should of course be most liberal.[41]

The same "right of self-consciousness, the moment of subjective freedom"[42] that requires that the laws be known to all also requires that judicial proceedings be open to the public. Again, these structures are based on the fundamental right of modern self-consciousness to find satisfaction in political institutions and not on any arguments about the "utility" of various political arrangements.[43] It might very well be, says Hegel, that leaving legal matters entirely in the hands of professionals, without any kind of a trial-by-one's-peers jury system, would function very well in practical terms, but this would violate the basic right of modern consciousness to be an active part of the political system.

The judicial system's sole function is to rectify deviations from the universality of the law that are brought before it. Once the conflicts of particular cases have been resolved and equilibrium has been restored, this legal system has no further concern for the welfare of the parties involved. The universality of the judicial system has a solely negative relationship to the individuals under that system. From the point of view of the legal system, it is a matter of indifference whether the parties flourish or not after they leave the tribunal, and they are thrown back upon their own resources. This abstract indifference is first superseded at the level of the police and the corporation. Here the welfare of the individual becomes a public concern. Indeed, for the first time a viewpoint is reached from which the individual's welfare is in its totality a social issue, and even the natural inequities that dominate the system of needs are mediated by social institutions.[44]

The police, or public authority, provides for the general welfare in a positive sense, beyond the redressing of individual wrongs. Welfare is treated as a right, not just as a contingent by-product of the workings of the system. In discussing Hegel's use of the concept of *Polizei* (police authority), Manfred Riedel notes that: "In the Jena lectures of 1805–6, he related the modern 'police' to the origin of politics, the *politeia* of classical Greek philosophy: 'The *police* here amounts to this— *politeia*, public life and rule, action of the whole but now degraded to the whole's action to provide public security of every type, protecting business against fraud.' "[45]

The public administration's first task is regulating in the common interest the essentials of economic production and exchange, though this should be done only indirectly, through the provision of basic services (roads, street lighting, and so on) and the policing of fair trade standards for basic goods. These standards come under the purview of the police because they are offered for sale to the general public, but this regulation should not be so extensive that it negates the general principle of free trade.[46] Hegel's interest in the education of the general public motivates his concern that society provide public education to as great a degree as possible, as well as his argument that the general social interest in education overrides the rights of parents who might otherwise choose to deny their children an education.[47]

The Problem of Poverty

Hegel raises the issue of poverty in civil society in the context of his discussion of the nature of the public authority rather than in the earlier discussion of the economic system and class divisions of the system of needs. The context in which Hegel discusses poverty is highly significant; the logic of the exposition of the *Philosophy of Right* is again the key to understanding its content. This discussion provides the best example of Hegel's political stance toward economic issues. Hegel is concerned with the effect of poverty on the degree of social integration rather than with poverty as an issue of economic injustice. He is concerned with relative rather than absolute levels of impoverishment.

To begin with, poverty is a social and not a natural phenomenon, and this fact is part of the general social consciousness.[48] "Against nature man can claim no right, but once society is established, poverty immediately takes the form of a wrong done to one class by another."[49]

In the modern world, poverty results directly from the internal dynamics of civil society. The drive to amass greater wealth and larger profits leads to a "double process of generalization." First, people are increasingly linked to each other by common needs that the progress of production itself generates. Second, the manufacture and distribution of the articles that will satisfy these needs takes place on an ever broader scale.[50] The success of this drive produces at one end of the social spectrum "conditions which greatly facilitate the concentration of disproportionate wealth in a few hands." At the same time, at the other end of the social spectrum "the result is the creation of a rabble of paupers."[51] The corollary to the generation of greater wealth and productivity "is the subdivision and restriction of particular jobs. This results in the dependence and distress of the class tied to work of that sort."[52]

Hegel's terminology in discussing the poor is extremely significant. When discussing class divisions in all other cases Hegel uses the term *Stände*, which signifies both "the classes of civil society and the Estates, which are the classes given a political significance."[53] It is only when discussing the poor that Hegel uses the term *Klasse* rather than *Stände*. The significance of the term *Klasse* is that it is a distinctively economic term, lacking the political and social connotations associated with *Stände*. The terminological distinction makes precisely the point of paramount importance to Hegel: poverty produces a segment of civil society disenfranchised from the political structure generated by civil society. This economic situation produces a segment of society whose consequent civil disenfranchisement entails the "inability to feel and enjoy the broader freedoms and especially the intellectual [*geistigen*] benefits of civil society."[54] Hegel's concern is not so much that the poor have insufficient income, though he does address that aspect of the problem, but more important that they are denied the kind of stable livelihood that is socially recognized and that would therefore allow them access to the mediating institutions that facilitate the transition from civil society to the state. What is destructive to society as a whole is not merely the fact of poverty but the existence of the "culture of poverty," as Avineri puts it.[55]

Hegel's emphasis on the consciousness of the citizens throughout his political philosophy serves him well here. He sees clearly that lacking a vocation in a society whose principle is that individuals must earn their living solely through their own efforts (and this is the principle of modern civil society) produces a certain kind of self-consciousness that makes it impossible to integrate individuals affected in this way into the society. A rabble of paupers is created when sufficient numbers of people fall below the standard of living of a given society—a standard that, again, is not natural but is generated by the society itself and depends more on a subjective sense of comparative social standing than on objective economic indicators. This group then loses the sense "of honesty and the self-respect which makes a man insist on maintaining himself by his own work and effort."[56] This self-respect and the consequent shame that would accompany the failure to make one's own way in society are identified by Hegel as "the subjective bases of society."[57] In this respect as well, the problem of poverty can be laid at the door of the very successes of civil society. It is only because the poor have internalized the values and standards of that society that they feel estranged from it.

Otherwise plausible solutions to the problem of poverty will not work because of the universal acceptance of the ideal of independent self-subsistence established by civil society. Charity and welfare programs, which might otherwise work as solutions, especially as the former appeals to the imperatives of subjective morality, "would violate the principle of civil society and the feeling of individual independence and self-respect in its individual members."[58] Hegel also argues that the solution of providing public works would simply intensify the dynamics of overproduction that produce poverty in the first place. His closing comment on poverty is that the solution that fits best with the principle of civil society that individuals remain independent "has turned out to be to leave the poor to their fate and instruct them to beg in the streets."[59] Although there is much of value in Hegel's emphasis on self-consciousness over material interest as a basis for political life, the drawbacks of the strict separation Hegel makes between these elements is evident here. Hegel's priorities are clearly reflected in the fact that he rejects solutions to the problem of poverty that might rectify the economic inequities but would violate the political principles of civil society, while he recommends a solution incapable of alleviating the economic problems of poverty but which respects the political ideals of civil society.

Hegel also mentions one other kind of attempt to resolve the economic tensions generated by the dynamics of production of civil society. The same "inner dialectic of civil society" that impels it to send some of its members out on the streets also impels it to send other of its members out on the seas to form colonies.[60] The growth of population alone provides impetus for colonization, but "it is due in particular to the appearance of a number of people who cannot secure the satisfaction of their needs by their own labour once production rises above the requirements of consumers."[61] As the forests of Germany would have absorbed the discontent of the French revolutionaries had they still flowered in their former abundance and as the wide-open spaces of the American frontier absorb that continent's malcontents and mitigate against political articulation of class conflicts, so colonization allows European nations to export their intransigent economic and political problems.

When colonization is carried out as an intentional public policy rather than merely by the emigration of private individuals, this too is undertaken by the public authority but should not detract from its "primary purpose" of maintaining a general order over the particularities of civil society.[62] In prescient anticipation of twentieth-century neocolonialism, Hegel notes that colonization works to the greatest benefit of the imperialist countries when they extend principles of political independence to the colonists rather than attempt to retain direct political control over them.[63]

In true dialectical fashion, the virtues of civil society are thus at the same time its defects. The dynamics of production that produce the wealth of that society also produce poverty: "Despite an excess of wealth civil society is not rich enough, i.e. its own resources are insufficient to check excessive poverty and the creation of a penurious rabble."[64] All attempts to check poverty are foiled by the principles of civil society itself, because any special programs to improve the lot of the poor violate the principles that everyone in civil society should be self-subsistent and that the laws of civil society should be applied to all with the same universality. Thus the abstractness of the law, which was supposed to be the basis for everyone being equally a part of the social order, ends up precluding the actual integration of everyone into society.

This is a major component of Hegel's critique of what he sees as the abstract sameness of the law as traditionally conceived. As we have seen, Hegel is indeed a proponent of the idea of the *Rechtstaat*, the state governed by codified, public law, but he denies that this legalism is sufficient as a basis for political society. To use Hegel's most general vocabulary, the standpoint of legalism is that of an understanding that keeps universals and particulars, or essences and appearances, rigidly separated. The universality of law is seen to preclude the ability to recognize particularity as being as essential to political order as universality. What is missing is precisely the series of mediations that would allow for the necessary integration of particular welfare and universal rights.

We end our discussion of civil society with a consideration of the same topic with which Hegel ends his analysis of civil society—the nature of the corporations. The corporations are the key mediating structures that effect the transition from civil society to the state, leading persons from an individualist to a collectivist consciousness. They transform the "natural" into the "rational" rights of earning one's living.[65]

The Corporations

In an essay titled "The Sources and Significance of Hegel's Corporate Doctrine," G. Heiman demonstrates that the roots of Hegel's corporatism lie in his reading of Roman law. The connection between the abstract legalism of Roman law and the divisive factionalism of Roman politics lies at the core of Hegel's analysis of ancient Rome.[66] Roman political theory recognized only one "universal," that of the state, which harshly imposed its will on the "abstract freedom of the individual." "In considering the Roman World, we have not to do with a concretely spiritual life, rich in itself; but the world-historical element in it is the *abstractum* of Universality, and the object which is pursued with soulless and heartless severity, is mere *dominion*, in order to enforce that *abstractum*."[67]

According to legend, Rome was founded on force. This element is never eliminated from Roman politics. The Roman citizen is a member of no communal organizations but is rather in all realms of life part of a rigid hierarchy of power—"a servant on the one side [toward the state], a despot on the other [toward his family]."[68] Even the ethical bonds of the family are dissolved into contractual relations under Roman law. Hegel attributes the lack of real political cohesion under the Roman emperors precisely to the lack of mediating organizations. "The Emperor *domineered* only, and could not be said to rule; for the equitable and moral medium between the sovereign and the subjects was wanting—the bond of a constitution and organization of the state, in which a graduation of circles of social life, enjoying independent recognition, exists in communities and provinces, which, devoting their energies to the general interest, exert an influence on the general government."[69]

As we noted earlier, the family is the first ethical community treated as a foundation of the state by Hegel. Hegel so strongly resists the idea that marriage is to be understood in contractual terms largely in virtue of the negative example of Roman law and life.

"As the family was the first, so the Corporation is the second ethical root of the state, the one planted in civil society."[70] It is this "plantedness" [*gegrundete*, or "groundedness"] that differentiates the corporation from the family. The family precedes civil society, and therefore economic considerations enter into the picture only upon the dissolution of the family, as it opens up onto civil society. But the corporation begins as an organ of civil society, and therefore its first function is an economic one; only further on does it begin to perform its political functions.

The first experiences individuals in civil society have in dealing with the corporations occur as the corporations exercise their right "to come on the scene like a second family for its members."[71] The corporations are voluntary organizations organized to represent particular areas of industry and commerce and even of cultural life. In their capacity as "second family" the corporation performs four particular tasks: (1) looking after the interests of its members within its province of specialization, (2) regulating the size of the membership, in accordance with both the members' own needs and general social needs, (3) protecting its members against contingent misfortunes, and (4) providing the education necessary to train new members.[72] The fact that these activities are carried out by official public bodies gives members of corporations a recognition and dignity they would otherwise lack. It is "recognized that he [the corporation member] belongs to a whole which is itself an organ of the entire society, and that he is actively concerned in promoting the comparatively disinterested end of this whole. Thus he commands the respect due to one in his social position."[73]

Membership in corporations provides a person with "evidence that he is a somebody"[74] because these bodies are formally recognized ("it is only by being authorized that an association becomes a Corporation").[75] For this reason, Hegel's dictum that "it is of the utmost importance that the masses should be organized"[76] can only partially be understood as tactical advice about the greater likelihood of being able to advance one's interests when organized as a political force. The political identity of the masses is of greater importance. One need only recall Hegel's general stance toward issues of self-consciousness, his insistence that consciousness of oneself as an agent only fully emerges when the objective consequences of one's activity are reflected back to one, to see that for Hegel questions of political organization can never be reduced simply to questions of means. His idealism requires that basic considerations relating to personal identity and self-consciousness are always involved in such issues for him.

The transition from the "natural" to the "rational" state is accomplished in the corporation because by accepting responsibility for the welfare of its members the corporation removes the aura of "personal opinion and contingency"[77] from life in civil society. It makes life "less idiosyncratic."[78] Here the dichotomy between individual welfare and universal right is overcome in that "particular welfare is present as a right and is actualized."[79]

Participants in the running of the affairs of the corporation receive a concrete political education in that they see how particular interests depend on the general welfare. This is a materialist doctrine of education. It is political education received not by the didactic inculcation of a particular political ideology but through participation in the mode of life that embodies that ideology. Hegel's analysis of civil society again reveals him at his most materialist moments. Throughout his discussion of civil society, Hegel refers to its "educative" effects, and it is this sort of practical education he has most in mind rather than any formal schooling.

Hegel is aware that his description of the corporations has strong affinities with the medieval guild system. He consequently takes pains to point out that his corporate doctrines are not inconsistent with modern political principles.[80] He therefore differentiates the privileges accorded to corporations from the privileges held by the feudal aristocracy. The latter were private exceptions to the public order; the former are public instantiations of that order. Hegel provides a historical overview of this issue of corporate organizations in modern times, including his critique of the French Revolution for doing away with them, in his essay titled "Proceedings of the Estates Assembly in the Kingdom of Wurtemberg, 1815–1816." It provides a useful summary of his views.

> The great beginnings of internal legal relationships in Germany which presaged the formal construction of the state are to be found in that passage of history where, after the decline of the old royal executive power in the Middle Ages and the dissolution of the whole into atoms, the knights, freemen, monasteries, nobility, merchants, and tradesmen formed themselves into societies and corporations to counteract this state of disorganization. . . . After the development of the supreme powers of the state had been completed in recent times, these subordinate communities and guilds were dissolved or at least deprived of their political role and their relation to internal constitutional law. Now, however, it would surely be time, after concentrating hitherto mainly on introducing organization into the circles of higher state authority, to bring the lower spheres back again into respect and political significance, and, purged of privileges and wrongs, to incorporate them as an organic structure in the state. A living interrelationship exists only in an articulated whole whose parts themselves form particular subordinate spheres. But, if this is to be achieved, the French abstractions of mere numbers and quanta of property must be finally discarded, or at any rate must no longer be made the dominant qualification or, all over again, the sole condition for exercising one of the most important political functions. Atomistic principles of that sort spell, in science as in politics, death to every rational concept, organization, and life.[81]

The "most important political function" Hegel is referring to here is that of voting, and we shall see Hegel's use of his doctrine of corporations to combat an atomistic view of voting procedures in the next chapter when we discuss his ideal of political representation. For the moment, we shall remain focused on the corporations' functions within civil society. In order to carry out these functions the corporations depend on the state in two ways: for the explicit public sanction that gives them legitimacy and for the state's function of regulating their interaction so that they do not "ossify, build themselves in, and decline into a miserable system of castes,"[82] which would become a factionalizing rather than integrating force in political life.

Corporations can play this key integrating role because they are simultaneously situated at the apogee of the orbits of the particular interests of civil society and at the perigee of the orbits of the universal interests of the state. Because in the modern world all citizens cannot directly participate in the affairs of the state, the corporations play an essential role in investing private interests with a public character, thereby providing the foundations of social cohesion. "Under modern political conditions, the citizens have only a restricted share in the public business of the state, yet it is essential to provide men—ethical entities—with work of a public character over and above their private business. This work of a public character, which the modern state does not always provide, is found in the Corporation."[83]

The class divisions of the Hegelian state, like those of the Platonic state, are intended to transform economic necessity into philosophic virtue. The corporations play a key role in this transformation. By allowing economic activities to take place under the umbrella of institutions organized by the state, the corporations restore a political dimension to these activities that is denied by the abstract universality of the sweep of modern history. The corporations enable civil society to be invested with a public character without being divested of its private character. They thus allow Hegel to fulfill his project of overcoming the anomie of modern life fostered by the individualizing tendencies of civil society without bringing about the anarchic situation he thought resulted from a direct politicization of life. Aside from their use in civil society discussed here, Hegel makes further use of the integrating functions of the corporation within the political structure of the state, as we shall see in the analysis of Hegel's doctrine of the state in the next chapter.

Notes

1. *PR*, §190A, p. 127.
2. *Ibid.*, §193, p. 128.
3. *Ibid.*, §197, p. 129.
4. *Ibid.*, §200, p. 130.
5. *Ibid.*, §202, p. 131.
6. *Ibid.*, §206, p. 132.
7. *Ibid.*, §207, p. 133.
8. *Ibid.*, §206A, p. 133.
9. George H. Sabine, *A History of Political Theory*, 3d ed. (New York: Holt, Rinehart and Winston, 1961), p. 637.
10. Jean-Jacques Rousseau, *On the Social Contract*, ed. Roger D. Masters, trans. Judith R. Masters (New York: St. Martin's Press, 1978), p. 78.
11. *Ibid.*, p. 81.

12. Paul Ricoeur, "The Political Paradox," in *Existential Phenomenology and Political Theory*, ed. Hwa Yol Jung (Chicago: Henry Regnery Company, 1972), p. 351.

13. *PH*, p. 85.

14. *Ibid.*, p. 85.

15. For a fuller treatment of Hegel on the United States, see George Armstrong Kelly, "Hegel's America," *Philosophy and Public Affairs* 2:1, Fall 1972, pp. 3–36.

16. *PR*, §299A, pp. 194–195.

17. This is noted by Paul Chamley in *Economie Politique et Philosophie chez Steuart et Hegel* (Paris: Librairie Dalloz, 1963), p. 55.

18. *PH*, p. 86.

19. See Chapter 2.

20. Peter Berger, "In Praise of Particularity: The Concept of Mediating Structures," in *Facing Up to Modernity* (New York: Basic Books, 1977), p. 55.

21. *Ibid.*, p. 134.

22. *Ibid.*, p. 135.

23. *Ibid.*, p. 138.

24. *Ibid.*, pp. 132–133.

25. *Ibid.*, p. 133.

26. *Ibid.*, p. 132.

27. *Ibid.*, pp. 135–136.

28. J. L. Talmon, *The Origins of Totalitarian Democracy* (New York: W. W. Norton, 1970).

29. *PR*, §238A, p. 276.

30. *Ibid.*, §246–248, pp. 151–152.

31. Hermann Lübbe, "Hegels Kritik der Politisierten Gesellschaft," *Filosoficky Casopis* 15:3, 1967, pp. 373–374 (my translation).

32. Rousseau, *On the Social Contract*, pp. 61–62.

33. Roberto Mangabeira Unger, *Knowledge and Politics* (New York: Free Press, 1976), p. 75.

34. *Ibid.*, pp. 305–306.

35. Jane Bennett, *Unthinking Faith and Enlightenment: Nature and the State in a Post-Hegelian Era* (New York: New York University Press, 1987), p. 88.

36. The standard debate is contained in the essays by Sidney Hook, Shlomo Avineri, and Z. A. Pelczynski in *Hegel's Political Philosophy*, ed. Walter Kaufmann (New York: Atherton Press, 1970). Cf. Charles Taylor, *Hegel* (Cambridge: Cambridge University Press, 1978), pp. 374–375.

37. This is emphasized by Herbert Marcuse in his analysis of Hegel's attitudes toward the *Burschenschaften*. See *Reason and Revolution: Hegel and the Rise of Social Theory* (Boston: Beacon Press, 1960), pp. 180–181. The fear of overdemocratization leading to tyranny was in the minds of many at the founding of the

American republic as well. Hamilton's statement that "if we incline too much to democracy, we shall soon shoot into a monarchy" expresses typical sentiments (In Constitutional Convention, June 26, 1787; quoted in Saul Padover, ed., *The Mind of Alexander Hamilton* [New York: Harper and Brothers, 1958], p. 434).

38. *PR*, §209A, p. 134.
39. *Ibid.*, §215A, p. 138.
40. *Ibid.*, §9216A, p. 139. Cf. G.W.F. Hegel, "The German Constitution," in *Hegel's Political Writings*, trans. T. M. Knox, ed. Z. A. Pelczynski (Oxford: Oxford University Press, 1969), pp. 159–164.
41. *PR*, Preface, p. 11.
42. *Ibid.*, §228A, p. 144.
43. *Ibid.*, §228A, p. 145.
44. *Ibid.*, §230, pp. 145–146.
45. Manfred Riedel, *Between Tradition and Revolution: The Hegelian Transformation of Political Philosophy*, trans. Walter Wright (Cambridge: Cambridge University Press, 1984), p. 152.
46. This is precisely the argument that Mill explicitly rejects in the last chapter of "On Liberty." See John Stuart Mill, *Utilitarianism, Liberty, and Representative Government* (New York: Everyman-Dutton, 1951), p. 202.
47. *PR*, §239, p. 148.
48. See Clark A. Kucheman, "Abstract and Concrete Freedom: Hegelian Perspectives on Economic Justice," *Owl of Minerva* 15:1, Fall 1983, pp. 23–44.
49. *PR*, §244A, pp. 277–278.
50. *Ibid.*, §243, p. 149.
51. *Ibid.*, §244, p. 150.
52. *Ibid.*, §243, pp. 149–160.
53. *Ibid.*, §303A, p. 198.
54. *Ibid.*, §243, p. 150.
55. Shlomo Avineri, *Hegel's Theory of the Modern State* (Cambridge: Cambridge University Press, 1974), p. 150. See also Iring Fetscher, *Hegel—Grösse und Grenzen* (Stuttgart: W. Kohlhammer, 1971), p. 70.
56. *PR*, §244, p. 150.
57. *Ibid.*, §245A, p. 150.
58. *Ibid.*, §245, p. 150.
59. *Ibid.*, §245A, p. 150.
60. *Ibid.*, §246, p. 151.
61. *Ibid.*, §248A, p. 278.
62. *Ibid.*, §249, p. 152.
63. *Ibid.*, §248A, p. 278. See David MacGregor, *The Communist Ideal in Hegel and Marx* (Toronto: University of Toronto Press, 1984).

64. *PR*, §245, p. 150.
65. *Ibid.*, §254, p. 154.
66. G. Heiman, "The Sources and Significance of Hegel's Corporate Doctrine," in *Hegel's Political Philosophy: Problems and Perspectives*, ed. Z. A. Pelczynski (Cambridge: Cambridge University Press, 1971).
67. *PH*, p. 279.
68. *Ibid.*, p. 287.
69. *Ibid.*, p. 317.
70. *PR*, §255, p. 154.
71. *Ibid.*, §252, p. 153.
72. *Ibid.*, §252, pp. 152–153.
73. *Ibid.*, §253, p. 153.
74. *Ibid.*, §253, p. 153.
75. *Ibid.*, §253A, p. 153.
76. *Ibid.*, §290A, p. 290.
77. *Ibid.*, §254, p. 154.
78. *Ibid.*, §253A, p. 154.
79. *Ibid.*, §255, p. 154.
80. See Anthony Black, *Guilds and Civil Society in European Thought from the Twelfth Century to the Present* (Ithaca, N.Y.: Cornell University Press, 1984), especially Chapter 17, "The Philosophy of the Corporation: Hegel."
81. G.W.F. Hegel, "Proceedings of the Estates Assembly in the Kingdom of Wurtemberg, 1815–1816," in *Hegel's Political Writings*, p. 263. Cf. *PR*, §290A, p. 291.
82. *Ibid.*, §255A, p. 278.
83. *Ibid.*, §255A, p. 278.

6

Public Opinion
and Its Representation

Hegel's political philosophy is idealist in the decisive sense that its primary focus is on the *consciousness* of the citizens of the modern state. This focus has two facets. First, Hegel argues that the consciousness of the citizens is a key factor in determining the success or failure of other functions normally associated with government: maintaining public law and order, securing the general welfare, providing for a common defense, and so on. Secondly, a key task facing the state is precisely to engender the kind of civil, ethical consciousness that makes public life possible and fruitful. The success of political institutions in furthering this consciousness therefore becomes a key criterion in judging their value.

Hegel presents his theory of the internal workings of the state under the heading of "Constitutional Law" in the section on "The State" in the *Philosophy of Right.* From the early discussions of patriotism and religion to the closing discussion of public opinion, Hegel's political philosophy remains focused here on the consciousness produced in the citizens through their participation in the institutions of modern political life. Hegel's theory moves between the two poles of the most natural, immediate expression of civic consciousness in the patriotic and religious standpoints to the most explicit, articulated expression of civic consciousness in the arena of public opinion. This chapter and the next will trace this theme through Hegel's text.

Before going through the particulars of the Hegelian state, it will be helpful to discuss the general context of Hegel's political ideals. We have seen that the individualism of civil society is to be replaced by the ethical community of the state. Again, Hegel's idea of community is rationalist, not romantic.[1] It advocates the integration of individuality and community, not the abnegation of the former in favor of the latter. Ethical community is established for Hegel when the categories with which people comprehend their relations with others reflect a commonality of interests and identities and when people intentionally direct their actions toward this commonality. It does not require that there be no disagreements or tensions concerning those interests and identities.

For purposes of exposition, it will be helpful to separate two dimensions of Hegel's attempt to realize ethical community before finally examining the somewhat unhappy interplay between these two dimensions. The first dimension is Hegel's attempt to directly inculcate in the citizens of the state the kind of ethical, political consciousness he argues for. In this regard, we shall look at Hegel's doctrines of patriotism, religion, and public opinion. Our concern here is with the interface of religious and political consciousness, with religion as a social phenomenon, not as theology.

The second dimension of Hegel's attempt to realize ethical community is his attempt to instantiate these ideals mediately through their embodiment in objective political institutions rather than directly in the subjective consciousness of the citizens. This latter project is distinctly Hegelian. Many misinterpretations of Hegel's political doctrines have resulted from a failure to appreciate this strain of Hegel's thought. In this context, we shall examine Hegel's accounts of the legislature, the bureaucracy, and the monarchy in order to see how the formation of political consciousness is central to the roles Hegel assigns to each. A discussion of neglected aspects of the function of the monarchy in Hegel's thought will demonstrate how international law and world history feed back into the mechanisms of the Hegelian state, serving as an external background for the internal political sovereignty exercised within the Hegelian state. We shall conclude by taking note of the problems in reconciling the individual and the institutional strains of Hegel's attempt to realize an ethical consciousness in and through the state.

Patriotism

Political consciousness finds its most immediate and natural expression in the patriotic attitude. Hegel's attitude toward patriotism is far from being a glorification of the exercise of state power. Patriotism is a part of daily, unreflective life. It is ordinary and commonplace. One misunderstands the fundamental nature of patriotism if one conceptualizes it in terms of supererogatory acts or acts that take place on the battlefield or in any other arena in which citizens are called upon to make extraordinary sacrifices for the state. Patriotism is not an act but an attitude. Far from eliciting the spirit of sacrifice, it rather entails the recognition that one's interests are being cared for by the state. "Patriotism is often understood to mean only a readiness for exceptional sacrifices and actions. Essentially, however, it is the sentiment which, in the relationships of our daily life and ordinary conditions, habitually recognizes that the community is one's substantive groundwork and end."[2]

Hegel understands patriotism to reflect rather than constitute the political order. This is an important distinction, because Hegel's comments on patriotism have been taken as a sign of his affinity with the German Romantic tradition of political theory, for which the political sphere is based on emotions and a natural affective harmony.[3] But in fact these remarks on patriotism serve to differentiate Hegel from Romanticism more than to demonstrate affinities. Hegel is an "organic" theorist of the state only when the tinge of naturalism is removed from organicism. Although sentiments or feelings cannot be the ground or basis of political bonds for Hegel, the same considerations that motivate his critique of the abstract legalism of contractarian and liberal traditions lead him to insist that the rational relationship between citizens and the state must also affect the sentiments and feelings of the citizens in an immediate, nonreflective way. Hegel's theory of patriotism is addressed to this dimension of political life. In the patriotic attitude the rational structure of political institutions penetrates down into the most mundane levels of life. Patriotism is to be found not when the citizen's will is bent to that of the state but when the citizen has truly internalized the rationality of the state to the extent that it is felt as one's own. This internalization is ethically justified by the rational deduction of the *Philosophy of Right*, not by the feelings of loyalty themselves. This is important because Hegel's remarks on patriotism have been used to feed charges that he is a totalitarian thinker. Understanding that for Hegel patriotism is ultimately based on rational judgment, not emotional identification, renders such charges less plausible. The justification for patriotism ultimately lies not in the opinions of the citizenry—"subjective assurance" in the passage quoted below—but in the knowledge of the philosopher ("truth"). "The political sentiment, patriotism pure and simple, is assured conviction with truth as its basis—mere subjective assurance is not the outcome of truth but is only opinion—and a volition which has become habitual.

In this sense it is simply a product of the institutions subsisting in the state."[4]

Patriotism, then, is not something to be resorted to only in times of crisis. It is the normal attitude of the citizens in a well-ordered state. In the same vein, Hegel's remarks on the "relation of the state to religion" begin with an admonition against seeing religion only as something to turn to for comfort in times of crisis.[5] The religious attitude, too, is one of the stable, permanent features of the consciousness of the citizens of the modern state.

Church and State

We noted earlier that Hegel's discussion of religion is situated in his treatment of the political institutions of the state rather than in the context of the individual rights of civil society. Here, again, the structural arrangement of Hegel's text offers important clues to his political doctrines. The liberal view of the relation between church and state conceptualizes religious beliefs under the general heading of individual freedoms of thought and expression. As such, they belong to a sphere of private, personal relations outside the authority of the state. For Hegel, however, the question of church-state relations is not one of delimiting the boundaries between individual rights and social authority but one of reconciling different kinds of social authority, of integrating overlapping communities. Religion for Hegel is by nature not merely private and personal but also collective and social.[6] It is inherently political, not merely civil. Not only does religion exist in intersubjective and institutional form (spiritual communities and churches) but religious doctrine by its nature claims application to the totality of reality, including ethical and political matters, and not merely to a personal domain of subjective conviction. "The essence of the relation between religion and the state can be determined, however, only if we recall the concept of religion. The content of religion is absolute truth."[7]

In his discussion of the relation of religion to the state Hegel notes that awareness of the claims of religion to absolute truth might lead one to hold that the claims of religion could not in any way be limited or encompassed by the state. Religious consciousness could always claim to be outside and above the laws of the state. From this point of view, maxims like the following seem sufficient to determine one's conduct in political affairs. "To the righteous man no law is given; only be pious, and for the rest, practise what thou wilt; yield to thine own caprice and passion, and if thereby others suffer wrong, commend them to the consolations and hopes of religion, or better still, call them irreligious and condemn them to perdition."[8]

It would seem that what is secular, finite, and limited, such as the state, would be in every way subordinate to what is divine, infinite, and unlimited. But this negative attitude toward the state misunderstands the proper nature of religious consciousness. One must remember that although the content of religion lays claim to absolute truth, it does so in a form that is limited—limited in much more telling ways than the supposed limitations of the state.

Religion is a relation to the absolute, but it is "a relation which takes the form of feeling, representative thinking, faith."[9] The "task of the world during the whole course of its history" has been to turn these subjective convictions into objective reality. This is the necessary "prodigious transfer of the inner into the outer, the building of reason into the real world."[10] To hold to a religious standpoint that bears only a negative relation to the present, real political world neglects this history and threatens the stability of the ethical world.

> Those who "seek guidance from the Lord" and are assured that the whole truth is directly present in their unschooled opinions, fail to apply themselves to the task of exalting their subjectivity to consciousness of the truth and to knowledge of duty and objective right. The only possible fruits of their attitude are folly, abomination, and the demolition of the whole ethical order, and these fruits must inevitably be reaped if the religious disposition holds firmly and exclusively to its intuitive form and so turns against the real world and the truth present in it in the form of the universal, i.e. of the laws.[11]

The subjective veil thrown over political institutions by the kind of religious thinking in which everything other than the undifferentiated unity of the Lord "becomes only accidental and transient"[12] (reminiscent of the "night in which all cows are black" of the *Phenomenology*) results in the same kind of fanaticism found in the secular, undifferentiated immediacy of the French Revolution.

> If religious feeling wished to assert itself in the state in the same way as it is wont to do in its own field, it would overturn the organization of the state, because the different organs of the state have latitude to pursue their own paths, while in religion everything is always referred back to the whole. If this whole, then, wished to engulf all the concerns of the state, this would be tantamount to fanaticism; the wish to have the whole in every particular

could be fulfilled only by the destruction of the particular, and fanaticism is just the refusal to give scope to particular differences.[13]

Fortunately, says Hegel, religion need not remain at this undifferentiated, subjective level. As we saw earlier, the path forward from this emotive level of religious consciousness is a historical one. The histories of religious and political forms of consciousness converge toward the idea of the "bourgeois-Christian" state.[14] The Reformation inaugurated the process of applying to the social, secular realm the principle, which Hegel sees as the essence of Christian doctrine, that "man is in his very nature destined to be free."[15] The account of the process that Hegel gives in his philosophy of history focuses on the process as one of increasing politicization of religious ideals. In the section of the *Philosophy of Right* on the relation between church and state under discussion here, Hegel focuses on this process as one of increasing spiritualization of politics. The state can no longer be regarded solely in mechanistic or legalistic terms. Nor can political rights and offices be seen as simply a conglomerate of individual, private rights and privileges. Any post-Reformation account of the state must see the state as being internally related to the ethical consciousness of individuals and as creating a spiritual community that in its concept of collective authority goes beyond any purely individualistic or legalistic framework. The consciousness of the citizens and their degree of apprehension of the principles upon which political life is based must be central to any such account. "The state, too, has a doctrine, since its organization and whatever rights and constitution are authoritative within it exist essentially in the form of thought as law. And since the state is not a mechanism but the rational life of self-conscious freedom, the system of the ethical world, it follows that an essential moment in the actual state is the mental attitude of the citizens, and so their consciousness of the *principles* which this attitude implies."[16]

An understanding of Hegel's views on the proper relation between church and state clarifies the general principles according to which politics for Hegel is related to the consciousness of the citizens. Hegel's most concrete, institutional instantiation of these principles occurs in his discussion of the political role of public opinion, to which we shall have recourse shortly. Almost all commentators on Hegel's political thought take note of the profound influence of the classical idea of the polis on Hegel's philosophy. In the polis, Hegel found a form of political organization in which citizens identified their own interests with those of the political order and saw themselves as integral parts of an enduring ethical community. For Hegel, the primary reason the polis cannot and should not be reintroduced into the modern political world is that it fails to do justice to the modern principle of subjectivity—the idea that individuals must be free to affirm the legitimacy of political institutions on the basis of their individual ethical consciousness.

What has usually been overlooked in accounts of the origins and development of Hegel's political philosophy is that he finds in the Christian, and especially Protestant, idea of the spiritual community the vehicle of transmission into the modern world of what remains valid in the classical conception. Hegel's abandonment of the standpoint of the individualism of civil society for the collectivism of the state is not a nostalgic, ahistorical leap back into the past, as it might seem to be if all one recalled of Hegel's philosophy of history was the idea that civil society is the distinctive achievement of the modern world. Hegel's idea of the state as an ethical community is rather grounded in that strain of world history to which an Enlightenment-inspired rationality is blind because reference to religion is anathema to the Enlightenment spirit. The spreading of a politically appropriate religious consciousness throughout the population over the course of modern history (see Chapter 3) is a necessary foundation for the realization of an ethical community in political institutions. Because religious consciousness, on the one hand, is rooted in the depths of individual subjectivity and, on the other hand, lays claim to encompass the totality of the objective world, it prepares the ground for and exemplifies the individual's ethical identification with the collective whole. The Protestant ideal of spiritual community does so, on Hegel's analysis, in a way that does not violate the right of subjectivity as the polis does. Hegel argues against any immediate identification of church and state. "Mention may also be made of the 'unity of state and church'—a favorite topic of modern discussion and held up by some as the highest of ideals. While state and church are essentially one in truth of principle and disposition, it is no less essential that, despite this unity, the distinction between their forms of consciousness should be externalized as a distinction between their special modes of existence."[17]

The kind of unity between citizens and the state required in the modern era is one that does not necessitate a homogeneous citizenry but one that is predicated on diversity.[18] In Hegelian terms, it is a mediated unity that preserves the sphere of particularity. Just as the universality of the state does not abolish economic differences in civil society, neither does it abolish doctrinal differences among various denominations. Hegel's theory in fact requires that there be multiple religious

institutions. Only in this way can the proper ethical disposition toward
the state develop. Given this diversity, the state can then encourage,
but not require, that citizens belong to some church, just as the state
should pursue policies that channel people into various corporations, so
that their integrating function can be fulfilled, without fear that any
one religious doctrine will impose itself on all.

The state attains "religious credentials"[19] because both church and
state are rational, ethical communities, not because theology dictates
policy. Hegel cites the greater freedom of scientific and academic inquiry that accompanies religious diversity and tolerance as an argument
in favor of a multiplicity of religions. Here, again, the guiding principle
of Hegel's approach to the question of how religion relates to politics
emphasizes rational rather than affective ties. Hegel's political theory
is so far from embracing any kind of theocracy that rather than seeing religious disharmony as threatening to political unity he argues that
the state's having reached its proper universality and self-consciousness
presupposed the "inward divisions" that have occurred in the history
of Christianity. "So far from its being or its having been a misfortune
for the state that the church is disunited, it is only as a result of that
disunion that the state has been able to reach its appointed end as a
self-consciously rational and ethical organization. Moreover, this disunion is the best piece of good fortune which could have befallen either
the church or thought so far as the freedom and rationality of either is
concerned."[20]

This is the essence of Hegel's attitude toward church-state relations
in regard to the claims of church and state on the consciousness of
the citizens. The "religious credentials" of the state do not deify or
sanctify the state, if by that one means that the state cannot be subject
to rational criticism. Instead, these credentials certify that the state
addresses the citizens' need to see themselves as part of an ethical whole
that reflects their collective consciousness rather than as merely part
of an external union of individuals that serves only the satisfaction
of their material needs. Significantly, although Hegel sees individual
morality (*Moralität*) as too subjective a foundation for the state, as
too easily leading to abstract fanaticism, he is willing to see the state
gain additional legitimacy as an ethical community (*Sittlichkeit*) from
recognition by another organized institution like the church.

Insofar as churches are publicly organized bodies, Hegel treats them
as corporations. Although questions of internal doctrine are left to each
church to determine, their external, worldly affairs come under political
regulation. Though Hegel emphasizes the civic aspects of religion, he

makes no attempt to establish any kind of Rousseauian civic religion. As we have seen, he argues against any such indoctrination as too direct, immediate an attempt at political indoctrination. The precise line between public regulation and independent autonomy of course "is indeterminate in extent,"[21] but Hegel maintains that this indeterminacy is exactly parallel to the degree of indeterminacy encountered in establishing the precise boundaries of any civil regulation in civil society and poses no special problems.

The Sphere of Public Opinion

Just as religion has its particular niche to fill in the well-ordered Hegelian state, so too does the sphere of public opinion have a particular, and especially important, role to play. It may seem a truism to say that public opinion has an important bearing on political life, yet this has particular significance for Hegel. Perhaps the best way to fully appreciate the significance of Hegel's analysis of public opinion is to approach the topic through the work of a modern social theorist who more than anyone else has built on and developed Hegel's analysis of public opinion. One of Jürgen Habermas's earliest works was *Strukturwandel der Öffentlichkeit* (*Structural Transformation of the Public Sphere*). The book was "first published in 1962 and reprinted four times since. With this work, the young philosopher and social theoretician, Jürgen Habermas, established his credentials. Originally written as a *Habilitationsschrift* for a small circle of scholars, *Strukturwandel der Öffentlichkeit* soon became a standard work which was to help shape the political consciousness of the emerging New Left in the 1960s."[22]

Part of the book contains a history of the concept of public opinion as it appears in the writings of numerous social theorists beginning with Plato but focusing more closely on the period from Hobbes to Tocqueville. A look at Habermas's analysis of the development of the concept of public opinion up to Hegel will be helpful in understanding Hegel's position as well as the importance of Hegel's theory for later social theorists like Habermas.

The concept of opinion, from the Latin *opinio*, retained the associations that accrued to the Greek *doxa*. For Plato, *opinion*, or *doxa*, is sharply differentiated from knowledge. Opinions are held by ordinary people and expressed in everyday speech. Opinions, no matter how fervently held, do not entitle one to input into the political process in the ideal state, which is the sole province of those who have knowledge— the philosophers. Politics cannot be based on opinions because they tend to be naive, biased, and incomplete. This is the sharpest kind of differentiation between the sphere of opinion and the sphere of politics. With these concepts as one's point of departure, no concept of "public opinion," of a politically relevant sphere of the opinions of ordinary citizens, can emerge.

For Hobbes, the opinions of the citizens may count in the "inner court" of conscience, but in the political realm the final word of the sovereign is not to be challenged. One finds in Locke the beginnings of a concept of public opinion, but in the final analysis the sphere of opinion remains marked off from that of politics. Public opinion has only an indirect influence on politics because it is grounded in the private opinions of "private men . . . who have not authority enough to make a law."[23] Only in the late eighteenth century does one see the emergence of a concept of "public" opinion. Only then do the collected opinions of the citizenry begin to be conceptualized as a public and political, rather than private and personal, domain.[24]

This change in the concept of public opinion reflects a change in the actual composition of the public. The eighteenth century saw the emergence of a literate, politically active public in the new institutions of political journals and pamphlets and in the salons. The concept "public opinion" comes to incorporate the recognition that in order to be politically efficacious, public opinion must be articulated through some public institutions. At the same time, and in counterpoint to this aspect of the concept that emphasizes the need for institutional articulation, the concept has always retained some reference to the immediate, unformed opinions of individuals. Rousseau's concept of the "public spirit" for the first time combines both these elements.

Rousseau has a well-deserved reputation as the champion of the natural wisdom of the people. For him, what is required for the expression of the infallible general will is simply that the question be correctly put to the assembled public. Rousseau's basic position is that protracted argument, and especially the existence of any intermediate associations in which public policy would be debated from the standpoint of particular interests outside the sovereign assembly, would only serve to distract and deceive the natural wisdom of the people expressed in the general will. At the same time, however, the general will is found not in the private personal judgments of the people but only in the collective assembly at which the citizens come together to listen to orations on public policy. But Rousseau does argue that the opinions of the people do need to be inspired by a legislator, casting doubt on Rousseau's original extolling of the virtues of the untutored intelligence of the people.

One finds the distinction needed for a clear, unambiguous concept of public opinion first articulated in the writings of Burke. Burke differentiates the immediate, natural opinions and volitions of the people from their educated, political voice. When Burke writes that "general opinion is the vehicle and organ of legislative omnipotence,"[25] he is referring neither to the human wisdom of the heart in Rousseauian terms nor to the unreflective force of tradition but to opinions formed in public, open dialogue, to the "real public wisdom and sagacity in shops and manufactories."[26]

So far Habermas has shown a progression from seeing opinion as a personal, apolitical matter to seeing it as arising from the natural, unmediated opinions of people but acquiring a political function. The first to discuss the formation of public opinion as a function of government rather than merely as an influence on it is Bentham. Bentham sees a reciprocal relationship between the process of making laws in Parliament and the formation of public opinion. On the one hand, Parliament is to make laws under the guidance of public opinion, which serves as a kind of check on the lawmakers. On the other hand, the public opinion that oversees Parliament is itself educated by the process of open discussion in Parliament, whose debates serve as a model for the proper conduct of the sphere of public opinion. The presuppositions for this conception of an interrelationship between Parliament and public opinion had been articulated by Guizot. According to Guizot, public discussion forces the authorities to seek the truth of a matter, preventing government by fiat. The publication of social research and reasoned argument in independent journals and other publications is supposed to set all this out before the public. The public press is also supposed to play a role in motivating citizens to seek the truth in political matters.[27]

As can be seen from the list of names referred to in the preceding historical sketch, the institutionalization of public opinion as a political force took place in England and France before it did in Germany. Habermas notes that Kant was the first in Germany to see public opinion as a force that could rationalize politics.[28] Kant does not expect enlightenment to come from ordinary common sense alone. He expressly looks to organized public opinion to further the aims of enlightenment. "It is difficult for each separate individual to work his way out of the immaturity which has become almost second nature to him. He has even grown fond of it and is really incapable for the time being of using his own understanding. . . . There is more chance of an entire public enlightening itself."[29]

Kant emphasizes the public nature of enlightened understanding to so great a degree that he even argues that the private use of one's reason, by which he means the use of one's reason in carrying out the duties of a particular task or position, can be restricted with less harm to the body politic than if the public use of reason were to be restricted. "The *public* use of man's reason must always be free, and it alone can bring about enlightenment among men; the private use of reason may quite often be very narrowly restricted, however, without undue hindrance to the progress of enlightenment. But by the public use of one's own reason I mean that use which anyone may make of it as a man of learning addressing the entire reading public."[30]

Kant has come a long distance from Rousseau's conception of natural human wisdom. In the above passage, it is noteworthy that the enlightened public is the literate, educated public and that enlightenment of the public is seen as a process, not as a given human capacity to reason. With this, the concept of public opinion becomes linked to the philosophy of history. Not only does the establishment of a politically relevant sphere of public opinion presuppose a process of education in Kant but it also achieves its effects as part of a historical process.

Habermas discerns two philosophies of history in Kant: what he calls the "official" and the "unofficial" versions.[31] In the "official" version, expressed above all in the essay "Idea for a Universal History with a Cosmopolitan Purpose,"[32] the natural course of history alone is sufficient to produce a moral politics. In the "unofficial" version, the natural course of history aided by a moral politics produces a public sphere that can permanently establish a moral politics by uniting the wills of all into a legal system. For this reason, denying the freedom of the public sphere denies the possibility of progress.[33] Furthermore, knowledge of this philosophy of history must become part of the knowledge of the sphere of public opinion itself, so that the knowledge of enlightenment can be widely circulated "up to the throne itself."[34]

With this background in mind, we may now turn to Hegel's own theory of public opinion. Given the issues raised by Habermas's historical overview, what stands out most clearly in Hegel's approach is his emphasis on the "public" nature of public opinion. This is what lies behind the putative anomaly, according to the traditional liberal logic, of Hegel dealing with the issues of freedom of speech and the press as the concluding segment of his discussion of the political institutions of the state, rather than under the heading of the individual freedoms of civil society.

In making the topic of public opinion a central topic of his political philosophy, Hegel shows himself to be an acute observer of developing trends in political society. As one analyst recently wrote: "Whether the historians have written of 'the supremacy of public opinion' or of a *naissance d'un monstre*, they have agreed that the latter part of the eighteenth century and the early nineteenth century saw changes in western Europe and elsewhere that signalled the arrival of public opinion as a significant force."[35]

To many thinkers, bringing up the issue of the expression of public opinion in the politicized way Hegel does raises the specter that what is being discussed is not the freedom of expression so much as limitation. For example, Ernst Bloch writes that the whole manner in which the will of the people is treated in Hegel's *Philosophy of Right* "has the sole task of letting the people know that they are ruled well; it [the manner in which the people are represented] is not an instrument for improving the will, but solely the point at which objective spirit is mediated to subjective consciousness."[36]

For Bloch, as well as for those who subscribe to the classical liberal individual-rights defense of rights of expression, discussing public opinion in the context of the functions of the state and the political formation of opinions means that one is more interested in the control of public opinion from above than in the expression of popular sovereignty from below. There is indeed much in Hegel to support such an estimation. We have seen, especially in his attitudes toward the French Revolution, that Hegel is no champion of direct popular sovereignty. And Hegel does say that public opinion contains so much that is false that much of it must be disregarded by any able legislator.[37] But a fairer estimation of Hegel's philosophy requires an understanding of the positive reasons why Hegel situates his discussion of public opinion in this context, in addition to seeing the drawbacks of this approach.

The standard individualist approach to defending freedoms of expression continues to treat political views as the private affairs of those who hold them. As Habermas's historical account of the concept of public opinion shows, in this approach the right to express one's views belongs to a separate sphere from any considerations of the possible impact of those views on actual political affairs. The right to speak is systematically separated from the right to be listened to, which does not enter into the picture at all.

However, when public opinion is treated not as a question of private right but as a question of public welfare, then the right to speak carries with it the right to speak in forums that have access to real political

power. This is a positive consequence of Hegel's political idealism, his
emphasis on the consciousness of the citizens. Rights to the expression
of public opinion follow not from individual, natural rights but from the
demand of modern consciousness to find recognition of itself in modern
political institutions. They are political rights, or rights of participation
in public discourse, not civil rights, or rights to noninterference by the
political state.

Hegel's understanding of the rights of modern political consciousness
leads him to affirm the necessity for institutionalized access to policy
makers by ordinary citizens, as well as a free press and public education. Only with these structures in place can all citizens feel that they
have had their say and been heard. At the same time, policy makers
must not let such a system of citizens' input degenerate into a system
of government by plebiscite or referendum, because public opinion is
too unstable for such a system to achieve the necessary political stability. Indeed, Hegel offers as a supporting argument for full freedom
of expression the idea that in a well-run political system much of what
is said by public opinion is rendered superfluous and innocuous by the
rationality of the debates and decisions of public officials.

> Freedom of public communication . . . is assured indirectly by the innocuous
> character which it acquires as a result principally of the rationality of the
> constitution, the stability of the government, and secondly of the publicity of
> Estates Assemblies. The reason why the latter makes free speech harmless is
> that what is voiced in these Assemblies is a sound and mature insight into the
> concerns of the state, with the result that members of the general public are
> left with nothing of much importance to say, and above all are deprived of the
> opinion that what they say is of peculiar importance and efficacy.[38]

Hegel's last remarks in the passage quoted above echo his remarks
in the Preface to the *Philosophy of Right* against the superficial view
that sees the idiosyncratic uniqueness of an idea as a sign of its profundity rather than recognizing that true profundity lies in seeing through
to the roots of widely shared views that form the basis of the social
fabric.[39]

Hegel's attitudes toward public opinion share the same ambivalence
we saw earlier in his attitudes toward the general political consciousness of his day. Public opinion is the repository of valid truths, yet
these truths are lost in a mass of scattered opinions. It is the task of
philosophy to sort out what is true and deserving of being preserved

from what is not. Here, Hegel has added to his analysis of the relationship between the ordinary discourse of everyday life and the task
of the philosopher the insight that this confrontation between philosophy and ordinary language can take place successfully only when the
encounter is mediated through established institutional recognition of
public opinion. This recognition brings articulated public opinion into
the light of the public forum. The forum itself then plays a pedagogical
role in further refining public opinion.

Recognition and Legitimacy

It would be well at this point to call attention to the deepest significance of what is at stake here in Hegel's analysis of public opinion
and to suggest why it is appropriate that it is the last topic he deals
with in discussing the institutions of the state. Throughout this study,
the importance of the *consciousness* of the citizens in Hegel's political
philosophy has been emphasized. What Hegel's political idealism successfully captures about the modern state is that modern politics, like
no other political system or theory earlier, is founded on the consciousness of the citizens. This is what is correct about contractarian political
theory, which bases political legitimacy on the will. But contractarian
theory mistakenly conceptualizes this will as a private, individual will
and thus fails to do justice to the need for this will to be an internal
part of the political system in which it finds recognition of its efficacy.
Individualistically based political theory leads either to a system in
which all individuals feel that their will must be immediately, directly
active and effective in ordering political life, or to a system in which
the essential element in politics is seen to be the private, personal interests of individuals, and the whole political sphere is seen as simply
a means to that end. The creation of an integrated, satisfying political
system that is subject to neither anarchy nor alienation, argues Hegel,
depends on a social, universal conception of the will that can serve as
a foundation for politics, and not on a private, particularist conception
of that will. Ultimately, what is at issue here is the Hegelian notion of
recognition as a basis for the legitimacy of political authority, in contrast to the liberal notion of consent. Hegel finds the standard liberal
notion of consent, as paradigmatically expressed in classical social contract theory, too volitional for it to play the foundational role assigned
to it in these theories. He attempts to found political legitimacy on
a more complex sociological analysis of the institutional arrangements

required for individuals to identify with and find an expression of their will in political institutions.

Hegel's criticism of contractarian theory's voluntarism would also extend to the updated, Rawlsian version of social contract theory.[40] Furthermore, Rawls's *A Theory of Justice* would invoke another line of criticism by Hegel.[41] The notion of consent embedded in the Rawlsian reformulation of social contract theory is not only voluntaristic but also hypothetical. It is a reconstruction of the logic of what political agents *would* rationally affirm behind a "veil of ignorance," positioned outside their present society. But for Hegel the citizen's identification with the society must be *actual*, not merely *hypothetical*. As we saw earlier, the logic of the *Philosophy of Right* is not only logical but also phenomenological, reflecting the lived experience of individuals. Rawlsian theory lacks this phenomenological content. The feeling of satisfaction of living within an ethical community must be in some way available to individuals other than philosophers.

The importance of this notion of "recognition," developed by Hegel as an aspect of the institutionalized rational will, as the legitimating concept of modern politics, and its advantage over the contractarian notion of consent, is nicely captured by Michael Oakeshott in the following passage.

> The only conditions of conduct which do not compromise the inherent integrity of a Subject are those which reach him in his understanding of them, which he is free to subscribe to or not, and which can be subscribed to only in an intelligent act of Will. The necessary characteristic of *das Recht* is not that the Subject must himself have chosen or approved what it requires him to subscribe to, but that it comes to him as a product of reflective intelligence and exhibiting its title to recognition.[42]

A crucial element in this Hegelian conception of politics is the conceptualization of public opinion in political terms, which has just been presented. Thus, although Hegel's concept of public opinion does carry with it the risk of authoritarian overtones that threaten to limit the free expression of opinion, it also carries with it the possibility of much greater integration of public opinion into the political process than the individualistic alternative. Indeed, it should be noted that the liberal defense of free speech usually put forward as the preferred alternative to Hegel's view has always recognized the right of the state to limit speech. Radical critics of liberalism have even argued that in different historical periods the degree of toleration of radical political speech in liberal societies seems to vary in inverse proportion to the degree of effectiveness of that speech.[43]

The importance of the idea that the modern state bases its legitimacy on the consciousness of the citizens can be illustrated by reference to Habermas's development of this concept. We noted that the historical overview of the concept of public opinion cited earlier appears in one of Habermas's earliest works. This political concept of public opinion is crucial to understanding the concepts of political legitimacy and of the legitimation crisis of the modern state, which Habermas develops in his later work.[44] It is only because the modern state depends for its legitimacy in its own self-understanding on the principle of the rational will of its citizens that a crisis of confidence in the system becomes a serious *internal* problem for the system itself and not a threat from without by a competing system. The "legitimation crisis" of modern states is differentiated from all previous forms of failures in the legitimating arguments of the system (for example, the arguments of religion, tradition, and so on) by the way in which the crisis of legitimacy enters into the logic of the system itself. By way of contrast, the denial of the divine right of kings was an external denial of the entire form of legitimating arguments of an earlier period and not an immanent critique and challenge to the authority of this or that monarch while remaining within the religious, authoritarian paradigm of argument. The universal rise of the principles of the modern state, however, means that all arguments for the legitimacy of one state over another remain within a logic that holds that the legitimacy of the political order is founded on the rational will of the citizens.

The point can be put in other idioms as well. It is widely understood that around the middle of the last century the term "democracy" shifted from having a primarily descriptive to having a primarily prescriptive meaning. That is to say, prior to this period, "democracy" was more or less consistently used to refer to a system of direct rule by the majority of the people and was as such argued for or against. After the mid-nineteenth century, "democracy" lost this specific cognitive content. Diverse political systems, from liberal capitalist democracy to communism, all advanced arguments designed to put forth their claims to being a true system of democracy. The principle underlying this change is what Hegel has in mind when he declares that in the modern world politics must be based on the will of all, and all that remains is to work out the more precise meaning of this principle. The unchallenged, universal acceptance of this very basic principle is what Hegel has captured in the basic tenets of his political philosophy and in his claim that the modern era has reached this decisive stage from which there can be no retreat. Hegel's attention is on the underlying deep level of continuity and agreement in the foundations of political discourse in the modern world that makes it possible, for example, to take competing systems like capitalism and communism and cast the arguments for each in terms acceptable to the other system, to speak of competing claims to realize political and economic democracy, and to construct a dialogue with shared basic assumptions in a way that could not have been constructed between monarchists and republicans, for example, in an earlier period. Every modern political system must in some sense claim to express "the voice of the people" and must at least give lip service to the idea of "popular sovereignty." Classical or medieval political systems, in contrast, had no such obligation.

Public opinion is the sphere in which the universal truths of the age find their particular voices to articulate them. It is here that what one commentator calls "the ascending and descending power structures,"[45] the voices of the many seeking political power from below and the voice of the state conferring legitimacy from above, most clearly meet in the consciousness of the citizens. This is the closest Hegel comes to answering a key question that has troubled many commentators on Hegel's political philosophy: precisely how much knowledge of the principles of political philosophy do the claims of Hegel's philosophy require one to attribute to the citizens of the Hegelian state?[46] Between the extreme poles of the claim that all Hegelian citizens must essentially be Hegelian philosophers and the claim that only the few true Hegelian philosophers in the state possess a satisfied consciousness, lies the Hegelian middle that claims that these principles are embodied in the institutions that constitute the Hegelian state and that these institutions are structured with an eye toward the creation of a rational sphere of public opinion open to all. A key criterion of Hegel's evaluation of all Hegelian political institutions is their effect on the consciousness of those who participate in them. Again, there is a necessary indeterminacy in the empirical application of these principles. That is to say, Hegel does not need to show that every empirical individual in the Hegelian state can give a full account of the rationale behind all political institutions and practices. To make such a demand misunderstands the nature of philosophy, which needs only provide the general principles on which society is to be ordered.

Legislative Debate and Representation

The institution that deals most directly with the formation of public consciousness in the Hegelian state and that in fact leads Hegel into his discussion of public opinion in the first place is the legislature, and so it is appropriate that we turn to an examination of the Estates Assembly.

The most important aspect of the Estates is their role in the formation of public political consciousness rather than their role in caring for the material interests of the citizens. Though the latter is an important function of the legislature, it is not to the legislature but to the bureaucracy that this latter is assigned as a primary task.

> The purpose of the Estates as an institution is not to be an inherent *sine qua non* of maximum efficiency in the consideration of state business, since in fact it is only an *added* efficiency that they can supply [see Paragraph 301]. Their distinctive purpose is that in their pooled political knowledge, deliberations, and decisions, the moment of formal freedom shall come into its right in respect of those members of civil society who are without any share in the executive. Consequently, it is knowledge of public business above all which is extended by the publicity of Estates debates.[47]

Although unorganized public opinion threatens to become mob rule rendering governance impossible (as in the extremes of Jacobinism), the Estates turn this potentially oppositional force into an integrative force in the society. "They [the Estates] prevent individuals from having the appearance of a mass or an aggregate and so from acquiring an unorganized opinion and volition and from crystallizing into a powerful bloc in opposition to the organized state."[48]

Note that Hegel does not argue that an *independent* volition is harmful to the state but only that an *unorganized* one is. The point here is not to stifle or co- opt dissent but to create an institutional channel for public dialogue. Lack of a channel for input into the political system is far more alienating and disruptive of political harmony than dissident opinions themselves. "In France freedom of speech has turned out far less dangerous than enforced silence, because with the latter the fear is that men bottle up their objections to a thing, whereas argument gives them an outlet and a measure of satisfaction, and this is in addition a means whereby the thing can be pushed ahead more easily."[49]

Given that in the modern world people insist that the political system fulfill their demand for the recognition of their subjective consciousness, the alternative to a representative assembly is violence. "When the multitude enters the state as one of its organs, it achieves its interests by legal and orderly means. But if these means are lacking, the voice of the masses is always for violence."[50]

The public business conducted by the Estates includes not only the passing of laws serving the "well-being and happiness"[51] of the citizens but also the extracting of services from the citizens for the state. It is a mark of the modern state that these services are all extracted through the medium of taxation rather than through tasks directly performed for the state by the citizens, with the exception of military service, which is a uniquely personal form of service. This permits one's service to the state to be mediated through one's subjective consciousness, because in the modern state one is, in Hegel's view, essentially free to choose the means through which one earns the money that goes to the state. The state does not infringe on the sphere of personal dignity by deciding for the individual what kind of work is to be done by the individual for the public welfare, argues Hegel.

> In these circumstances [for example, Plato's *Republic*, feudal monarchies, the building of Egyptian and Eastern public monuments] the principle of subjective freedom is lacking, i.e. the principle that the individual's substantive activity . . . shall be mediated through his particular volition. This is a right which can be secured only when the demand for service takes the form of a demand for something of universal value, and it is this right which has brought with it this conversion of the state's demands into demands for cash.[52]

Hegel proposes that the legislature should consist of two houses. In this way, each of the classes of civil society can attain its appropriate political significance. One house is to represent the agricultural class and membership in this body is fixed by birth. Here the social concept of private property developed by Hegel in the "Abstract Right" section of the *Philosophy of Right* has its most direct impact on the form of institutions in the Hegelian state.[53] The idea that property is family property comes to mean in this class that this property is not entirely subject to the individual prerogative of any member of the landed class. It must be handed down according to the rules of primogeniture in order to assure that there is in the state a fixed, substantial class that comes into direct relation to the state without having its fortunes depend on "the state's capital, the uncertainty of business, the quest for profit, and any sort of fluctuation in possessions. It is likewise independent of favour, whether from the executive or the mob."[54]

Hegel here seeks to use property to "anchor" the state, as Alan Ryan puts it.

He contrasts the *Weltanschauung* of the agriculturalist, who plants the seed and waits patiently for the harvest in an attitude of trust and gratitude, with the busy-ness of the businessman, who constantly has to keep an eye on his assets to maximize his profits from them. Equally the agriculturalist is socially and geographically immobile; it is *this* place he lives in, cultivates, and loves, and no other will do in exchange. . . . Hegel, of course, knew that he was describing an ideal type and not the much more varied empirical reality. But it was enough to distinguish the traditionalist, communal, pious outlook of the countryside from the rationalist, self-centered and secular outlook of the town. Apart from anything else, here was Hegel's way of making the old point that money breeds the world of easy come, easy go, while land stays put and its owner with it. There is more, too, including a hint of the standard nineteenth-century English view that the ties of master and man in the country were paternal and caring on the one side and deferential and grateful on the other, whereas the callous cash nexus did not link employer and employee so much as set them at one another's throats.[55]

Seen in historical perspective, this is the same kind of nostalgia for which Hegel criticizes Plato when he attempts to conceptualize a form of the Greek polis already in the process of being rendered obsolete by the growing commercialization of Athens. The noncommercial aristocracy on which this description of Hegel's depends was already a rapidly vanishing breed when this was written. Like Plato, too, Hegel sees internal strife among the aristocracy over property as a serious threat to the stability of the state. Nonetheless, Hegel's underlying principle, that in the interests of greater social stability a way should be found to have at least one segment of the government not committed to the proposition that the business of government is business, can be separated from the specific class Hegel pinpointed to embody this idea. The "deep structure" principle guiding Hegel's construction seems more valid than the institution that serves as its repository.

Hegel's most distinctive contribution to the question of how legislative representation is best to be achieved comes in his discussion of the other house of the Estates, whose members are elected by the business class. (It is tempting to use the terms "Upper" and "Lower" houses—that is, "Lords" and "Commons"—for these institutions as some commentators do, but it is noteworthy that Hegel makes no such differentiation. Because both houses are equally essential, no hierarchy obtains between them.)[56] Although the members of the landed class are directly present in the Assembly in their own persons, the members of the commercial class are represented by their deputies. Hegel's doctrine of the nature of this representation is the key to understanding how the Estates are to facilitate the growth of political reconciliation and identity out of the economic diversity of civil society.

Hegel's doctrine of representation is derived from his concept of political mediation discussed earlier. In order to prevent the alienation and anomie that continually threaten to dominate modern political life, it is essential that individuals interact with the state not as isolated individuals, who would be overwhelmed by the scale and complexity of the modern state, but as members of organizations that ensure that their members have attained a stable political identity. The state is thus not a conglomerate of individuals but "an organization each of whose members is in itself a group."[57] Hegel argues that the representatives of the commercial class must be chosen through the organizations that give that class social cohesion and enable it to have political status and impact. To disperse these associations at election time by having each individual vote for deputies-at-large would destroy the political integration the corporations have achieved. Representatives are elected as representatives of specific corporations and other associations.

> Since these deputies are the deputies of civil society, it follows as a direct consequence that their appointment is made by the society as a society. That is to say, in making the appointment, society is not dispersed into atomic units, collected to perform only a single and temporary act, and kept together for a moment and no longer. On the contrary, it makes the appointment as a society, articulated into associations, communities, and Corporations, which although constituted already for other purposes, acquire in this way a connexion with politics.[58]

Hegel's concept of representation mediates between what Hannah Pitkin, in an insightful analysis, calls the "Burkean" and "liberal" concepts of representation.[59] What is again striking about Hegel's theory is his use of a nonliberal schema for the attainment of the ends of liberal doctrine. As Pitkin puts it, on the Burkean model: "The member [of Parliament] is to pursue the interest of his constituency rather than do its bidding; the characteristic feature of the Burkean approach is that such a contrast is possible and even highly meaningful."[60]

Hegel's doctrine of election to the Assembly through corporations rather than through direct universal suffrage is a form of functional representation that assumes this Burkean distinction. Like Burke, he argues that representatives are chosen for their insight into the affairs of the nation as a whole, seen from the perspective of the interests of their constituency. Although they are elected because the electors have confidence in their judgment, once they are in office they are not bound by the will of their constituency but are to follow their own judgment. The Assembly is not a congregation that simply records the votes of delegates delivering opinions developed in separate political bodies in isolation from each other. It is a deliberative body whose rationality emerges from the discussions in its chambers. Consequently, the delegates must have the freedom to have their insight shaped by parliamentary debate.

> Since deputies are elected to deliberate and decide on public affairs, the point about their election is that it is a choice of individuals on the strength of confidence felt in them, i.e. a choice of such individuals as have a better understanding of these affairs than their electors have and such also as essentially vindicate the universal interest, not the particular interest of a society or a Corporation in preference to that interest. Hence their relation to their electors is not that of agents with a commission or specific instructions. A further bar to their being so is the fact that their assembly is meant to be a living body in which all members deliberate in common and reciprocally instruct and convince each other.[61]

For Burke and Hegel, it is essential that all branches of society have their interests represented. Hegel argues that leaving the matter simply to universal suffrage not tied to already organized interests does not insure that this will happen. For both, the essential point is that each particular point of view on the universal be represented in public deliberations. The point is the completeness of public debate, not a competition of power among different interests. Therefore both are not so much concerned with the numerical distribution of representatives among different groups as they are with the simple requirement that each constituency be represented. "It is obviously of advantage that the deputies should include representatives of each particular main branch of society (e.g. trade, manufactures, &c., &c.)—representatives who are thoroughly conversant with it and who themselves belong to it. The idea of free unrestricted election leaves this important consideration entirely at the mercy of chance."[62]

Seen in this light, it becomes clear that Hegel's criticism of direct universal suffrage is that it does not assure sufficiently equitable representation of all elements of society, not that it gives too great a voice to

the people. In fact, Hegel argues that one of the flaws of undifferentiated universal suffrage is that in large states it will encourage political
abstention and apathy, "since the casting of a single vote is of no significance where there is a multitude of electors."[63] As Shlomo Avineri
points out, "Hegel is thus among the first political theorists to recognize that direct suffrage would create a system very different from that
envisaged by the advocates of such a system of direct representation."[64]
"Thus the result of an institution of this kind is more likely to be the
opposite of what was intended; election actually falls into the power
of a few, of a caucus, and so of the particular and contingent interest
which is precisely what was to have been neutralized."[65]

These same concerns figure prominently in Hegel's other political
writings, in which he often criticizes what are to him simply abstract
age and property qualifications for voting— qualifications that do not
take into account the properly political concerns that Hegel's theory
addresses. For Hegel, mass universal suffrage, in which isolated individuals vote for at-large representatives, rather than voting for their
deputies as recognized members of Estates and corporations, leaves voting as just a civil and not yet a political practice. In the "Proceedings
of the Estates Assembly in the Kingdom of Wurtemberg, 1815–1816,"
Hegel writes:

> Provisions of the kind which presuppose a nation as a mass rather than a
> state and divide it generally by numbers into particular masses and by age
> and a specified property qualification into two classes cannot possibly be called
> politicalinstitutions. They do not suffice to strip the people's share in national
> affairs of its democratic formlessness or to attain the end of not leaving to
> chance the acquisition of fit deputies for a National Assembly. A political
> institution cannot be content with the mere demand that something ought to
> happen, with the hope that it will happen, with barring certain factors which
> might impedeits happening. It deserves its name only when it is so organized
> that what ought to happen does happen.[66]

The same ideas figure in Hegel's criticisms of the proposed reforms
in his essay on "The English Reform Bill" of 1831,[67] and it is these passages in which Sidney Hook so egregiously saw something "ominous."[68]
Hegel's ambivalences about public opinion and direct, unmediated
democracy mirrored those of much progressive thought of his period.[69]
Hegel's concern that the Estates continue to function as a vehicle to
channel the consciousness and input of the citizens into the political
system is why the Burkean model does not exhaust Hegel's doctrine of

representation. The further element corresponds to the "liberal" concept of representation, to recall Pitkin's distinction between Burkean and liberal models. On the logic of Burke's concept of representation, the process of electing representatives seems almost superfluous. What matters here is that the electors' objectively measurable interests are being advanced, not that their subjectively held opinions are being validated. As Pitkin describes the interests that the Burkean representative is said to represent: "These interests are largely economic. . . . To a very great extent, these interests are conceived of as "unattached"; it is not the interest of farmers but the agricultural interest—an objective reality for Burke apart from any individuals it might affect."[70]

Hegel cannot accept in the Burkean doctrine this distance from the consciousness of the electorate. As we have seen, for Hegel the primary task of the Estates Assembly is to ensure the identification of the citizens with the political process, to be the institutionalization of the citizens' active role in politics. Hegel sides with the liberal concept of representation in insisting that what is being represented is not "unattached interests," but "people who have interests."[71]

For Hegel, the chief qualifying asset representatives bring to their deliberations is not any privileged insight into the general welfare, though it is to be hoped that electors are looking for this quality in their representatives, but the confidence of their constituency, who feel that their interests are being looked after. This is a decidedly subjective criterion, in contrast to Burke, who argues that the representatives should be demonstrably better educated and cultured than their constituents. In the final analysis, no political theory so thoroughly based on the will as is Hegel's can result in a Burkean conservatism.

Notes

1. See Michael A. Mosher, "Civic Identity in the Juridical Society: On Hegelianism as Discipline for the Romantic Mind," *Political Theory* 11:1, February 1983, pp. 117–132.
2. *PR*, §268A, p. 164.
3. H. S. Reiss, "Introduction," in *The Political Thought of the German Romantics* (Oxford: Basil Blackwell, 1955).
4. *PR*, §268A, pp. 163–164.
5. *Ibid.*, §270, p. 165.

6. See John E. Smith, "Hegel's Reinterpretation of the Doctrine of Spirit and Religious Community," in *Hegel and the Philosophy of Religion: The Wofford Symposium*, ed. Daniel E. Christensen (The Hague: Martinus Nijhoff, 1970).

7. *PR*, §270A, pp. 165–166.

8. *Ibid.*, §270A, p. 167.

9. *Ibid.*, §270A, p. 166.

10. *Ibid.*, §270A, p. 167.

11. *Ibid.*, §270A, p. 167.

12. *Ibid.*, §270A, p. 166.

13. *Ibid.*, §270A, p. 284.

14. See Karl Löwith, *From Hegel to Nietzsche* (New York: Anchor, 1967), pt. 2, chap. 1; and Lucio Colletti, *Marxism and Hegel* (London: New Left Books, 1973), chap. 12.

15. *PH*, p. 417.

16. *PR*, §270A, p. 170.

17. *Ibid.*, p. 173. Knox sees this as specifically aimed against "Romantics like Friedrich von Schlegel and Adam Muller," p. 366.

18. This is why Kojève's characterization of the Hegelian state as "homogeneous" is misleading. Alexandre Kojève, *Introduction to the Reading of Hegel*, ed. Allan Bloom, trans. James H. Nichols, Jr. (New York: Basic Books, 1969), pp. 95–97.

19. *PR*, §270A, p. 172.

20. *Ibid.*, §270A, p. 174.

21. *Ibid.*, §270A, p. 169.

22. Peter Uwe Hohendahl, "Jürgen Habermas: 'The Public Sphere' (1964)," *New German Critique* vol. 1, no. 3, Fall 1974, p. 45.

23. Quoted in Jürgen Habermas, *Strukturwandel der Öffentlichkeit* (Neuwied and Berlin: Luchterhand, 1976), p. 115.

24. Habermas is not alone in placing the rise of "public opinion" in this period. A contemporary, C.-C. de Rulhiere, is approvingly quoted by Crane Brinton in placing the rise of "the empire of public opinion" in prerevolutionary Paris. See "Reflections on the Alienation of the Intellectuals," in *Generalizations in Historical Writing*, ed. Alexander V. Riasanovsky and Barnes Riznik (Philadelphia: University of Pennsylvania Press, 1963), p. 213. For a survey of the influence of that aspect of Habermas's work under discussion here, see Peter Uwe Hohendahl, "Critical Theory, Public Sphere, and Culture: Jürgen Habermas and His Critics," *New German Critique*, No. 16, Winter 1979, pp. 89–118.

25. Quoted in Habermas, *Strukturwandel der Öffentlichkeit*, p. 117.

26. *Ibid.*, p. 118.

27. *Ibid.*, p. 125.

28. *Ibid.*, pp. 125–127.

29. Immanuel Kant, "An Answer to the Question: 'What is Enlightenment?'" in *Political Writings*, ed. Hans Reiss, trans. H. B. Nisbet (Cambridge: Cambridge University Press, 1977), pp. 54–55. Quoted in Habermas, *Strukturwandel der Öffentlichkeit*, p. 129.

30. Kant, *Political Writings*, p. 55.

31. Habermas, *Strukturwandel der Öffentlichkeit*, pp. 141–142.

32. Kant, *Political Writings*, pp. 41–53.

33. Cf. John Christian Laursen, "The Subversive Kant," and Onora O'Neill, "The Public Use of Reason," *Political Theory* 14:4, November 1986, pp. 584–603 and pp. 523–551.

34. Quoted in Habermas, *Strukturwandel der Öffentlichkeit*, p. 142.

35. J.A.W. Gunn, *Beyond Liberty and Property: The Process of Self-Recognition in Eighteenth-Century Political Thought* (Kingston, Canada: McGill-Queen's University Press, 1983), p. 260.

36. Ernst Bloch, "Der Schwur auf den Styx. Der zweideutige Kosmos in Hegels Rechtsphilosophie," in *Materialien zu Hegels Rechtsphilosophie*, vol. 2, ed. Manfred Riedel (Frankfurt am Main: Suhrkamp, 1975), pp. 433–434.

37. *PR*, §317–318, pp. 204–205.

38. *Ibid.*, §319, pp. 205–206.

39. *Ibid.*, Preface, pp. 2–4.

40. Cf. Carole Pateman, *The Problem of Political Obligation: A Critique of Liberal Theory* (Berkeley: University of California Press, 1985).

41. John Rawls, *A Theory of Justice* (Cambridge: Harvard University Press, 1971).

42. Michael Oakeshott, *On Human Conduct* (Oxford: Clarendon Press, 1975), p. 260. Cited in Patrick Riley, *Will and Political Legitimacy: A Critical Exposition of Social Contract Theory in Hobbes, Locke, Rousseau, Kant, and Hegel* (Cambridge: Harvard University Press, 1982), p. 143.

43. See Herbert Marcuse, Robert Paul Wolff, and Barrington Moore, Jr., *A Critique of Pure Tolerance* (Boston: Beacon Press, 1965). The earlier, contractarian version of liberalism with which Hegel was familiar is more susceptible to this strain of criticism than some later versions, though the individualist base is never abandoned. For example, some of Hegel's suggestions come close to John Dewey's "social conception of intelligence" in works like *Liberalism and Social Action* (New York: Capricorn, 1963).

44. See Jürgen Habermas, *Legitimation Crisis*, trans. Thomas McCarthy (Boston: Beacon Press, 1975); and *Communication and the Evolution of Society*, trans. Thomas McCarthy (Boston, Beacon Press, 1979), chap. 5.

45. G. Heiman, "The Sources and Significance of Hegel's Corporate Doctrine," in *Hegel's Political Philosophy: Problems and Perspectives*, ed. Z. A. Pelczynski (Cambridge: Cambridge University Press, 1971), p. 135.

46. See Robert B. Pippin, "Hegel's Political Argument and the Problem of Verwirklichung," *Political Theory* 9:4, November 1981, pp. 509–532.

47. *PR*, §314, p. 203.

48. *Ibid.*, §302, p. 197.

49. *Ibid.*, §317A, p. 294.

50. *Ibid.*, §302A, pp. 292–293.

51. *Ibid.*, §299, p. 194.

52. *Ibid.*, §299A, p. 195.

53. See Chapter 4.

54. *PR*, §306, p. 199.

55. Alan Ryan, "Hegel and Mastering the World," chap. 6 in *Property and Political Theory* (New York: Basil Blackwell, 1984), pp. 138–139.

56. See, for example, Charles Taylor, *Hegel* (Cambridge: Cambridge University Press, 1978), pp. 445–446; Raymond Plant, *Hegel* (Bloomington: Indiana University Press, 1973), p. 176; Eugene Fleischmann, *La Philosophie Politique de Hegel* (Paris: Librairie Plon, 1964), p. 325; Shlomo Avineri, *Hegel's Theory of the Modern State* (Cambridge: Cambridge University Press, 1974), p. 161; Pelczynski *Hegel's Political Philosophy*, p. 25.

57. *PR*, §304A, p. 198.

58. *Ibid.*, §308, p. 200.

59. Hannah Fenichel Pitkin, *The Concept of Representation* (Berkeley: University of California Press, 1972).

60. *Ibid.*, p. 176.

61. *PR*, §309, p. 201.

62. *Ibid.*, §311A, p. 202. Cf. Pitkin on Burke, *The Concept of Representation*, p. 187: "The interests are only discovered in Parliament, through debate. But their discovery presupposes the participation of representatives of every interest so that all considerations will be brought to light in the debate. For Burke this has nothing to do with compromise among the wishes of conflicting groups; government is a matter of reason and not of will. But reason needs deliberators from every relevant point of view."

63. *PR*, §311A, p. 203.

64. Avineri, *Hegel's Theory*, p. 163.

65. *PR*, §311A, p. 203.

66. G.W.F. Hegel, *Hegel's Political Writings*, trans. T. M. Knox (Oxford: Oxford University Press, 1969), p. 265.

67. *Ibid.*, pp. 295–330, especially pp. 317–321.

68. Sidney Hook, "Hegel Rehabilitated?" in *Hegel's Political Philosophy*, ed. Walter Kaufmann (New York: Atherton Press, 1970), p. 61.

69. See Gunn, "Public Spirit to Public Opinion," chap. 7 in *Beyond Liberty and Property*, pp. 260–321.

70. Pitkin, *The Concept of Representation*, p. 174.
71. *Ibid.*, p. 190.

7

The Rational State

The Civil Service

Having explored the aspects of the Hegelian state chiefly concerned with subjective consciousness, we now turn to those aspects focusing on objective interests. Hegel finds in the executive rather than in the legislative branch a group of people who are to look after the objective interests of all groups in the society, disregarding the subjective consciousness of those affected by their decisions. Hegel turns here to the civil bureaucracy and the ministers of government.[1] This is the only group that identifies its interest directly with that of the state. These people are uniquely suited to this task by virtue of their background and training. Their identification with the public good is secured through their receiving a salary from the state and through the countervailing pressures exerted by the monarchy, the corporations, and public opinion, which prevent the civil service from ossifying into a class with its own interests.[2] This is the group that most stringently embodies the principle of meritocracy.

> Individuals are not appointed to office on account of their birth or native personal gifts. The *objective* factor in their appointment is knowledge and proof of ability. Such proof guarantees that the state will get what it requires; and since it is the sole condition of appointment, it also guarantees to every citizen the chance of joining the class of civil servants.[3]

Although both the civil servant class of the state and the public authority of civil society deal with the activities of the commercial class, the former is differentiated from the latter because its task is the execution of the general laws of the state rather than the regulation of particular conflicts arising from civil society. Again, the distinction is not easy to draw in all cases and there are clearly overlapping areas.

Hegel admits that the precise organization of the executive is a "difficult task"[4] because it must respect the autonomy of the institutions of civil society and at the same time subsume these institutions under the supervision of the supervenient universality of the state. "Particular interests which are common to everyone fall within civil society and lie outside the absolutely universal interest of the state proper. . . . On the other hand, however, these circles of particular interests must be subordinated to the higher interests of the state."[5]

Although it tends to the interests of the business class, the bureaucracy is insulated from the immediate pressures of civil society. To this end, appointments to public office are not to be contracts that must be periodically renewed but appointments conditional for their perpetuation only on the fulfillment of the duties involved. The executive branch is organized into various departments, whose heads are in direct contact with the monarch. All the institutions of the Hegelian state are in some sense to converge toward the monarch.

The entire analysis of Hegel's political philosophy developed in this study leads to an interpretation of the Hegelian state that holds that the more important of the three branches of the state are the legislature and the crown and that minimizes the importance of the executive branch in the Hegelian state. This follows from the interpretation of the basic intentions of Hegel's political philosophy that argues that Hegel's basic concern in his political theory is with the consciousness rather than with the material well-being of the citizens.

This is not to say that the material well-being and the economic activities of the citizens are disregarded in the Hegelian state. On the contrary, these aspects of life are the chief concern of the entire sphere of civil society and of the bureaucracy within the state proper. But it is to say that when Hegel posits the political state as a sphere higher than civil society, he is indicating that these materialistic concerns are secondary to the more important question of the political consciousness and identity of the citizens in the modern political world, for reasons which have to do with the historical development of consciousness to this level, as outlined earlier.

This interpretation is corroborated by the relative amounts of space Hegel devotes to the three branches of the state in the *Philosophy of Right*, as well as by his own statements in the *Philosophy of Right* regarding the specific functions of these institutions. It is noteworthy that this relative valuation of the importance of the branches of the Hegelian state vis-à-vis each other directly contradicts much of the standard commentary on Hegel, much of which, in some cases under

Weberian influence, looks to the bureaucracy as the major institution in the Hegelian state, as the key agent of Hegelian rationality. Thus, for example, Georg Ahrweiler in *Hegels Gesellschaftslehre* writes: "The bureaucracy is without a doubt the most important authority for the realization of political autonomy against social interests and interest groups."[6]

Similarly, George Sabine expressed the traditional view when he wrote: "The key to . . . Hegel's constitutionalism was the high importance that he attached to an official governing class, the 'universal class' as he called it. . . . It represents the general will and the 'reason' of society. . . . In comparison with the part assigned to officialdom, both representative institutions and the monarchy played a minor role in Hegel's theory of constitutionalism, in spite of the mystical reverence that he gave to the monarchy."[7]

As this study has attempted to demonstrate, interpretations of Hegel's political philosophy along these lines import into Hegel's conceptual scheme a concept of instrumental rationality and a concept of material interests that are foreign to Hegel's philosophy and that miss the importance Hegel attaches to the concept of subjectivity in the political sphere.

Sovereignty and Monarchy

The structure of the state is said by Hegel to follow from the philosophical concept of the free, rational will alone. "The state must be treated as a great architectonic structure, as a hieroglyph of the reason which reveals itself in actuality. Everything to do with mere utility, externality, and so forth, must be eliminated from the philosophical treatment of the subject."[8]

The constitution of the state articulates a structure that must be understood as one totality. The three branches of the state are not to be thought of as competing powers, on the "balance of power" model of much of U.S. constitutional law theory, for example. Competing power centers produce no real political sovereignty, no focus for state authority with which the citizens can identify. This focus in the Hegelian state is the constitutional monarchy. It is only through the reference of all public authority back to the final decision-making will of the monarch that, for Hegel, the state can be said to exercise legitimate sovereignty and not just mere power. Sovereignty requires that all the autonomous power centers of a society converge toward a single point of public authority. In the Hegelian system, the office of the crown is deduced from the concept of political sovereignty.

> In feudal times . . . not only was the monarch not sovereign at all, but the state itself was not sovereign either. For one thing, the particular functions and powers of the state and civil society were arranged . . . into independent Corporations and societies, so that the state as a whole was rather an aggregate than an organism; and, for another thing, office was the private property of individuals, and hence what they were to do in their public capacity was left to their own opinion and caprice.[9]

To understand how Hegel envisages the relationship between the monarchy and the other branches of government, one may have recourse to his understanding of the standard mode of division of the branches of government. "Mention is usually made of three powers, the legislative, the executive, and the judiciary; of these the first corresponds to universality and the second to particularity, but the judiciary is not the third moment of the concept, since the individuality intrinsic to the concept lies outside these spheres."[10]

One need only compare this with Hegel's schematization of the "three substantive divisions" of his idea of the state to see that the monarchy has taken the place of the judiciary in the standard scheme of things. The divisions of the Hegelian state are

(a) the power to determine and establish the universal—the Legislature;
(b) the power to subsume single cases and the spheres of particularity under the universal—the Executive;
(c) the power of subjectivity, as the will with the power of ultimate decision—the Crown. In the crown, the different powers are bound into an individual unity which is thus at once the apex and basis of the whole, i.e. of constitutional monarchy.[11]

The substitution of the crown for the judiciary follows from the Hegelian distinction between civil society and the state. On the standard liberal model, the judiciary is of course part of the state apparatus. However, because it deals with the harmonization of individual, material interests and not with the determination of universal principles related to the political identity of the citizens, for Hegel the judiciary is part of civil society. This leaves a gap in the structure of the state, for there is still a need to connect the particular (executive) and the universal (legislative) branches. But a way must be found to do this that is consonant with the level of universality and subjectivity reached by the state, that does not represent a regression back to the level of civil society. This unifying moment must be established as an institution independent of the other branches, so that "all determinations of the Idea receive their due." Hegel, as is well known and much criticized, finds all this in the final "I will" of the monarch.[12] His reading of the historical development of political consciousness tells him that in all ages people have looked for a final, unconditional sign of decision as the ultimate basis of political right, but only in the modern period has this aspect of consciousness come into its own within the political system. Previously, one could witness people "deriving the last word on great events and important affairs of state from oracles, a 'divine sign' (in the case of Socrates), the entrails of animals, the feeding and flight of birds, etc. It was when men had not yet plumbed the depths of self-consciousness or risen out of their undifferentiated unity of substance to their independence that they lacked strength to look within their own being for the final word."[13]

For Hegel, then, it is a sign of the maturation of spirit that this "final word" is now understood as uttered by the human will rather than sought in nature or religion. It is the triumph of the spirit that this apotheosized will has now been symbolically internalized into the political system as its apex. This marks the autonomy of politics from nature, religion, or tradition—an autonomy strenuously achieved through the course of human history. The search for the "final word" reflects consciousness seeking an unconditioned grounding for universal authority. The monarch's "I will" ends this quest and makes possible the self-grounding of political obligation. For this reason, Hegel can say of "the development of the state to constitutional monarchy" that "the history of this genuine formation of ethical life is the content of the whole course of world-history."[14]

Although this will must be situated within the political system, it must also be insulated from the shifting pressures and contingencies of that system, because it could not otherwise provide the necessary substantiality and permanency. Monarchy must therefore be not elective but hereditary.[15] In this way, the personal, contingent characteristics of the personality of the monarch are seen to be irrelevant. What counts is the office itself—the institutionalization of the principle of human subjectivity. In a sense, Hegel here builds on yet another concept of representation, different from either of the two modern concepts of representation described earlier as Burkean and liberal. In medieval political theory, the monarch was often said to literally represent the people in that in his person he "re-presented" the political community to the people in embodied, objective form. Many modern European states that have retained a constitutional monarchy justify it using some such concept of "symbolic representation." It is said of these monarchs, or of heads of state in general when the office is separated from that of head of government, that they "represent or embody, that is, are symbols for the unity of the people of the state; as flags, coats of arms, national anthems are in a more material and functional way."[16]

This theory of symbolic representation is markedly different from the concept of the "charismatic" leader, to which it bears only surface resemblance. First, the locus of identification is with the office, not the person. Second, and more important, the basis of the ties between the monarch and the citizens is philosophical, not psychological. The monarch serves as a focus of identification with the state for the citizens because of the rationality embodied in the office as it is situated vis-à-vis the other institutions Hegel describes, not because of any emotional or "charismatic" appeals to the people. The role of the monarch is mediated through the entire political structure of the Hegelian state. It is not an external, emotional tie to the ruler. Given Hegel's problematic, the question is whether this relationship between the citizens and the monarch is too mediated to have the effect on the consciouness of the citizens that Hegel attributes to it. Hegel himself admits that "the conception of the monarch is therefore of all conceptions the hardest for ratiocination, i.e., for the method of reflection employed by the understanding."[17]

Because the method of the understanding is attributed by Hegel to most of the citizens of the state as their mode of thinking, it would seem that most citizens would lack the philosopher's Rosetta stone required to decipher this particular "hieroglyph of reason." After all, in the exposition of the role of the monarch given just above, we had recourse to much of the relatively esoteric presuppositions and terminology of Hegel's philosophy, and one could hardly attribute this knowledge to the majority of the citizens in the Hegelian state.

Hegel goes into considerable detail in discussing specific tasks that fall to the monarch, most of which consist of giving his seal of approval to political appointments and decisions of cabinet ministers, and the like. If all is functioning well, the monarch should be called upon to do no more than "say 'yes' and dot the 'i'."[18] The power to pardon criminals, however, is by its nature so intimately tied up with the subjective, nonsystematic use of state power in the lives of particular individuals that it falls under the discretionary power of the crown.[19]

The details of these arrangements need not concern us here. However, there is another aspect to the office of the crown with which we should concern ourselves. Although it is hard to see how the monarch could function internally in a way that would lead the citizens to perceive and identify with the rationality of the state as Hegel suggests, there is another function of the monarch in which the suggestion that the monarchy serves to institutionalize and convey to the citizenry an appropriate political consciousness is more plausible. This is the monarch's role as the focus of recognition vis-à-vis other states in the conduct of foreign affairs.

Foreign Relations

The sovereignty of the state vis-à-vis other states is the complement to the sovereignty of the state vis-à-vis its own citizens. Too little attention has been paid to the fact that all the institutions of the state that we have analyzed so far comprise only one half of the topic of "Constitutional Law" in the *Philosophy of Right*. The other half is "Sovereignty vis-à-vis foreign States." The monarch is the pivot between these two sides of constitutional law.

It may seem odd that Hegel discusses international relations in the context of constitutional law, because the major thrust of Hegel's analysis of international relations is to deny that relations between sovereign states can be brought under any obligatory, enforceable law. In an argument specifically aimed against the Kantian idea of international law expressed in Kant's essay "Perpetual Peace," Hegel insists that because "every state is sovereign and autonomous against its neighbors,"[20] it and its neighbors are "in a state of nature in relation of each other."[21] There is no universal court of appeal among states representing a higher authority to which they can appeal to resolve disputes. Consequently, though states may sign treaties to which Hegel affirms they are morally bound, in the final analysis it remains a state's prerogative to interpret the clause of any treaty and abrogate its obligations. "Since there is no power in existence which decides in face of the state what is right in principle and actualizes this decision, it follows that so far as international relations are concerned we can never get beyond an 'ought'. The relation between states is a relation between autonomous entities which make mutual stipulations but which at the same time are superior to these stipulations."[22]

Despite the fact that the principles of national sovereignty preclude the establishment of any international legal system, there is nonetheless a system of less formal international relations among nations. Each nation recognizes the integrity and autonomy of other nations. On Hegel's analysis, each nation's internal sovereignty is logically prior to this recognition by other nations, and so although this system of mutual recognition among nations does not establish sovereignty, it does solidify it. The logical priority of internal over external sovereignty is Hegel's most systematic way of expressing ideas we have come across earlier—the idea that a constitution cannot be imposed on a people externally but must grow out of the historical experiences of that people and the idea that a political system presupposes an economic system on whose integrating mechanisms it can build.[23]

The idea that existence as an independent, autonomous being involves recognition by others is a familiar Hegelian theme. "A state is as little an actual individual without relations to other states (see Paragraph 322) as an individual is actually a person without *rapport* with other persons."[24]

The state enters world history as one state among others. Through the sovereign individual within the state, the monarch, the recognition the state gains from other states is mediated to the consciousness of the citizens in the state. To have recourse again to Pitkin's analysis of the kind of symbolic representation earlier attributed to the monarch, the other sovereign states of the world function as a kind of audience before which the sovereignty of the state is affirmed. "Some writers have argued that representation can exist only where there is a third party or audience . . . what German theorists call an *Addressat*, before whom representation can take place. . . . The representative of a business, for instance, has to represent his firm before another firm, which constitutes the third factor: if that were not the case there would be no need for his services. Or consider the diplomat, who represents his country before a foreign government."[25]

Though it captures some of Hegel's symbolism, the paragraph above is too broad to be directly applied to Hegel's argument. The monarch is more than just a diplomat. The main reason the conduct of foreign affairs falls to the monarch is for internal rather than external considerations, because the complexity of international relations must not be allowed to shatter the internal unity of the state. Every state must speak with only one voice to other states, not primarily to avoid chaos in international affairs but to cement unity at home. "The state's tendency to look abroad lies in the fact that it is an individual subject. Its relation to other states therefore falls to the power of the crown. Hence it directly devolves on the monarch, and on him alone, to command the armed forces, to conduct foreign affairs through ambassadors etc., to make war and peace, and to conclude treaties of all kinds."[26]

The causal priority of domestic over foreign political considerations throughout Hegel's analysis of international relations follows from his concept of the sovereignty of the modern state. This does not mean, however, that there is no feedback mechanism by which the conduct of foreign affairs and the recognition of the sovereignty of the state by other states can enter into the consciousness of the citizens. Rather, it is precisely here that the monarchy as the transition from internal to external sovereignty has a key role to play. In a sense, the monarch is the only world-historical individual in the modern era, because there are no further new fundamental principles to be announced by any world-changing figures in the modern age. In the paragraph in which he introduces the concept of "world-historical actions" in the *Philosophy of Right*, Hegel explicitly refers the reader back to his deduction of the monarchical principle. "All actions, including world-historical actions, culminate with individuals as subjects giving actuality to the substantial (see Remark to Paragraph 279)."[27]

The focus on the "I will" of the monarchy in Hegel's account of the internal sovereignty of the state, coupled with the determining role of the monarchy in relations with other states as the state enters the domain of world history, are intended to orient the citizens toward understanding the ultimate significance of their actions in historical terms. It is Hegel's only, and in the final analysis insufficient, attempt to directly inculcate a historical consciousness within the state.

Ultimately, the institution of the monarchy within Hegel's system may be understood to be an attempt to fuse the idea of Plato's philosopher-ruler with the idea of the pedagogic state of German idealism. The philosophical insight and pedagogic goals attributed by Plato to the person of the philosopher are transferred by Hegel to the institutions of the state as a whole, with the result that the monarch remains as only a symbolic figurehead of this philosophical rationality. Insofar as the monarch reflects back to the individuals of the state their own fully developed nature as historical/political agents, Hegel's monarch stands midway between Machiavelli's *Prince* and Antonio Gramsci's *Modern Prince*.[28]

This attempt fails, however, at least as far as the consciousness of the citizens is concerned, because, as stated earlier, the symbolism of the monarchy remains too esoteric, too much in need of technical philosophical decoding, to have the required impact on the citizens. In its most

general terms, the intent of Hegel's construction here has been summarized by one commentator as follows: "Knowledge of the destiny of
man, of the meaning of history, and insight into logicality immanent
in life are, however, not merely essential prerequisites for reasonable
political action; as assimilated in the general consciousness of a nation
and appropriately put to use, this knowledge and insight also mediately
ensure the ethical strength of a nation as a whole."[29]

War

There is another way in which the mechanisms of the historical process impinge on the lives of the citizens, in far more dramatic fashion
than through the exemplar of the decision-making capacities of the
monarch. The analysis of patriotism as Hegel sees it, presented earlier,
should serve to remove the tinge of much of the misinterpretation of
Hegel's analysis of the role of war in history. It is neither a paean to
the military virtues nor an advocacy of war as an ethical policy for a
nation. It is rather an attempt to systematically identify the role war
has and will continue to play in world history, given the impossibility
of a Kantian perpetual peace.

In terms of the problematic of this study, the most relevant aspect of
Hegel's analysis of war is the way in which he holds that war confirms
the infinite authority of the state by demonstrating the finitude of the
finite.[30] In concrete terms, war shows the transience of property rights,
and even the right to life itself of each individual, in contrast to the
enduring substance of the state that lasts through the devastation of
war. The obligation of individuals to risk their lives to defend the state
in times of crisis, an obligation conceded even by contractarian theories
in which the preservation and security of life and property is supposed
to be the basis of the political bond, demonstrates the insufficiency of
theories that attempt to account for the origins and purpose of the state
solely in these terms. War is the living refutation by *via negationis* of
contractarian or economistic theories of the state.[31]

The End of History

Finally, the *Philosophy of Right* ends with a recapitulation of the
course of world history, the ultimate arena in which the nature of the
state is revealed. The inclusion of world history in the *Philosophy of
Right* brings us full circle. Political philosophy ends with history, just as

this study has attempted to show that it begins with history. For this Hegelian circle to close, history itself must have in some sense ended; otherwise the historicity of politics could not yet be known, because philosophy only brings to conceptual cognition that which has already developed in the world. It remains to determine the meaning that can be given to the proposition that history has in some sense come to an end.

One approach taken by some on this score is to attempt to in effect deny that Hegel is committed to an "end-of-history" thesis and to argue that the owl of Minerva, which takes wing at dusk in the *Philosophy of Right*, only announces the end of a particular historical epoch, albeit this epoch is a watershed of note. This characterizes the standard left-wing Hegelian position that developed after Hegel's death. This camp argued that the attempt by Hegel in the *Philosophy of Right* to absolutize his own era betrayed the dialectical dynamics that are more fundamental to his system. More recently, in the last chapter of *Hegel's Theory of the Modern State*, Shlomo Avineri collects the passages in which Hegel makes reference to possible future developments in America, Russia, and so on, to argue that the Hegelian system is not as closed as one would think, that philosophy painting grey in grey implies that a new canvas is soon to be at hand. But in the final analysis, Avineri admits that these asides fly in the face of too many statements Hegel makes to the effect that history has reached its final end in the modern era. These statements are much more consistent with Hegel's system than his scattered remarks about the future.[32]

If Hegel's philosophy does then seem to require a commitment to some form of the end-of-history thesis, a minimalist reading of this claim seems most plausible. Such a reading draws on the contrast between history and nature, referred to several times earlier in the course of this study. History, hitherto conceived of as a force opposed to human agency, a kind of fate that happens to or acts on people, is now seen to be fully a product of human agency. In this view, to announce the end-of-history is another way of announcing the advent of fully self-conscious human action. This is the appropriation of the end-of-history concept made by Sartre and by Marcuse when he says that the Marxian analogue to the Hegelian contrast between all previous history and the end of history (the beginning of this end being heralded by the French Revolution) is the break Marx envisaged between the prehistory and the coming history of humanity signaled by the communist revolution. Here the contrast is between human beings acting under (relatively) blind necessity as opposed to human beings freely and consciously creating their own collective destiny.

One can discern a progression of this kind—a progression referred to by Hegel as the progress of spirit as it wins its freedom from nature—in the history of political philosophy. Rousseau is the first major figure in this history to offer anything approaching a modern philosophy of history. For Rousseau, this history is propelled by a teleology, based on natural need, implicit in the original state of nature itself. For Kant, history straddles the boundary between the realm of natural necessity and that of self-legislated freedom. History is the story of what "nature has willed,"[33] yet at the same time we are justified in seeking in it evidence of humanity's own self-willed moral perfectibility. It is in Hegel's work that for the first time human history is systematically severed from natural history. Now, it can be said without controversy that Hegel's end-of-history thesis entails at least this much. But this much can already be gleaned from the *Phenomenology*. The question remains whether there is any further specifically political meaning to the end-of-history thesis in the *Philosophy of Right*.

This further political meaning of the end of history has already been alluded to earlier, but it bears repeating here. Hegel's theory commits him to the position that the basic principles of the modern era—the principles of the universal nature of political right in the modern world, of the fully developed rationality of the state, and of the subjective, self-conscious nature of political action in the modern world—cannot be replaced or superseded by any future developments without negating his entire conceptual edifice. This does not mean that nothing of significance will happen after Hegel's own period, but it does mean that whatever is to happen in the political world will be a development of these basic principles and that no fundamentally new principles will be put into practice on any meaningful scale. On this level of generality, the claim is plausible and is in fact not far from the common understanding of the basic framework of political discourse in the world today (for example, the universal acceptance of "democracy" as *the* political paradigm, adduced above). The plausibility of this view depends on applying the distinction between the deep structure of Hegelian political philosophy, that is, interpreting the *Philosophy of Right* as a systematic presentation of the basic categories of modern political theory and practice, and the surface structure of Hegel's theory, that is, interpreting the *Philosophy of Right* as a tract that recommends certain political institutions on various grounds. The interpretation of the end-of-history thesis suggested here requires that one insist that it is *only* the basic categories of political theory that Hegel absolutized as valid for all future political philosophy and not his specific institutional recommendations. Although this interpretation admittedly departs from the letter of Hegel's presentation, once one accepts the proposition that Hegelian philosophy does require some version of an end-of-history thesis, it seems preferable to the alternative. Without some such distinction between the basic categories of Hegelian political philosophy and their institutional actualization, one would have to commit Hegel to such absurdities as the proposition that aristocratic primogeniture is absolutely essential to any state for all time to come.

Deep and Surface Structures in the *Philosophy of Right*

Hegel can and should be faulted for not consistently adhering to the distinction between basic principles and their institutional realization, for often presenting his specific institutional recommendations as necessarily being the only possible institutional arrangements deducible from his basic principles rather than as being more or less fitting instantiations of them. The attempt to combine one's philosophical principles and their real-world applications in a single book results in a work as complex and as much an interpreter's nightmare as if Plato had written the *Republic* and the *Laws* as a single book or as if Rousseau had done the same with the *Social Contract* and the *Government of Poland*.[34]

Perhaps the distinction between the programmatic and the pragmatic dimensions of Hegel's political philosophy is suggested in the full title of the work itself. In the original German, the title is *Grundlinien der Philosophie des Rechts oder Naturrecht und Staatswissenschaft im Grundrisse* (*Outlines* of the Philosophy of Right or Natural Law and Political Science in *Outline* [emphasis added]). Because Hegel was not noted for his modesty as a philosopher (this could hardly be said of a thinker who claimed that his work represented "the exposition of God as he is in his eternal essence before the creation of nature and a finite mind"),[35] one may ask why what seems to be a complete enough work is designated as only an "outline." Of course, a simple answer to this question is given by Hegel in the opening sentence of the book—it was prepared for use as a textbook to be accompanied by his lectures at the University of Berlin.[36] But a comparison with the titles of the other works Hegel published in his lifetime suggests a deeper reason. Neither the *Science of Logic* nor the *Phenomenology of Spirit* are referred to in their titles as outlines of their subject matter, but the *Encyclopaedia* is. In other words, the introduction to the system, which recapitulates what has come before from a scientific standpoint, and that part of the system whose exposition is atemporal and nonhistorical are not qualified by being designated as "outlines," while those parts of the system whose content, at least in part, refers to the historical developments of the current epoch are.

This suggests that the reason for the "outline" qualifier is not any personal limitation of Hegel's as an individual trying to present the entire scope of a vast subject—for this kind of disclaimer is given by Hegel at the close of his Preface to the *Phenomenology*, whose title is not qualified in this sense—but rather that it represents a limitation of Hegel's political period itself.[27] Standing near the beginning of the first fully rational, self-conscious political period in history, it is only the basic principles, the outlines, of the universal rational state that are visible. The details of that outline have yet to be developed historically. Hegel's political philosophy, then, fills in this outline as well and fully as possible, given the material historically at hand. This is not a departure from Hegel's philosophical methodology, because his political rationalism is committed to the proposition that there is material at hand in the present historical epoch to rationally fill out this basic framework—that there is a rose in the cross of the present. At the same time, although the basic outline must hold good for all time, there is nothing to preclude the possibility that future developments will provide better institutional instantiations for these basic conceptions than those recommended in the *Philosophy of Right*.

The above interpretation of the way in which the essentials of the course of history can be said to ground the *Philosophy of Right* seems to accord best with everything else that has been said in this study about the historical basis of Hegel's political philosophy. It justifies neither too much nor too little of the principles of the Hegelian state and turns the *Philosophy of Right* neither into a deification of the Prussian state nor into an a priori deduction of the form of an eternal utopia.

The integration of a historical dimension into political philosophy in a deep, systematic way is Hegel's most lasting contribution to the history of political philosophy. After Hegel, political philosophy remained much more self-conscious about its own historical origins than previously. However, political philosophy did not develop along Hegelian lines. As this study has attempted to demonstrate, the frameworks subsequently developed by Marxism and liberalism have eclipsed the Hegelian framework to such an extent that they have clouded the interpretation of Hegel's own thought. Perhaps the best way to end this study would be to attempt a brief internal critique of Hegel's political philosophy as a whole.

This study has argued that the key criterion in any such internal evaluation of Hegel's political philosophy would have to be the self-consciousness of the citizens of the Hegelian state, the degree to which they could be expected to have met the standards for an explicit political identity that Hegel sets. As he says: "Since the state is not a mechanism but the rational life of self-conscious freedom, the system of the ethical world, it follows that an essential moment in the actual state is the mental attitude of the citizens, and so their consciousness of the *principles* which this attitude implies."[38]

We have seen during the course of this study why criticisms to the effect that the economic problems of civil society are not truly solved or that the Hegelian state does not rest on the unequivocal defense of individual natural rights miss the central point of Hegelian political theory, though these criticisms are valid in their own terms and important. From a Hegelian perspective, the success of the Hegelian state must stand or fall with the citizens' awareness of the principles that define that state.

In the final analysis, it must be said that Hegel's political philosophy is more effective as a critical perspective on other views than as a positive construct of its own principles. Hegel makes important and sound criticisms of the economistic and individualistic perspectives he criticizes. The mechanisms of transition from these perspectives in civil society to the level of the state could be expected to function reasonably well. That is to say, one could expect that through the political education they would receive through their participation in the institutions of civil society the citizens of the Hegelian state would to some extent realize the drawbacks Hegel identifies in an individualist, materialist sense of self. And they could even be expected to have a vague sense of searching for an ethical community that would foster an enlarged ocnse of self. But the criticism made earlier of the role Hegel expected the institution of the monarchy to fulfill could be extended to apply to the project of the Hegelian state as a whole. The symbolism of the articulated structure of the Hegelian state is simply too much in need of philosophical interpretation to expect that it would penetrate the consciousness of ordinary citizens to the extent that Hegel's theory demands it must.

Of course, Hegel has institutional substitutes for this lack of philosophical consciousness, such as religion and organized public opinion. These factors and the role that this study has argued they play in the

Hegelian state refute at least one version of the judgment just made: the idea that each and every citizen of the Hegelian state must have a philosopher's understanding of the principles of the state. As I have argued, Hegel does not need to show this. It is enough if he can simply show that the philosophical principles of the state are manifest in the institutional functioning of the state. Perhaps simply showing that the higher officials in the political institutions of the Hegelian state have a general understanding of the political principles involved would be enough to meet the Hegelian criteria for a properly functioning, ethical state. Though it is indeed possible that they might develop such an understanding, there is simply not enough in the Hegelian state to ensure they they will. And as Hegel himself says, a political theory must not merely make it possible that what should happen will happen, it must bring it about that what should happen will happen. Thus, although the Hegelian project remains important and the Hegelian perspective on other political philosophies remains valuable, Hegel himself failed to adequately realize his project.

As I suggested earlier, the mismatch between the general principles of Hegel's *Philosophy of Right* and the particular instantiations of those principles may well be, even on Hegel's own terms, a function of the period in which he lived—a period at the beginning of a new era in political philosophy. If this is so, then the historical dimensions of Hegel's theory remain the key to understanding Hegel, even to the point of understanding the reasons for his shortcomings.

Notes

1. Lewis Hinchman identifies this as Hegel's "Hamiltonianism." Lewis P. Hinchman, *Hegel's Critique of the Enlightenment* (Tampa: University of South Florida Press, 1984), pp. 258–263.

2. *PR*, §205, p. 132 and §295–297, pp. 192–193.

3. *Ibid.*, §291, p. 190.

4. *Ibid.*, §290, p. 190.

5. *Ibid.*, §288, p. 189.

6. Georg Ahrweiler, *Hegels Gesellschaftslehre* (Darmstadt und Neuwied: Luchterhand, 1976), p. 147 [My translation].

7. George H. Sabine, *A History of Political Theory*, 3d ed. (New York: Holt, Rinehart and Winston, 1961), pp. 662–663.

8. *PR*, §279A, p. 288.

9. *Ibid.*, §278A, p. 180.

10. *Ibid.*, §272A, p. 286.

11. *Ibid.*, §273, p. 176.

12. Ludwig Siep calls this a "theory of the personalized state will." "Person and Law in Kant and Hegel," in *The Public Realm: Essays on Discursive Types in Political Philosophy,* ed. Reiner Schurmann (Albany: State University of New York Press, 1989), p. 101. Many see Hegel's monarch as the embodiment of the totalitarian state. See F. R. Cristi, "The *Hegelsche Mitte* and Hegel's Monarch," *Political Theory* 11:4, November 1983, pp. 601–622.

13. *PR.*, §279A, p. 184.

14. *Ibid.*, §273A, p. 176.

15. *Ibid.*, §280–281, pp. 184–186.

16. Hannah Fenichel Pitkin, *The Concept of Representation* (Berkeley: University of California Press, 1972), p. 93. Cf. Charles Taylor, *Hegel* (Cambridge: Cambridge University Press, 1978), pp. 389–399. A similar concept can be found in Hobbes. See Thomas Hobbes, "De Cive," in *Man and Citizen,* ed. Bernard Gert (New York: Anchor-Doubleday, 1972), chap. 6, sec. 19, p. 188: "By him who hath the supreme power, and no otherwise, the city hath a will, that is, can either will or nill"; and chap. 12, sec. 8, p. 250: "The people is somewhat that is one, having one will, and to whom one action may be attributed: none of these can properly be said of a multitude. . . . And in a monarchy, the subjects are the multitude, and (however it seem a paradox) the king is the people." Peter Steinberger, in *Logic and Politics: Hegel's Philosophy of Right* (New Haven: Yale University Press, 1988), p. 230, interprets this as a thesis about the actuality of state political action, not merely its representation: "Louis XIV's claim that 'L'état c'est moi' is, I believe, adopted by Hegel as an analytically true principle of political society."

17. *PR*, §279A, p. 182.

18. *Ibid.*, §280A, p. 289.

19. *Ibid.*, §282, pp. 186–187.

20. *Ibid.*, §331, p. 212.

21. *Ibid.*, §333, p. 213.

22. *Ibid.*, §330A, p. 297.

23. *Ibid.*, §274A, p. 179 and pp. 286–287; §332, p. 213.

24. *Ibid.*, §331A, p. 212.

25. Pitkin, *The Concept of Representation,* pp. 105–106.

26. *PR*, §329, p. 212.

27. *Ibid.*, §348, p. 218.

28. Antonio Gramsci, *The Modern Prince and Other Writings,* trans. Louis Marks (New York: International Publishers, 1975); Niccolo Machiavelli, *The Prince,* trans. and ed. Robert M. Adams (New York: W.W. Norton, 1977).

29. Wilhelm Seeberger, "The Political Significance of Hegel's Concept of History," trans. K. R. Dove and C. R. Dove, *The Monist,* 48:1, January 1964, p. 94.

30. Cf. *Logic*, p. 443: "The non-being of the finite is the being of the absolute."
See Michael Allen Gillespie. "Death and Desire: War and Bourgeoisification in
the Thought of Hegel," in *Understanding the Political Spirit: Investigations from
Socrates to Nietzsche*, ed. Catherine H. Zuckert (New Haven: Yale University
Press, 1988), pp. 153–179.

31. For a full account of Hegel on war, see Shlomo Avineri, *Hegel's Theory of the
Modern State* (Cambridge: Cambridge University Press, 1974), chap. 10; and
"The Problem of War in Hegel's Thought" in *Perspectives on Political Philoso-
phy*, vol. 2, *Machiavelli through Marx*, ed. David K. Hart and James V. Downton,
Jr. (New York: Holt, Rinehart and Winston, 1971).

32. Avineri, *Hegel's Theory*, pp. 234–238.

33. Kant, "Idea for a Universal History with a Cosmopolitan Purpose," in *Political
Writings*, ed. Hans Reiss (Cambridge: Cambridge University Press, 1977), p. 43.

34. For this analogy, I am indebted to Peter Steinberger for his remarks in *Logic and
Politics*, pp. 242–243.

35. *Logic*, p. 50. In a private conversation, Herbert Marcuse once referred to this as
the greatest case of chutzpah in the history of philosophy.

36. *PR*, p. 1.

37. *Phen.*, p. 130.

38. *PR*, §270A, p. 170.

8

Contemporary Applications
of Hegel's Philosophy of Politics

Up to this point, this study has been concerned with interpreting Hegel's philosophy as he articulated it. In this final chapter, I shall approach Hegel in a more speculative fashion. I shall briefly consider the appropriation and impact, both actual and potential, of Hegelianism in certain key areas of contemporary political theory. My remarks here are intended merely to suggest the beginnings of certain lines of thought—they need to be developed much more fully. I shall consider three areas to which Hegel has particular relevance: (1) society and civil society, (2) law, and (3) feminism. All three areas speak, in different ways, to a widely shared perception that we now stand at a historical turning point in regard to the liberalism that has dominated Western political discourse for so long.

Society and Civil Society

The core of Hegel's relevance to contemporary political debates is his concept of civil society. Hegel's use of this concept to overcome the dichotomy between statism and individualism is of particular importance. When various reform movements had not yet brought forth the tangible results they have now achieved, one commentator wrote: "The most fundamental idea shared by popular movements East and West is the principle of 'civil society.' "[1]

The sphere of "civil society" has been central to the "new social movements" of recent years.[2] To understand recent events in Eastern Europe, one must understand that there the state is challenged *not* in the name of the individuals and their individual rights of Western liberalism but rather by and in the name of "society." The difference

is not just rhetorical. "Society" here means the sphere identified by
Hegel as "civil society," the local and specific associations into which
people organized themselves and through which they claim their political identities: unions, churches, neighborhoods, regional associations,
workers councils, political parties, and so on. The reform effort is to
create a sphere, a mode of action, that is public and political and yet
not identified with the state. This re- formation gives form to public
political opinion, in the Hegelian sense of "public opinion" articulated
earlier, that is, a "public opinion" not just as a collection of singular,
individual voices but as a collective of individuals who share a kind of
identity, a sort of "solidarity."

The banner of Solidarity in Poland is one flag under which these new
social forces have rallied. The image of the forum has been adapted by
some Eastern European states, such as East Germany and Czechoslo-
vakia, giving rise to a New Forum and Civic Forum, as the new political forces named themselves. These movements captured the Hegelian
sense in which, in contrast to liberalism, rights of speech and association
are understood not as *civil* rights, that is, rights of a natural freedom
from the state, but rather as *political* rights, that is, social rights of
participation *in* the political sphere. Even in the Soviet Union, "glasnost" means more than simply "openness" in the sense of a new honesty
and disclosure on the part of the state. It also carries with it the connotations of the German *Öffentlichkeit*, literally "openness," but also
used in modern political theory to designate the "public sphere," an
autonomous arena of public discourse not immediately identifiable or
integrated with the state. Pierre Rosanvallon invokes the concept of
"civil society" and its attendant public social sphere to argue that the
heart of any democratic regime is the translucency of the exercise of
power under that regime. In contrast to the inaccessible and therefore
unaccountable exercise of power in totalitarian regimes, here glasnost,
publicity, openness become, in Rosanvallon's phrase, "social visibility."[3]

The idea of establishing as a measure of the degree to which a society
is truly democratic the degree to which the exercise of authority in that
society is visible or translucent seems promising. G. A. Cohen refers to
a similar idea as "the yearning for transparent human relations."[4]

Such a measure seems particularly useful as a critical analytical tool
that would render the nature and degree of capitalist coercion more
visible. In contrast to the more public, naked display of power typical of authoritarian or Stalinist-style regimes, capitalist liberal regimes
tend to exercise power behind and through the more hidden hand of
economic power. The ideal of a civil society structured so as to make

visible its own lines of authority is an illuminating regulatory ideal. It derives from the Hegelian doctrine of political idealism this study has emphasized, that is, Hegel's conception of politics being aimed at developing the citizens' self-consciousness as political agents. As we have seen in Hegel's critique of the political economy of his day, civil society is unfree because it does not comprehend its own mechanisms. This is why basing politics on capitalist economics cannot lead to freedom, because action remains under the dictatorship of the hidden hand.

Thus the political freedoms people are struggling for today in Eastern Europe do not necessarily carry with them the economistic, laissez-faire assumptions and overtones their articulation in Western liberalism carries. They are much more compatible with a social democratic welfare state. Hegel's theory here provides exceptionally appropriate analytical tools through which to conceptualize this new civic "open society."

I have just argued that Hegelian political theory is most useful for comprehending recent political developments by using his concept of civil society to show the commonalities between European reform movements in the East and West. This stands in sharp contrast to another recent attempt to use Hegel as interlocutor in East-West dialogue: Francis Fukuyama's essay "The End of History?" that attempts to deploy Hegel to demonstrate the superiority of West over East.[5] Given the notoriety it achieved, a brief critical look at this article's central thesis seems appropriate.

Fukuyama invokes Hegel to provide a philosophical foundation for the deepest meaning of the ostensible definitive, irreversible triumph of liberalism he sees in the world. To do this, he must trace these liberal ideals back to the French Revolution, as any interpretation of Hegel that wishes to invoke his political philosophy in historical context must do, for reasons explained in this study. But Fukuyama reveals the fundamental inadequacy of his essay every time he refers to these triumphant liberal ideals purportedly announced by the French Revolution. He always refers to them in the same way: "the ideas of liberty and equality."[6] Glaringly absent is the third of the revolution's triumvirate: fraternity. I shall argue that Fukuyama needs to omit this to make his case. Noticing the omission undermines his argument. Indeed, it refutes it.

Let us recall what was said earlier about Hegel's views of the modern age. I argued that what Hegel meant by the ascendancy of the political principles of modernity was a claim about the legitimating paradigm of all regimes in the modern world. Hegel attempts to establish that they must base their legitimacy on the claim that they embody the rational wills of their citizens. All modern regimes, whether liberal, communist, populist, and so on, must claim to in some sense represent the "will of the people," to be in some sense "democratic."[7]

To the revolutionaries, "fraternity" stood for an ideal of community. The omission of the "fraternity" ideal is an attempt to mask what has emerged in contemporary political theory as the primary defect of liberalism: its lack of community.[8] As we have seen, liberalism's atomistic individualism is a primary target of Hegelian political theory. Fukuyama's reading of the revolution is so truncated as to amount to a falsification of the historical record. Only on the basis of his markedly truncated reading of the revolution can Fukuyama claim that liberalism is the true and sole heir of the modern political era inaugurated by the revolution. He obliterates Hegel's critique of liberalism.[9] Remembering fraternity as part of this modern ideal makes it clear that not only is liberalism not the sole inheritor of the ideals of 1789, it is at best only a partial heir, heir to only two-thirds of that heritage. Marxism, which Fukuyama attempts to portray as alien to that tradition, embodies it as well. Marxism and liberalism are sibling rivals for the mantle of that tradition.

In sharp contrast to Fukuyama, who wants to establish Marxism as alien and "other" to liberalism, Hegel's theory demonstrates the sibling nature of the rivalry between Marxism and liberalism. My objection to Fukuyama can be put simply. He attempts to use Hegel's end-of- history thesis to prove that one side has won the contest, when what Hegel means by it is the claim, at once both simpler and deeper, that we are all now engaged in contestation over realizing the same basic ideals.[10] Fukuyama's use of the only-game-in-town metaphor is a misuse and abuse of it. The point is not that "our" game is better than "theirs" but that we're all playing the same one.

I shall use one final metaphor to illustrate the inadequacy of Fukuyama's formulation on this score before raising another issue. In a nice twist of the *Geist*, Fukuyama's essay appeared in the year of the revolution's bicentennial. That summer saw a celebration of the revolution, presided over by a socialist president of France, culminating in a spectacular parade down the Champs Elysee in Paris. Nations from all over the world were represented in that parade, including a wide range of regimes. They all claimed the heritage of the revolution. Hegel's point was that all of their claims were legitimate, at least at the level of generality at which the end-of-history thesis obtains. It is sometimes said that World War II settled the dispute between left- and right-wing Hegelianism in favor of the left.[11] In the same way, that parade may be said to have settled the question of Fukuyama's appropriation of Hegel—against Fukuyama.

Civil society is the arena of mediation between public and private, the stage "between," the sphere of "difference." Hegel identifies the achievement of the autonomy of this "society" as the distinctive achievement of modernity. This autonomy of "society," first brought to full conceptualization by Hegel, is the precondition for modern social theory. For modern social theory is distinctively "sociological," and it is the hallmark of modern sociological theory that it conceptualizes society as an ontologically separate and identifiable object of investigation.

The legitimacy of sociology as an autonomous discipline depends on the claim that it is reducible or assimilable neither to psychology on the one hand nor to political science on the other. Its object of investigation is neither the psychological states of individuals nor the formal structures of the state. One of the core problematics of sociological theory, the "structure/agency" question, is generated precisely because sociology is in this way situated *between* structure and agency. Its subject for analysis stands between the willed intentions of individuals and the given structures of the state.[12] Hence the attribution of agency to a particular subject is rendered problematic.[13] Hegel's thesis about modernity is particularly relevant to the foundations of sociology because sociology understands itself as having a particular historical point of departure. It distinguishes itself from anthropology through its understanding of the "society" it investigates as distinctively "modern," that is, post–French and post–Industrial Revolution.[14]

Hegel's decisive step is his expansion of civil society beyond the "System of Needs" to include the "external state" or the "state as the Understanding conceives it," that is, the "Administration of Justice" and the "Police."[15] This renders classical political economy inadequate to conceptualize these political dimensions of civil society that transcend the economistic, individualist standpoint of the market. Hence there is a new need for a new modern kind of *society*. This must be a systematic body of thought based on the logic of categories based on a public sphere situated between the market and the state, that is, a socio-logy. This is the ground of modern sociology.

This sphere of the "social" is the ground of modern social theory in general, even outside the discipline of sociology as narrowly defined, extending to social theory in philosophy, political science, and so on. The most contentious issues in Western political life today are precisely the "social" issues—those issues whose solutions lie in a fundamental reconceptualization of the dichotomy of the individual and the state inherited from classical political theory.

Within academia, the "social" sphere is the province of the relatively recent field of "social philosophy." In the lead article of a special issue of the *Journal of Social Philosophy* devoted to "The Agenda for Social Philosophy in the Nineties," Robert Paul Wolff identifies as "the most intractable and the philosophically most interesting" of what he specifies as the three "major tasks facing social theory in the coming decade" (the other two being the rapprochement of Marx and Freud in a theory of personality and the updating of Marx's economics for a theory of capitalism) "the working out of the ontological status of society, as an object of investigation. . . . Even as late as the end of the eighteenth century, society does not figure as an independent category of being—a kind of thing *sui generis*, not to be reduced to, or explained in terms of, either nature or the individual."[16]

As we have seen, Hegel's theory offers an important perspective on "the ontological status of society." When Herbert Marcuse published *Reason and Revolution* in 1941, his landmark work on Hegel, he gave it the subtitle *Hegel and the Rise of Social Theory.* He meant by "the rise of social theory" primarily what the Marxist tradition has always taken the famous Eleventh Thesis on Feuerbach to mean: that philosophy as abstract, contemplative theory (the Greek *theoria*) came to an end after Hegel, and that henceforth philosophy must be practiced as (critical) social, political theory. But to associate Hegel with the rise of social theory has another meaning as well. It signifies the rise of "society" as an object to be independently theorized. In this fundamental and groundbreaking sense Hegel is the first social theorist of modernity.

Law

In an address to the conference on "Hegel and Legal Theory," held at the Cardozo School of Law on March 27–29, 1988, Cornel West argued that

The increasing interest in Hegel among legal scholars can be attributed to three recent developments. First, there is a slow but sure historicist turn in legal studies. . . . Second, there are a growing number of serious reexaminations of the basic assumptions and fundamental presuppositions of dominant forms of liberalism. . . . Third, a new emerging subject matter has seized the imagination of some legal theorists: the complex *cultures* of liberal society. . . . In this context, Hegel emerges as an enabling figure principally owing to his profound historicist sense, his penetrating critique of liberalism, and his illuminating insights about the kinds of *Sittlichkeit* requisite for a stable and harmonious modern society.[17]

Probably the issue of most pressing practical concern in the triad mentioned by West is the concept of *Sittlichkeit* and the critique of liberal individualism that accompanies it. The discourse of individual rights is the foundation of American law, yet it has recently come under fire by a line of criticism very similar to Hegel's for, among other things, subverting the ideal of community. But Hegel figures here not just as ammunition for the critique. Increasingly, some are turning to Hegel as a model for the construction of a new communitarian or dialogic model for the legal system.[18]

Rather than pursue the lines of inquiry noted above, about which much has already been written,[19] I would like to pursue another Hegelian line of influence on contemporary legal discourse that derives from the interpretation of Hegel's political idealism presented by this study. In the discussion of the sovereignty of the state, we saw how Hegel's doctrine of political sovereignty required that political authority be self-grounded rather than being derived from the spheres of morality, religion, or any other source. This self-grounding of political authority is the source of both the role Hegel assigns to the monarchy in his system, for it is symbolized by the monarch's "I will," and his ascription of a kind of divinity to the state, for Hegel follows the Western philosophical tradition in seeing independent self- creation in such theological terms.[20]

Of particular relevance here is how idealist theories of law have continued to embody such a conception. Perhaps the best example of this is to be found in Ronald Dworkin's *Law's Empire*, in which he speaks of the "integrity" of the law as the foundation of its "empire."[21] For Dworkin, jurisprudential decisions are made by recourse neither to moral principles above the law nor to the sort of sociological considerations about the consequences of decisions appropriate to the formation of public policy but by reference to the internal logic of the law itself. This explains the distinctive nature of legal reasoning and the penultimate role of precedent within it. The key is to see the law's idea of its own autonomy and unity as its motive force.[22] According to idealist theories of law like Hegel's and Dworkins's, legal right and authority and decision making are self-grounding. Thus, in his idealist concept

of sovereignty, Hegel can be seen to have articulated the law's understanding of itself as an autonomous system of logic. Of course, this view
is challenged by more materialist theories of law, which see this idealist view of law as at best reflecting the law's official self-understanding
rather than being the real truth of the substance and operation of law.
But an understanding of the sources and philosophical impulses behind
Hegel's notion of sovereignty can provide an important contribution to
contemporary legal discourse.[23]

Feminism

The theme of Hegelian feminism or feminist Hegelianism will strike
many as being farfetched, to say the least. Some will no doubt regard
it as an oxymoronic conjunction of contradictory terms. Among the
major philosophers of the nineteenth century, probably only Nietzsche
and Schopenhauer have a more antifeminist reputation.

Hegelian metaphysics, to take just one facet of this issue as an example, is generally taken as the highest expression of the hierarchical
dichotomies between mind and matter, activity and passivity, and reason and emotion basic to the mainstream of Western ideology that have
so thoroughly redounded to the detriment of women. The oft-quoted
statement "The difference between men and women is like that between
animals and plants" has not endeared Hegel to anyone with feminist
or even mildly profeminist sympathies and places him squarely, if not
paradigmatically, in the high court of Western patriarchy.[24] The title
of a 1970 essay by Italian feminist Carla Lonzi expresses a widespread
feminist response to Hegel quite nicely: "Let's spit on Hegel."[25] One
should note that this is not only a gesture of feminist disdain for
the mainstream of Western philosophy, which some feminists call the
"malestream," but also a Mediterranean gesture of defiance against
Northern European cultural hegemony.

Still, Nietzsche's chauvinism, for example, has not prevented him
from emerging as a major figure in at least one strain of contemporary
feminism—postmodernist feminist discourse. It may on occasion be
possible to disengage a philosopher's patriarchal pronouncements on
"the woman question" and that theorist's other explicit statements on
questions of gender and gender equity from other theoretical strains
in the philosopher's thought that may be more hospitable to feminist
appropriations.

I would like here to briefly interrogate Hegel's political philosophy
from two distinct, but related, points of view. The first is what I

call "feminist Hegelianism." There are many different schools of Hegel interpretation. Each, whether Marxist, theological, Existentialist, and so on, selectively highlights certain themes, texts, and problems in the Hegelian corpus, according to its particular interests and predilections. Though not yet articulated as such among the community of scholars on Hegel, I believe there is now a sufficient body of writing on Hegel from feminist perspectives that one may begin to speak of a feminist reading of Hegel, with its own distinctive key texts, problematics, and emphases. This is what I designate as "feminist Hegelianism." Second, there is what I call the question of "Hegelian feminism." Here, one may refer to the progression of feminist scholarship regarding other key figures in the history of Western patriarchal thought. Freud, for example, was by no means a feminist. Indeed, much early feminist thought developed expressly as a reaction against Freud, particularly in the United States. Yet, psychoanalytic feminism is today one of the most important streams of contemporary feminist thought. Similarly, although Hegel himself was certainly no feminist, one may still ask what sort of feminism would result from the sympathetic application of the Hegelian framework to feminist concerns. The result would be a "Hegelian feminism." This is not an attempt to transmute Hegel into a feminist in spite of himself, *malgre lui*, but an attempt to reach into what has been referred to throughout this study as the "deep" structure of Hegel's thought to penetrate past the surface sexism, if such it be.

We may begin by looking once again at the central concept of "civil society," but this time with the question of gender in the foreground. We had occasion to note earlier in passing that the individuals who emerge from the family into civil society are male. For Hegel, as for so many others, women's proper place is in the home, not in the sphere of the economy or political life. Despite everything said earlier about Hegel's rejection of a "naturalistic" interpretation of civil society, in this case he reverts to precisely such a view, as the "natural" difference between the sexes enters into the structure of civil society. Having made a decisive contribution to the conceptualization of the family in the history of political theory by conceptualizing the family as an ethical institution, Hegel's consignment of women back into the sphere of "nature" undermines his achievement. He reifies the split between public and private and between production and reproduction that his theory was on the way to overcoming.[26]

Hegel's lapse in this regard would reasonably be expected to produce an analogous lapse in the consciousness of the male individuals now within civil society. The family was supposed to have imbued them

with an "ethical" consciousness, a consciousness that habituates them
to thinking of themselves as part of a larger unit. Now it turns out
that this consciousness is gender-blind. What was earlier referred to
as the citizens' "socialization for citizenship" requires them to accept
the gendered nature of their socialization, to accept without significant
ethical qualm that the parenting they received was mothering and not
fathering and that their sisters are denied privileges and prerogatives
available to them. But it would seem that the principles of civil society would generate such qualms. The principle of civil society, that
here we are dealing with "man as such," that is, simple personhood,
with categories such as race, nationality, and religion explicitly declared
irrelevant, would seem to require gender equity.

Patricia Jagentowicz Mills argues that, for Hegel,

> woman is confined to the family, the sphere of first nature, while man moves
> into the realm of second nature or self-conscious political life. Since, according
> to Hegel, to be human is to have direct access to the sphere of second nature,
> and since woman does not have this direct access, one can only conclude that
> woman is not truly human in the Hegelian system. Hegel himself does not
> acknowledge this contradiction. . . .
>
> For Hegel, the family is a "preserve," a refuge or "haven in a heartless
> world," but he fails to point out that this refuge is maintained at the cost
> of women's self-conscious development: she never achieves self-consciousness,
> never becomes an "I." However, even though Hegel has an inadequate concept
> of the family, he does recognize it as an autonomous sphere of life, a domain
> which has its own specific and unique logic.[27]

I have argued that for Hegel's project to work successfully, the citizens of the Hegelian state must have some consciousness of the continuing progression of their education and socialization (*Bildung*). But
the denial of the salience of gender just discussed means that they have
now been rendered oblivious to an essential aspect of their *Bildung*.
Thus, in addition to reservations I voiced earlier, the Hegelian project
may be thrown into doubt at this point.

It will be useful to recall here another point at which Hegel's political
philosophy has been criticized. I argued earlier that Hegel's remarks on
war were not intended as a glorification of war, as some have argued,
but as a pointed reminder of the finitude of the finite, as a criticism
of contractarian theories that construct justifications of the state from
the standpoint of the considerations of property rights in the sphere of
civil society. According to Hegel's doctrine of the historical and ethical

significance of war, civil society must be shaken out of its illusions of permanence, so to speak. What is the connection between this Hegelian view of war and the neglect of the question of gender and gender equity in the family and civil society?

The connection is this: the forgetting of the actual gendered circumstances of life in the family required for males to be members in good standing and good faith of civil society is the precondition for the illusion of self-subsistence and autonomy these individuals have about themselves from which war must liberate them. Were consciousness of reproductive processes involving the bestowing of life fully integrated into civic consciousness, violence would not be required to loosen citizens' ties to their possessive individualism. Modern consciousness' "forgetting" of birth engenders the "reminder" of death. When viewed through the lens of feminist theory, Hegel's philosophy thus, despite itself, reveals a central tenet of radical feminist theory—the intrinsic connection between masculine self-identity, the repression of the importance of women's reproductive labor, and violence. One commentator raises this issue in connection with the psychoanalytic thesis about the male Oedipal need to reject the early identification with the mother in the family. "Hegel's theory of the state and war is a rational rendering of male psychic needs for differentiation as a mode of achieving identity, i.e., a reflection of the fact that masculinity means separation from the primary other."[28]

Clearly a primary concern in feminist Hegelianism is the question of Hegel's views on women's natures, roles, and rights.[29] But bringing feminist theory to bear on Hegel means more than simply looking at Hegel's writings on women. Using gender as an analytical category through which to interpret Hegel casts new light on the entire Hegelian corpus, revealing unexpected linkages between hitherto seemingly disparate elements of the Hegelian system—in the example just given, between Hegel on the family and Hegel on war.

We may recall that Marx's critique of Hegel's *Philosophy of Right* is able to move back and forth between the critique of the text and the critique of the actual society under investigation because Marx believed that in some fundamental sense Hegel correctly theorized fundamental aspects of that society, only in an unconscious, "inverted" fashion, in some cases *malgre lui*. Had Hegel simply been *wrong*, Marx's critique could not have had as simultaneous targets both Hegel's philosophy and the society he philosophized about. Feminist Hegelianism may in some ways adopt the same stance toward Hegel. It is worthwhile engaging with him because in some ways he theorized patriarchy correctly, *malgre lui*. Without in any way making Hegel into a prefigurative feminist before the fact, feminist Hegelianism may in some cases be able to explicate Hegel as, if by no means a theorist *of* patriarchy, then a theorist who illuminatingly *reveals* patriarchy.[30]

Interesting and illuminating use is already being made of Hegel by various feminist theorists. One should note that in one very significant sense Hegelianism is already present at the foundations of contemporary feminism. Simone de Beauvoir's *The Second Sex* is inconceivable without its Hegelian philosophical foundation.[31] The dialectics of lordship and bondage, desire and otherness remain essential for contemporary social thought. These themes are central, for example, to Jessica Benjamin's *The Bonds of Love: Psychoanalysis, Feminism, and the Problem of Domination*.[32] Judith Butler's *Subjects of Desire: Hegelian Reflections in Twentieth- Century France* traces the influence of this Hegelian theme on such figures as Jean-Paul Sartre, Jacques Lacan, Gilles Deleuze, and Michel Foucault.[33] In "Hegel and Feminism," Susan M. Easton writes: "In seeking to explain and transcend the subordination of women in advanced industrial societies, Hegel's *Phenomenology* is arguably the most significant text, offering a rich harvest of concepts for feminist theory. Its analysis of the dynamics of domination and subordination in the master-slave dialectic raises issues which lie at the heart of the feminist critique of patriarchy."[34]

The *Phenomenology* is of course a key text for many Hegel interpretations. Yet other texts are uniquely highlighted by feminist Hegelianism. Hegel's analyses of Sophocles' *Antigone*, for example, in the *Philosophy of Right*, *Philosophy of History*, *Phenomenology*, and *Aesthetics* are prominent in many if not most feminist readings of Hegel.[35] In the same vein, his writings on the family and his early writings on love are receiving renewed attention.[36] His distinctive theory of "society" discussed above is also relevant to feminist theory, for when the "social" emerged as a distinctive sphere in the nineteenth century, both it and the new field of "sociology" associated with it were strongly linked to the feminine and to women's reform movements.[37] And Hegel's philosophy of nature figures in writings dealing with themes related to ecofeminist concerns.[38]

As I have argued elsewhere, in my view a Hegelian-inspired feminism would incorporate the following themes:

the dialectic between individual consciousness and social structure, a thoroughly historical epistemology, a non-dualistic metaphysics, an understanding of gender, class, and other differences as being constituted through interaction rather than consisting of isolated "roles," the priority of political over moralistic or economistic theory, a probing of the relations between state power and cultural hegemony, a program for reaching unity through difference rather than through sameness, a tolerance of if not preference for ambiguity and contradiction, and an orientation toward process over end product.[39]

Hegel might also be invoked on particular issues, in addition to broader themes, approaches, and problematics. For example, the campaign for Wages for Housework has been controversial within feminist circles.[40] It is clear that a Hegelian-based feminism would be committed to and capable of carrying out a deep and thorough critique of this position. It would argue against it as precisely the reduction of all relations to those appropriate to civil society that Hegel's system warns against.

It has been my intention here merely to point to some present and future directions in Hegelian political theory. All of the above stands in need of further development. The current period seems to me a propitious time for such further development of Hegelianism.

Notes

1. Jefferson Morley, "On 'Civil Society,'" *The Nation*, May 7, 1988, p. 630.
2. See John Keane, ed., *Civil Society and the State: New European Perspectives* (London: Verso, 1988); and Michael Walzer, "The Idea of Civil Society," *Dissent*, Spring 1991, pp. 293–304.
3. Pierre Rosanvallon, "The Decline of Social Visibility," in Keane, *Civil Society*.
4. G. A. Cohen, "Karl Marx and the Withering Away of Social Science," in *Marx, Justice, and History*, ed. Marshall Cohen, Thomas Nagel, and Thomas Scanlon (Princeton: Princeton University Press, 1980), p. 309.
5. Francis Fukuyama, "The End of History?" *The National Interest* 16, Summer 1989, pp. 3–18. For a fuller critical analysis of Fukuyama's Hegelianism, see Philip T. Grier, "The End of History, and the Return of History," *Owl of Minerva* 21:2, Spring 1990, pp. 131–144.
6. *Ibid.*, p. 6.
7. See Chapter 6, in the section "Recognition and Legitimacy."
8. Michael J. Sandel's *Liberalism and the Limits of Justice* (Cambridge: Cambridge University Press, 1982) is paradigmatic.
9. See the excellent recent study by Steven B. Smith, *Hegel's Critique of Liberalism: Rights in Context* (Chicago: University of Chicago Press, 1989).

10. See Barry Cooper, *The End of History: An Essay on Modern Hegelianism* (Toronto: University of Toronto Press, 1984).

11. Ernst Cassirer, *The Myth of the State* (New Haven: Yale University Press, 1971), p. 249. Cited by Steven B. Smith, "Hegel's Idea of a Critical Theory," *Political Theory* 15:1, February 1987, p. 122. Cassirer attributes the comment to Hajo Holborn, "The Science of History," in *The Interpretation of History*, ed. Joseph R. Strayer (Princeton: Princeton University Press, 1943), p. 62.

12. See Anthony Giddens, *Profiles and Critiques in Social Theory* (Berkeley: University of California Press, 1982).

13. For an interpretation of Hegel's philosophy of action with reference to this question, see A. S. Walton, "Hegel: Individual Action and Social Context," in *Hegel's Philosophy of Action*, ed. Lawrence S. Stepelevich and David Lamb (Atlantic Highlands, N.J.: Humanities Press, 1983), pp. 75–92.

14. Anthony Giddens, *Sociology: A Brief but Critical Introduction* (New York: Harcourt Brace Jovanovich, 1982).

15. Cf. Andrew Arato, "A Reconstruction of Hegel's Theory of Civil Society," *Cardozo Law Review* 10:5–6, March/April 1989, pp. 1363–1388.

16. Robert Paul Wolff, "Social Philosophy: The Agenda for the Nineties," *Journal of Social Philosophy* 20:1–2, Spring/Fall 1989, p. 13.

17. Cornel West, "Hegel, Hermeneutics, Politics: A Reply to Charles Taylor," *Cardozo Law Review* 10:5–6, March/April 1989, pp. 871–875.

18. For Hegel's critique, see Smith, *Hegel's Critique*. For a model of an alternative invoking Hegel, see Drucilla Cornell, "Toward a Modern/Postmodern Reconstruction of Ethics," *University of Pennsylvania Law Review* 133:2, January 1985, pp. 291–380; and "Taking Hegel Seriously: Reflections on Beyond Objectivism and Relativism," *Cardozo Law Review*, 7, 1985, p. 139.

19. See *Cardozo Law Review* 10:5–6, March/April 1989, pts. 1 and 2, pp. 847–1931. (Special Issue on "Hegel and Legal Theory.")

20. For a different view of the nature and significance of the Hegelian thesis of the self-determined nature of political philosophy, see Richard Dien Winfield, *Reason and Justice* (Albany: State University of New York Press, 1988).

21. Ronald Dworkin, *Law's Empire* (Cambridge: Harvard University Press, 1986).

22. See Harry Brod, "Law Thinking Itself: The Idealism of International Law," review of *International Legal Structures*, by David Kennedy, *Cardozo Law Review* 10:5–6, March/April 1989, pp. 1879–1885.

23. For a classic view of Hegel's philosophy of law in the context of the philosophical tradition, see Huntington Cairns, *Legal Philosophy from Plato to Hegel* (Baltimore: The Johns Hopkins Press, 1949). For another, more modern, view of Hegel on law, see Michael H. Mitias, *Moral Foundation of the State in Hegel's "Philosophy of Right": Anatomy of an Argument* (Amsterdam: Editions Rodopi, 1984).

24. *PR*, 166A, p. 263.

25. Carla Lonzi, "Let's Spit on Hegel," in *Italian Feminist Thought: A Reader*, ed. Paola Bono and Sandra Kemp (New York: Basil Blackwell, 1991), pp. 40–59.

26. For a fundamental and groundbreaking articulation of the importance of this theme for feminist theory expressed within the idiom of the Hegelian-Marxist tradition, see Mary O'Brien, *The Politics of Reproduction* (Boston: Routledge & Kegan Paul, 1981).

27. Patricia Jagentowicz Mills, *Woman, Nature, and Psyche* (New Haven: Yale University Press, 1987), pp. xiii–xiv.

28. Jo-Ann Pilardi Fuchs, "On the War Path and Beyond: Hegel, Freud, and Feminist Theory," *Women's Studies International Forum* 6:6, 1983, p. 571.

29. In addition to other works cited in this section, see also Genevieve Lloyd, *The Man of Reason: "Male" and "Female" in Western Philosophy* (Minneapolis: University of Minnesota Press, 1984); Lawrence A. Blum, "Kant's and Hegel's Moral Rationalism: A Feminist Perspective," *Canadian Journal of Philosophy* 12:2, June 1982, pp. 287–302; and Joan Landes, "Hegel's Conception of the Family," *Polity* 14:1, 1981, pp. 5–28.

30. Gila J. Hayim, "Hegel's Critical Theory and Feminist Concerns," *Philosophy and Social Criticism* 16:1, 1990, p. 11. Carole Pateman treats Hegel in this vein in *The Sexual Contract* (London: Polity Press, 1988), pp. 173–183.

31. Simone de Beauvoir, *The Second Sex*, trans. and ed. H. M. Parshley (New York: Alfred A. Knopf, 1953).

32. Jessica Benjamin, *The Bonds of Love: Psychoanalysis, Feminism, and the Problem of Domination* (New York: Pantheon, 1988).

33. Judith P. Butler, *Subjects of Desire: Hegelian Reflections in Twentieth-Century France* (New York: Columbia University Press, 1987).

34. Susan M. Easton, "Hegel and Feminism," in *Hegel and Modern Philosophy*, ed. David Lamb (London: Croom Helm, 1987), p. 42.

35. For the story of prefeminist responses to Hegel on *Antigone*, see Martin Donougho, "The Woman in White: On the Reception of Hegel's *Antigone*," *Owl of Minerva* 21:1, Fall 1989, pp. 65–89. *Antigone* figures prominently in Easton, "Hegel and Feminism," and Mills, *Woman, Nature, and Psyche*, as well as in Heidi M. Raven, "Has Hegel Anything to Say to Feminists?" *Owl of Minerva* 19:2, Spring 1988, pp. 149–168; Luce Irigaray, "The Eternal Irony of the Community," in *Speculum of the Other Woman*, trans. Gillian C. Gill (Ithaca, N.Y.: Cornell University Press, 1985), pp. 214–226; and Christopher J. Arthur, "Hegel as Lord and Master," in *Socialism, Feminism and Philosophy: A Radical Philosophy Reader*, ed. Sean Sayers and Peter Osborne (New York: Routledge, 1990), pp. 27–45.

36. See Joanna Hodge, "Women and the Hegelian State," in *Women in Western Political Philosophy*, ed. Ellen Kennedy and Susan Mendus (London: Wheatsheaf

Books, 1987); and Benjamin R. Barber, "Spirit's Phoenix and History's Owl *or* The Incoherence of Dialectics in Hegel's Account of Women," *Political Theory* 16:1, February 1988, pp. 5–28.

37. See Denise Riley, *"Am I That Name?": Feminism and the Category of "Women"* *in History* (Minneapolis: University of Minnesota Press, 1988).

38. See Jane Bennett, *Unthinking Faith and Enlightenment: Nature and the State in* *a Post-Hegelian Era* (New York: New York University Press, 1987); and Edith Wyschogrod, *Spirit in Ashes: Hegel, Heidegger, and Man-Made Death* (New Haven, Yale University Press, 1985). See also Isaac D. Balbus, *Marxism and* *Domination: A Neo-Hegelian, Feminist, Psychoanalytic Theory of Sexual, Polit-* *ical, and Technological Liberation* (Princeton: Princeton University Press, 1982); and Mary O'Brien, "Hegel: Man, Philosophy, and Fate" in her *Reproducing the* *World: Essays in Feminist Theory* (Boulder: Westview Press, 1989).

39. Harry Brod, "Pornography and the Alienation of Male Sexuality," *Social Theory* *and Practice* 14:3, Fall 1988, pp. 280–281.

40. Mariarosa Dalla Costa and Selma James, *The Power of Women and the Subver-* *sion of the Community* (Bristol, England: Falling Wall Press, 1972).

References

Works by Hegel in German Original

Grundlinien der Philosophie des Rechts. Ed. Eva Moldenhauer and Karl Markus Michel. Frankfurt am Main: Suhrkamp, 1970.

Phänomenologie des Geistes. Ed. Johannes Hoffmeister. Hamburg: Felix Meiner, 1952.

Die Philosophie des Rechts: Die Mitschriften Wannenmann (Heidelberg 1817/18) und Homeyer (Berlin 1818/19). Ed. Karl-Heinz Ilting. Stuttgart: Klett Cotta, 1983.

Philosophie des Rechts: Die Vorlesung von 1819/20 in einer Nachschrift. Ed. Dieter Henrich. Frankfurt am Main: Suhrkamp, 1983.

Schriften zur Politik und Rechtsphilosophie. Ed. Georg Lasson. Leipzig: Felix Meiner, 1923.

Vorlesungen über Rechtsphilosophie. 4 vols. Ed. Karl-Heinz Ilting. Stuttgart-Bad Cannstatt: Frommann-Holzboog Verlag, 1973.

Wissenschaft der Logik. 2 vols. Ed. Georg Lasson. Hamburg: Felix Meiner, 1967.

Works by Hegel in English Translation
[Abbreviations used in notes given in brackets]

Early Theological Writings. Trans. T. M. Knox. Philadelphia: University of Pennsylvania Press, 1971.

The Encyclopaedia of the Philosophical Sciences. Pt. I, *Logic.* Trans. William Wallace. Oxford: Oxford University Press, 1972. [*Enc. I*]

Hegel and the Human Spirit. Trans. Leo Rauch. Detroit: Wayne State University Press, 1983.

Hegel's Idea of Philosophy. Trans. Quentin Lauer. New York: Fordham University Press, 1974.

Hegel's Phenomenology of Spirit. Trans. A. V. Miller. New York: Oxford University Press, 1977. [*Phen.*]

Hegel's Political Writings. Trans. T. M. Knox. Oxford: Oxford University Press, 1969. [*Polit.*]

Hegel's Science of Logic. Trans. A. V. Miller. New York: Humanities Press, 1969. [*Logic*]

Lectures on the History of Philosophy. 3 vols. Trans. E. S. Haldane and Frances H. Simson. New York: Humanities Press, 1974.

Lectures on the Philosophy of Religion. 3 vols. Trans. E. B. Spiers and J. Burdon Sanderson. New York: Humanities Press, 1974.

Logic of Hegel. 2d ed. Trans. William Wallace. Oxford: Oxford University Press, 1072.

Natural Law. Trans. T. M. Knox. Philadelphia: University of Pennsylvania Press, 1975.

On Art, Religion, Philosophy. Ed. J. Glenn Gray. New York: Harper and Row, 1970.

Phenomenology of Mind. Trans. J. B. Baillie. New York: Harper and Row, 1967. [*PM*]

Philosophy of History. Trans. J. Sibree. New York: Dover Publications, 1956; [*PH*] and P. F. Collier, 1901, pp. 25–38 (Edward Gans's "Preface to the First Edition").

Philosophy of Mind. Trans. William Wallace. Oxford: Clarendon Press, 1973.

Philosophy of Right. Trans. T. M. Knox. London: Oxford University Press, 1971. [*PR*]

"Prefatory Lectures on the Philosophy of Law." Trans. Alan S. Brudner. *Clio* 8, 1978, pp. 48–70.

Reason in History. Trans. Robert S. Hartman. Indianapolis: Bobbs-Merrill, 1976.

System of Ethical Life and First Philosophy of Spirit. Ed. and trans. H. S. Harris and T. M. Knox. Albany: State University of New York Press, 1979.

The Berlin Phenomenology. Ed. and trans. M. J. Petry. Dordrecht: D. Reidel Publishing Company, 1981.

Three Essays, 1793–1795. Ed. and trans. Peter Fuss and John Dobbins. Notre Dame: University of Notre Dame Press, 1984.

Other Works

Ahrweiler, Georg. *Hegels Gesellschaftslehre.* Darmstadt and Neuwied: Luchterhand, 1976.

Arato, Andrew. "A Reconstruction of Hegel's Theory of Civil Society." *Cardozo Law Review* 10:5–6, March/April 1989, pp. 1363–1388.

Arendt, Hannah. *The Human Condition.* Chicago: University of Chicago Press, 1974.

Aristotle. *Politics*. Ed. and trans. Ernest Barker. New York: Oxford University Press, 1962.

Arthur, Christopher J. "Hegel as Lord and Master." In *Socialism, Feminism, and Philosophy: A Radical Philosophy Reader*, ed. Sean Sayers and Peter Osborne. New York: Routledge, 1990.

Avineri, Shlomo. *Hegel's Theory of the Modern State*. Cambridge: Cambridge University Press, 1974.

⸻. "The Problem of War in Hegel's Thought." In *Perspectives on Political Philosophy*. Vol. 2, *Machiavelli Through Marx*, ed. David K. Hart and James V. Downton, Jr. New York: Holt, Rinehart and Winston, 1971.

⸻, ed. *Karl Marx on Colonialism and Modernization*. New York: Anchor-Doubleday, 1969.

Balbus, Isaac D. *Marxism and Domination: A Neo-Hegelian, Feminist, Psychoanalytic Theory of Sexual, Political, and Technological Liberation*. Princeton: Princeton University Press, 1982.

Barber, Benjamin R. "Spirit's Phoenix and History's Owl *or* The Incoherence of Dialectics in Hegel's Account of Women." *Political Theory* 16:1, February 1988, pp. 5–28.

Beauvoir, Simone de. *The Second Sex*. Trans. and ed. H. M. Parshley. New York: Alfred A. Knopf, 1953.

Beck, Lewis White. "The Reformation, the Revolution, and the Restoration in Hegel's Political Philosophy." *Journal of the History of Philosophy* 14:1, January 1976, pp. 51–61.

Benjamin, Jessica. *The Bonds of Love: Psychoanalysis, Feminism, and the Problem of Domination*. New York: Pantheon, 1988.

Bennett, Jane. *Unthinking Faith and Enlightenment: Nature and the State in a Post-Hegelian Era*. New York: New York University Press, 1987.

Berger, Peter. "In Praise of Particularity: The Concept of Mediating Structures." In *Facing Up to Modernity*. New York: Basic Books, 1977.

Bienenstock, Myriam. "The Logic of Political Life: Hegel's Conception of Political Philosophy." In *Knowledge and Politics: Case Studies in the Relationship Between Epistemology and Political Philosophy*, ed. Marcelo Dascal and Ora Gruengard. Boulder: Westview Press, 1989.

Black, Anthony. *Guilds and Civil Society in European Thought from the Twelfth Century to the Present*. Ithaca, N.Y.: Cornell University Press, 1984.

Blum, Lawrence A. "Kant's and Hegel's Moral Rationalism: A Feminist Perspective." *Canadian Journal of Philosophy* 12:2, June 1982, pp. 287–302.

Bonar, James. *Philosophy and Political Economy*. New York: Humanities Press, 1967.

Brinton, Crane. "Reflections on the Alienation of the Intellectuals." In *Generalizations in Historical Writing*, ed. Alexander V. Riasanovsky and Barnes Riznik. Philadelphia: University of Pennsylvania Press, 1963.

Brod, Harry. "The 'Spirit' of Hegelian Politics: Public Opinion and Legislative Debate from Hegel to Habermas." In *Hegel's Philosophy of Spirit*, ed. Peter Stillman. Albany: State University of New York Press, 1987.

———. "Law Thinking Itself: The Idealism of International Law." Review of *International Legal Structures*, by David Kennedy. *Cardozo Law Review* 10:5–6, Marvh/April 1989, pp. 1879-1885.

———. "Pornography and the Alienation of Male Sexuality." *Social Theory and Practice* 14:3, Fall 1988, pp. 265-284.

Butler, Clark. "Technological Society and Its Counterculture: An Hegelian Analysis." *Inquiry* 18, 1975, pp. 195-212.

Butler, Judith P. *Subjects of Desire: Hegelian Reflections in Twentieth-Century France*. New York: Columbia University Press, 1987.

Cairns, Huntington. *Legal Philosophy from Plato to Hegel*. Baltimore: Johns Hopkins Press, 1949.

Cardozo Law Review 10:5–6, March/April 1989. (Special issue on "Hegel and Legal Theory.")

Cassirer, Ernst. *The Myth of the State*. New Haven: Yale University Press, 1971.

Chamley, Paul. *Economie Politique et Philosophie chez Steuart et Hegel*. Paris: Librairie Dalloz, 1963.

Christensen, Daniel E., ed. *Hegel and the Philosophy of Religion: The Wofford Symposium*. The Hague: Martinus Nijhoff, 1970.

Cohen, G. A. "Karl Marx and the Withering Away of Social Science." In *Marx, Justice, and History*, ed. Marshall Cohen, Thomas Nagel, and Thomas Scanlon. Princeton: Princeton University Press, 1980.

Cole, Charles W. "The Heavy Hand of Hegel." In *Nationalism and Internationalism: Essays Inscribed to Carlton J. H. Hayes*, ed. Edward Mead Earle. New York: Columbia University Press, 1950.

Colletti, Lucio. *From Rousseau to Lenin: Studies in Ideology and Society*. New York: Monthly Review Press, 1972.

———. *Marxism and Hegel*. London: New Left Books, 1973.

Connolly, William, ed. *Legitimacy and the State*. New York: New York University Press, 1984.

Cooper, Barry. *The End of History: An Essay on Modern Hegelianism*. Toronto: University of Toronto Press, 1984.

Cornell, Drucilla. "Taking Hegel Seriously: Reflections on Beyond Objectivism and Relativism." *Cardozo Law Review* 7, 1985, p. 139.

———. "Toward a Modern/Postmodern Reconstruction of Ethics." *University of Pennsylvania Law Review* 133:2, January 1985, pp. 291-380.

Costa, Mariarosa Dalla, and Selma James. *The Power of Women and the Subversion of the Community*. Bristol, England: Falling Wall Press, 1972.

Cristi, F. R. "The *Hegelsche Mitte* and Hegel's Monarch." *Political Theory* 11:4, November 1983, pp. 601–622.

Dewey, John. *Liberalism and Social Action*. New York: Capricorn, 1963.

Donougho, Martin. "The Woman in White: On the Reception of Hegel's *Antigone*." *Owl of Minerva* 21:1, Fall 1989, pp. 65–89.

Dworkin, Ronald. *Law's Empire*. Cambridge: Harvard University Press, 1986.

Easton, Susan M. "Hegel and Feminism." In *Hegel and Modern Philosophy*, ed. David Lamb. London: Croom Helm, 1987.

Fackenheim, Emil L. *The Religious Dimension in Hegel's Thought*. Bloomington: Indiana University Press, 1967.

Farr, James. "'So Vile and Miserable an Estate': The Problem of Slavery in Locke's Political Thought." *Political Theory* 14:2, May 1986, pp. 262–289.

Fetscher, Iring. *Hegel—Grösse und Grenzen*. Stuttgart: W. Kohlhammer, 1971.

Fleischmann, Eugene. *La Philosophie Politique de Hegel*. Paris: Librairie Plon, 1964.

Fuchs, Jo-Ann Pilardi. "On the War Path and Beyond: Hegel, Freud, and Feminist Theory." *Women's Studies International Forum* 6:6, 1983, pp. 565–572.

Fukuyama, Francis. "The End of History?" *The National Interest* 16, Summer 1989, pp. 3–18.

Garaudy, Roger. *Marxism in the Twentieth Century*. New York: Charles Scribners Sons, 1970.

Giddens, Anthony. *Profiles and Critiques in Social Theory*. Berkeley: University of California Press, 1982.

———. *Social Theory and Modern Sociology*. Stanford: Stanford University Press, 1987.

———. *Sociology: A Brief but Critical Introduction*. New York: Harcourt Brace Jovanovich, 1982.

Gillespie, Michael Allen. "Death and Desire: War and Bourgeoisification in the Thought of Hegel." In *Understanding the Political Spirit: Philosophical Investigations from Socrates to Nietzsche*, ed. Catherine H. Zuckert. New Haven: Yale University Press, 1988.

———. *Hegel, Heidegger, and the Ground of History*. Chicago: University of Chicago Press, 1984.

Gooch, G. P. *Germany and the French Revolution*. New York: Russell and Russell, 1966.

Gramsci, Antonio. *The Modern Prince and Other Writings*. Trans. Louis Marks. New York: International Publishers, 1975.

Grier, Philip T. "The End of History, and the Return of History." *Owl of Minerva* 21:2, Spring 1990, pp. 131–144.

Gunn, J.A.W. *Beyond Liberty and Property: The Process of Self-Recognition in Eighteenth-Century Political Thought.* Kingston, Canada: McGill-Queen's University Press, 1983.

Habermas, Jürgen. *Communication and the Evolution of Society.* Trans. Thomas McCarthy. Boston: Beacon Press, 1979.

———. *Knowledge and Human Interests.* Trans. Jeremy J. Shapiro. Boston: Beacon Press, 1972.

———. *Legitimation Crisis.* Trans. Thomas McCarthy. Boston: Beacon Press, 1975.

———. "Nachwort," *G.W.F. Hegel, Politische Schriften.* Ed. Hans Blumenberg et al. Frankfurt am Main: Suhrkamp, 1966.

———."The Public Sphere: An Encyclopedia Article (1964)." Trans. Sara Lennox and Frank Lennox. *New German Critique* 3, Fall 1974, pp. 49–55.

———. *Strukturwandel der Öffentlichkeit.* Neuwied and Berlin: Luchterhand, 1976. (Translated by Thomas Burger with Fredrick Lawrence as *The Structural Transformation of the Public Sphere.* Cambridge: MIT Press, 1989.)

———. *Theory and Practice.* Trans. John Viertel. Boston: Beacon Press, 1974.

Hayim, Gila J. "Hegel's Critical Theory and Feminist Concerns." *Philosophy and Social Criticism* 16:1, 1990, pp. 1–21.

Heidegger, Martin. *Being and Time.* Trans. John Macquarrie and Edward Robinson. New York: Harper and Row, 1962.

Henrich, Dieter. *Hegel im Kontext.* Frankfurt am Main: Suhrkamp, 1975.

Hinchman, Lewis P. *Hegel's Critique of the Enlightenment.* Tampa: University of South Florida Press, 1984.

Hobbes, Thomas. *Leviathan.* Ed. C. B. MacPherson. Middlesex: Penguin Books, 1968; reprint 1975.

———. *Man and Citizen.* Ed. Bernard Gert. New York: Anchor-Doubleday, 1972.

Hodge, Joanna. "Women and the Hegelian State." In *Women in Western Political Philosophy,* ed. Ellen Kennedy and Susan Mendus. London: Wheatsheaf Books, 1987.

Hohendahl, Peter Uwe. "Critical Theory, Public Sphere, and Culture: Jürgen Habermas and his Critics." *New German Critique* 16, Winter 1979, pp. 89–118.

———."Jürgen Habermas: 'The Public Sphere' (1964)."*New German Critique*, vol. 1, no. 3, fall 1974, pp. 45–48.

Holborn, Hajo. "The Science of History." In *The Interpretation of History,* ed. Joseph R. Strayer. Princeton: Princeton University Press, 1943.

Horkheimer, Max, and Theodor W. Adorno. *Dialectic of Enlightenment.* Trans. John Cumming. New York: Herder and Herder, 1972.

Houlgate, Stephen. "World History as the Progress of Consciousness: An Interpretation of Hegel's Philosophy of History." *Owl of Minerva* 22:1, Fall 1990, pp. 69–80.

Huxley, Aldous. "Words and Behavior." In *Collected Essays*. New York: Bantam, 1960.

Hyppolite, Jean. *Genesis and Structure of Hegel's Phenomenology of Spirit.* Trans. Samuel Cherniak and John Heckman. Evanston: Northwestern University Press, 1974.

————. *Studies on Marx and Hegel.* Trans. John O'Neill. New York: Harper and Row, 1973.

Irigaray, Luce. *Speculum of the Other Woman.* Trans. Gillian C. Gill. Ithaca, N.Y.: Cornell University Press, 1985.

Kant, Immanuel. *Gessammelte Schriften.* vol. 19, PrAkAus.

————. *Political Writings.* Ed. Hans Reiss; trans. H. B. Nisbet. Cambridge: Cambridge University Press, 1977.

Kaufmann, Walter, ed. *Hegel's Political Philosophy.* New York: Atherton Press, 1970.

Keane, John, ed. *Civil Society and the State: New European Perspectives.* London: Verso, 1988.

Kelly, George Armstrong. "Hegel's America," *Philosophy and Public Affairs* 2:1, Fall 1972, pp. 3–36.

————. *Hegel's Retreat from Eleusis.* Princeton: Princeton University Press, 1978.

————. *Idealism, Politics, and History: Sources of Hegelian Thought.* Cambridge: Cambridge University Press, 1969.

Kojève, Alexandre. *Introduction to the Reading of Hegel.* Ed. Allan Bloom; trans. James H. Nichols, Jr. New York: Basic Books, 1969.

Kolb, David. *The Critique of Pure Modernity: Hegel, Heidegger, and After.* Chicago: University of Chicago Press, 1986.

Kucheman, Clark A. "Abstract and Concrete Freedom: Hegelian Perspectives on Economic Justice." *Owl of Minerva* 15:1, Fall 1983, pp. 23–44.

Landes, Joan. "Hegel's Conception of the Family." *Polity* 14:1, 1981, pp. 5–28.

Laursen, John Christian. "The Subversive Kant." *Political Theory* 14:4, November 1986, pp. 584–603.

Leiss, William. *The Domination of Nature.* Boston: Beacon Press, 1974.

Lloyd, Genevieve. *The Man of Reason: "Male" and "Female" in Western Philosophy.* Minneapolis: University of Minnesota Press, 1984.

Locke, John. *The Second Treatise of Government.* Ed. Thomas P. Peardon. Indianapolis: Bobbs-Merrill, 1952.

————. *Two Treatises of Government.* rev. ed. Ed. Peter Laslett. New York: New American Library, 1965.

Loewenberg, Robert J. "John Locke and the Antebellum Defense of Slavery." *Political Theory* 13:2, May 1985, pp. 266–291.

Lonzi, Carla. "Let's Spit on Hegel." In *Italian Feminist Thought: A Reader*, ed. Paola Bono and Sandra Kemp. New York: Basil Blackwell, 1991.

Löwith, Karl. *From Hegel to Nietzsche*. New York: Anchor, 1967.

Lübbe, Hermann. "Hegels Kritik der Politisierten Gesellschaft." *Filosoficky Casopis* 15:3, 1967, pp. 363–374.

Lukács, Georg. *The Young Hegel*. Trans. Rodney Livingstone. London: Merlin Press, 1975.

MacGregor, David. *The Communist Ideal in Hegel and Marx*. Toronto: University of Toronto Press, 1984.

Machiavelli, Niccolo. *The Prince*. Trans. and ed. Robert M. Adams. New York: W. W. Norton, 1977.

MacIntyre, Alasdair, ed. *Hegel: A Collection of Critical Essays*. Notre Dame: University of Notre Dame Press, 1976.

MacPherson, C. B. *The Political Theory of Possessive Individualism*. London: Oxford University Press, 1964.

Mah, Harold. "The French Revolution and the Problem of German Modernity: Hegel, Heine, and Marx." *New German Critique* 50, Spring/Summer 1990, pp. 3–20.

Maker, William, ed. *Hegel on Economics and Freedom*. Macon, Ga.: Mercer University Press, 1987.

Maletz, Donald J. "Hegel on Right as Actualized Will." *Political Theory* 17:1, February 1989, pp. 33–50.

Mandelbaum, Maurice. *History, Man, and Reason: A Study in Nineteenth-Century Thought*. Baltimore: Johns Hopkins Press, 1971.

Marcuse, Herbert. *Hegels Ontologie und die Theorie der Geschichtlichkeit*. Frankfurt am Main: Vittorio Klostermann, 1975. (Translated by Seyla Benhabib as *Hegel's Ontology and the Theory of Historicity*. Cambridge: MIT Press, 1987.)

———. *Reason and Revolution: Hegel and the Rise of Social Theory*. Boston: Beacon Press, 1960.

———. *Studies in Critical Philosophy*. Boston: Beacon Press, 1973.

Marcuse, Herbert, Robert Paul Wolff, and Barrington Moore, Jr. *A Critique of Pure Tolerance*. Boston: Beacon Press, 1969.

Marks, Elaine and Isabelle de Courtivron, ed. *New French Feminisms*. New York: Schocken, 1981.

Marx, Karl. *Critique of Hegel's Philosophy of Right*. Ed. Joseph O'Malley. Cambridge: Cambridge University Press, 1970.

———. *Writings of the Young Marx on Philosophy and Society*. Ed. Lloyd D. Easton and Kurt H. Guddat. New York: Doubleday, 1967.

Mill, John Stuart. *Utilitarianism, Liberty, and Representative Government*. New York: Everyman-Dutton, 1951.

Mills, Patricia Jagentowicz. *Woman, Nature, and Psyche*. New Haven: Yale University Press, 1987.

Mitias, Michael H. *Moral Foundation of the State in Hegel's "Philosophy of Right": Anatomy of an Argument*. Amsterdam: Editions Rodopi B. V., 1984.

Moore, Stanley. *Marx on the Choice Between Socialism and Communism*. Cambridge: Harvard University Press, 1980.

Morley, Jefferson. "On 'Civil Society.' " *The Nation*, May 7, 1988, p. 630.

Mosher, Michael A. "Civic Identity in the Juridical Society: On Hegelianism as Discipline for the Romantic Mind." *Political Theory* 11:1, February 1983, pp. 117–132.

O'Brien, Mary. *The Politics of Reproduction*. Boston: Routledge & Kegan Paul, 1981.

Olafson, Frederick A., ed. *Society, Law, and Morality: Readings in Social Philosophy*. Englewood Cliffs, N.J.: Prentice-Hall, 1961.

O'Neill, Onora. "The Public Use of Reason." *Political Theory* 14:4, November 1986, pp. 523–551.

Padover, Saul, ed. *The Mind of Alexander Hamilton*. New York: Harper and Brothers, 1958.

Pateman, Carole. *The Problem of Political Obligation: A Critique of Liberal Theory*. Berkeley: University of California Press, 1985.

———. *The Sexual Contract*. London: Polity Press, 1988.

Pelczynski, Z. A., ed. *Hegel's Political Philosophy: Problems and Perspectives*. Cambridge: Cambridge University Press, 1971.

———. *The State and Civil Society: Studies in Hegel's Political Philosophy*. Cambridge: Cambridge University Press, 1984.

Peperzak, Adriaan Th. *Philosophy and Politics: A Commentary on the Preface to Hegel's Philosophy of Right*. Dordrecht: Martinus Nijhoff, 1987.

Perkins, Robert L., ed. *History and System: Hegel's Philosophy of History*. Albany: State University of New York Press, 1984.

Piper, Adrian M. S. "Property and the Limits of the Self." *Political Theory* 8:1, February 1980, pp. 39–64.

Pippin, Robert B. "Hegel's Political Argument and the Problem of Verwirklichung." *Political Theory* 9:4, November 1981, pp. 509–532.

———. "The Rose and the Owl: Some Remarks on the Theory-Practice Problem in Hegel." *The Independent Journal of Philosophy*, 3, 1979, pp. 7–16.

Pitkin, Hannah Fenichel. *The Concept of Representation*. Berkeley: University of California Press, 1972.

Plant, Raymond. *Hegel*. Bloomington: Indiana University Press, 1973.

———. "Hegel's Social Theory: Parts I and II." *New Left Review*, nos. 103–104, May-June, and July-August, pp. 79–92, 103–113.

Plato. *The Laws of Plato*. Trans. Thomas L. Pangle. New York: Basic Books, 1980.

———. *Republic*. Trans. Francis MacDonald Cornford. New York: Oxford University Press, 1973.

Polin, Raymond. "Philosophie du Droit et philosophie de l'Histoire chez Hegel d'apres 'les Principes de la philosophie du Droit' de 1821." In *Hegel: L'Esprit Objectif: L'Unite de L'Histoire*. Lille: Actes du IIIème Congres International de l'association Internationale pour l'étude de la philosophie de Hegel, 1968.

Quelquejeu, Bernard. *La Volonté dans la Philosophie de Hegel*. Paris: Editions du Seuil, 1972.

Raven, Heidi M. "Has Hegel Anything to Say to Feminists?" *Owl of Minerva* 19:2, Spring 1988, pp. 149–168.

Rawls, John. *A Theory of Justice*. Cambridge: Harvard University Press, 1971.

Reiss, H. S., ed. *The Political Thought of the German Romantics*. Oxford: Basil Blackwell, 1955.

Ricoeur, Paul. "The Political Paradox." In *Existential Phenomenology and Political Theory*, ed. Hwa Yol Jung. Chicago: Henry Regnery Company, 1972.

Riedel, Manfred. *Between Tradition and Revolution: The Hegelian Transformation of Political Philosophy*. Trans. Walter Wright. Cambridge: Cambridge University Press, 1984.

———. *Bürgerliche Gesellschaft und Staat bei Hegel*. Neuwied and Berlin: Luchterhand, 1970.

———. *Studien zu Hegels Rechtsphilosophie*. Frankfurt am Main: Suhrkamp, 1969.

———. *Theorie und Praxis im Denken Hegels*. Frankfurt am Main: Ullstein, 1976.

———, ed. *Materialien zu Hegels Rechtsphilosophie*. 2 vols. Frankfurt am Main: Suhrkamp, 1975.

Riley, Denise. *"Am I That Name?": Feminism and the Category of "Women" in History*. Minneapolis: University of Minnesota Press, 1988.

Riley, Patrick. *Will and Political Legitimacy: A Critical Exposition of Social Contract Theory in Hobbes, Locke, Rousseau, Kant, and Hegel*. Cambridge: Harvard University Press, 1982.

Ritter, Joachim. *Hegel and the French Revolution: Essays on the "Philosophy of Right."* Trans. Richard Dien Winfield. Cambridge: MIT Press, 1982.

———. *Metaphysik und Politik: Studien zu Aristoteles und Hegel*. Frankfurt am Main: Suhrkamp, 1977.

———. *Subjektivität*. Frankfurt am Main: Suhrkamp, 1974.

Rosen, Stanley. *G.W.F. Hegel: An Introduction to the Science of Wisdom*. New Haven: Yale University Press, 1974.

Rosenzweig, Franz. *Hegel und der Staat*. 2 vols. Munich: Verlag R. Oldenbourg, 1920.

Rousseau, Jean-Jacques. *The Government of Poland*. Trans. Willmoore Kendall. Indianapolis: Bobbs-Merrill, 1972.

———. *On the Social Contract*. Ed. Roger D. Masters; trans. Judith R. Masters. New York: St. Martin's Press, 1978.

———. *The Social Contract and Discourses*. Trans. G. D. H. Cole. New York: Everyman Dutton, 1950.

Royce, Josiah. *Lectures on Modern Idealism*. New Haven: Yale University Press, 1967.

———. *The Spirit of Modern Philosophy*. Boston: Houghton Mifflin Company, 1920.

Rubinoff, Lionel, ed. *Tradition and Revolution*. Toronto: Macmillan of Canada, 1971.

Ryan, Alan. *Property and Political Theory*. New York: Basil Blackwell, 1984.

Sabine, George H. *A History of Political Theory*. 3d ed. New York: Holt, Rinehart and Winston, 1961.

Salvadori, Massimo, ed. *European Liberalism*. New York: John Wiley and Sons, 1972.

Sandel, Michael J. *Liberalism and the Limits of Justice*. Cambridge: Cambridge University Press, 1982.

Sartre, Jean-Paul. "An Interview (1970)." In *Phenomenology and Existentialism*, ed. Robert C. Solomon. New York: Harper and Row, 1972.

Schochet, Gordon J. *Patriarchalism in Political Thought*. New York: Basic Books, 1975.

Seeberger, Wilhelm. "The Political Significance of Hegel's Concept of History." Trans. K. R. Dove and C. R. Dove. *The Monist* 48:1, January 1964, pp. 76–96.

Sestanovich, Stephen. "Response to Fukuyama." *The National Interest* 16, Summer 1989, pp. 32–35.

Shklar, Judith N. *Freedom and Independence: A Study of the Political Ideas of Hegel's Phenomenology of Mind*. Cambridge: Cambridge University Press, 1976.

———. "Hegel and the French Revolution: An Epitaph for Republicanism." *Social Research* 56:1, Spring 1989, pp. 233–261.

Smith, Steven B. *Hegel's Critique of Liberalism: Rights in Context*. Chicago: University of Chicago Press, 1989.

———. "Hegel's Idea of a Critical Theory." *Political Theory* 15:1, February 1987, pp. 99–126.

Steinberger, Peter J. *Logic and Politics: Hegel's Philosophy of Right*. New Haven: Yale University Press, 1988.

Stepelevich, Lawrence S. and David Lamb, eds. *Hegel's Philosophy of Action*. Atlantic Highlands, N.J.: Humanities Press, 1983.

Stern, Alfred. "Hegel et les idées de 1789." *Revue Philosophique de la France et de l'Etranger* 128, July-December 1939, pp. 353-363.

Stillman, Peter G. "Hegel's Analysis of Property in the *Philosophy of Right*." *Cardozo Law Review* 10:5-6, March/April 1989, pp. 1031-1072.

————, ed. *Hegel's Philosophy of Spirit*. Albany: State University of New York Press, 1987.

Talmon, J. L. *The Origins of Totalitarian Democracy*. New York: W. W. Norton, 1970.

Taylor, Charles. *Hegel*. Cambridge: Cambridge University Press, 1978.

————. *Hegel and Modern Society*. Cambridge: Cambridge University Press, 1979.

Theunissen, Michael. *Die Verwirklichung der Vernunft: Zur Theorie-Praxis-Diskussion im Anschluss an Hegel*. Philosophische Rundschau, Beiheft 6, 1970.

Toews, John Edward. *Hegelianism*. Cambridge: Cambridge University Press, 1980.

Travis, D. C., ed. *A Hegel Symposium*. Austin: University of Texas Press, 1962.

Tucker, Robert C., ed. *The Marx-Engels Reader*. New York: W. W. Norton and Company, 1972.

Unger, Roberto Mangabeira. *Knowledge and Politics*. New York: Free Press, 1976.

Verene, Donald Phillip, ed. *Hegel's Social and Political Thought*. New Jersey: Humanities Press, 1980.

Walzer, Michael. "The Idea of Civil Society." *Dissent*, Spring 1991, pp. 293-304.

Weber, Shierry M. "Individuation as Praxis." In *Critical Interruptions: New Left Perspectives on Herbert Marcuse*, ed. Paul Breines. New York: Herder and Herder, 1972.

Weiner, Richard R. *Cultural Marxism and Political Sociology*. Beverly Hills: Sage Publications, 1981.

West, Cornel. "Hegel, Hermeneutics, Politics: A Reply to Charles Taylor." *Cardozo Law Review* 10:5-6, March/April 1989, pp. 871-875.

Winfield, Richard Dien. *Reason and Justice*. Albany: State University of New York Press, 1988.

Wolff, Robert Paul. "Social Philosophy: The Agenda for the Nineties." *Journal of Social Philosophy* 20:1-2, Spring/Fall 1989, pp. 4-17.

Wood, Allen W. *Hegel's Ethical Thought*. Cambridge: Cambridge University Press, 1990.

Wyschogrod, Edith. *Spirit in Ashes: Hegel, Heidegger, and Man-Made Death*. New Haven: Yale University Press, 1985.

About the Book and Author

This valuable book makes a significant contribution to the current revival of interest in Hegel. Brod demonstrates the central unifying role the collective historical social consciousness plays in Hegel's thought. But far from leading to totalitarian conclusions, this emphasis upon the social actually leads Hegel toward a "third way" between the anarchic individualism of unregulated market structures and the repressive collectivism of unopposed state power. Similarly, Hegel can be seen as a potentially moderating influence on his two quarrelsome offspring, Marxism and liberalism. Hegel emerges here as a thinker with relevance for our own time, with lessons for current communitarian critiques of liberalism, the revolutions in Eastern Europe, modern jurisprudence, and feminist theory. A virtue of Brod's treatment is its clarity and lack of jargon. Hegel receives a welcome demystification that leaves his political philosophy stronger and more viable rather than diminished.

Harry Brod is associate professor of women's and gender studies and philosophy at Kenyon College. He is the editor of *The Making of Masculinities: The New Men's Studies, A Mensch Among Men: Explorations in Jewish Masculinity,* and the forthcoming *Theorizing Masculinities.* Brod has held fellowships at the Hegel Archives at the Ruhr-Universität Bochum and at Harvard Law School and has taught at the University of Southern California, California State College at San Bernardino, the University of California at San Diego, and Palomar College.

Index